P9-BUG-666

YOUTH MINISTRY

BOOKS BY LAWRENCE O. RICHARDS

A New Face for the Church

Creative Bible Study

How I Can Be Real

How Far I Can Go

How I Can Experience God

How I Can Make Decisions

How I Can Fit In

69 Ways to Start a Study Group

Three Churches in Renewal

Reshaping Evangelical Higher Education
(with Marvin K. Mayers)

A Theology of Christian Education

A Theology of Church Leadership
(with Clyde Hoeldtke)

A Theology of Personal Ministry
(with Gib Martin)

A Theology of Children's Ministry

Discipling Resources Series
(with Norman Wakefield)

The Believer's Promise Book

The Believer's Guidebook

Expository Dictionary of Bible Words

YOUTH MINISTRY

its renewal in the local church

REVISED EDITION

Lawrence O. Richards

Zondervan Publishing House • Grand Rapids, MI

MINISTRY RESOURCES LIBRARY
is an imprint of
Zondervan Publishing House
1415 Lake Drive S.E.
Grand Rapids, Michigan 49506

Library of Congress Cataloging in Publication Data

Richards, Larry, 1931–
Youth ministry.

Includes bibliographical references and indexes.
1. Church work with youth. I. Title.

BV4447.R46 1985 259'.2 85–22779

ISBN 0–310–32010–0

Edited by Michael G. Smith and Gerard Terpstra

Designed by Louise Bauer

Printed in the United States of America

85 86 87 88 89 90 / 10 9 8 7 6 5 4 3 2 1

Contents

Table of Figures

Preface to the Revised Edition

Youth culture changes. Youth ministry remains much the same. In revising this book I have been guided by each of these realities.

My first edition of *Youth Ministry* analyzed and explored characteristics of youth culture at a particular point in time. In this edition, I have turned away from examining youth culture in a specific time period to look instead at several continuums along which youth culture shifts. And I have suggested some implications of each continuum for the practice of ministry with youth. My goal is to help youth workers to be sensitive to those significant, but shifting, aspects of youth culture that have a practical impact on the shape and form of ministry. My hope is that as youth culture undergoes its shifts—as it most certainly will—youth workers will be able to shift approaches along with it.

The first edition of *Youth Ministry* did more than analyze a particular generation of young people. It attempted to present a paradigm of ministry itself: a framework for working with young people that integrated adolescent development with a ministry built on relationships. This framework remains essentially the same. It has been modified in only a few areas where my own thinking has changed. And I remain convinced that the greatest contribution this book has made and will continue to make is in the *framework* it provides for ministry with youth.

I am excited that so many fine tools and resources have been developed since I first wrote this book. They are available from such sources as Youth Specialties (San Diego), Group (Loveland, Colorado), and the Son Power line of Scripture Press, to name just a few. Youth workers of this century will look to such sources for fresh and updated ideas. And they should. But it is with the firm conviction that tools are useful only within the framework provided by a biblical philosophy of ministry itself that I offer this revised form of *Youth Ministry*.

Larry Richards

Preface to the Original Edition

"Renewal" is a word we often hear today. It is a word that calls both for a new approach to life in the church and for a return to New Testament patterns of ministry.

In both these senses, this book on youth ministry is a renewal book. In it I seek to draw from Scripture and to explore principles on which youth ministry can be confidently based. And in it I develop what seems to me a distinctive approach to ministering with youth.

The book itself is divided into several parts. The first explores contemporary youth culture and hopefully will help you understand some of the ways of thinking and feeling about life that are characteristic of young people today.

Part two looks at youth as a time of life. Hopefully it will help you identify with adolescents. Although they are persons like you and me, they are under special pressures that we need to understand. The latter half of part two is a vital one, taking a look at leadership in biblical perspective. As I suggest there, this may be the most important part of the book, for it certainly examines a critical ministry area. Perhaps effectiveness in ministry does depend more on this one thing, *who you are as a leader,* than on any other factor.

The third part explores the primary processes of ministry. This is the heart of the book, attempting to explain those processes in which youth and adults must become involved to grow toward maturity as Christians.

Part four looks at programming and discusses both the structures (agencies, meetings, activities) of youth ministry and the organizing of youth for ministry.

The final and very brief section, part five, considers the goal and the result of an effective youth ministry: growth, together.

Together these chapters develop a philosophy of youth ministry, presenting a basic approach to youth ministry with an explanation of *why* we approach ministry as we do, and suggestions on *what* to do and *how* to do it. Although older teens (the senior high group) are primarily in mind as I write this book, the principles are also valid for, and have direct application to, young teens and college-age youth, with exceptions noted in the text.

Beginning with part two, this book will deal successively with the elements contained in the following diagram:

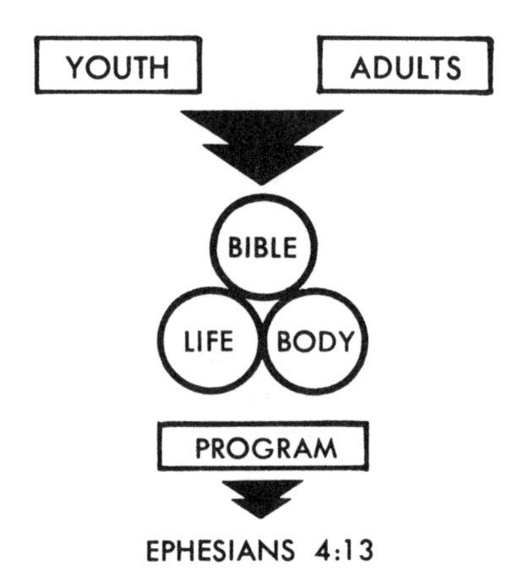

It is, I suppose, always rewarding to finish a book. As I complete this one I do so with the feeling that it may be the most significant book I have yet written. For, more than any other, it develops a pattern for ministry, one which I am convinced is both distinctively biblical and productive of exciting renewal—a renewal we desperately need, and need now.

Lawrence O. Richards

YOUTH MINISTRY

Part One

YOUTH IN OUR CULTURE

CHAPTERS

1. ADOLESCENCE
2. YOUTH CULTURE
3. CHRISTIAN "EDUCATION" OF YOUTH

1

ADOLESCENCE

"I can't remember any basic decision, actually," says an eighteen-year-old college freshman, thinking back over her life as a high schooler. "I just lived a day at a time and did what seemed right and most fun at the time. A lot of times, though, what I did or didn't do depended on whether my dad would approve." Adolescence is probably like this for most young people. But much more can be said about adolescence. Consequently, many different theories have emerged about this vitally significant time of life.

Technically, adolescence is most often described as a period of time: a time of transition that extends from about age twelve to age twenty-five in men, and to twenty-one or so in women. It is also defined in other ways. It is the period that stretches from the beginning of puberty, through a long process of education, until the person is able to take his or her place as a responsible individual in the adult world.

Adolescence is often seen as occurring in stages. In early adolescence young people are keenly aware of their physical selves. During this time they begin to develop the capacity to think abstractly, and they often experience emotional ups and downs.

Middle adolescence, usually seen as the period from age fifteen to eighteen, is associated with the development of a sense of personal identity and a growing struggle with sexuality. The character of friendships shift and deepen, and relationships become more important to the individual.

Late adolescence includes the period in which a person begins a marriage and a job or continues his or her education in a college or vocational school. During these years individuals are facing and making the choices that will shape their entire future.

These basic and simple facts about adolescence are common knowledge. We all know them and accept this general picture of adolescent development. But as we approach the exigencies of youth ministry, it is important to realize that we are likely to come to these basic facts with quite different perspectives. In fact, our different views of youth and our feelings about adolescence as a time of life are sure to color our approach to young people. So we need to look at a few common notions about adolescence, examine some evidence from research, and see whether we can develop a consensus that will help to guide us.

NOTIONS ABOUT ADOLESCENCE

We are familiar with most of the notions about adolescence. One notion that has been with us for a hundred years or so is that adolescence is a stormy period. Young people are viewed as unpredictable, moved by strong emotions they can't understand or control. The young person is not stable; dramatic personality shifts can be expected.

A parallel view sees adolescence as a unique period because it is a time of restructuring the personality. The child suddenly disappears, and before the adult can emerge, a whole new identity must be formed. During this period the young person must learn the roles he or she will play in adulthood. Sexual identity, moral orientation, identity with the values of the larger society are all seen as taking place in this period.

Others have argued that adolescence is unique because it is marked by the formation of a youth culture separate from and often antagonistic toward the general culture. This youth culture is thought to be in rebellion against adult norms and values.

Each of these common orientations to adolescence sees this time of life as unique, set apart from other periods of human development. Each agrees it is, in Anna Freud's phrase, an "interruption of peaceful growth" and a time of "emotional upsets and structural upheavals."[1]

---

[1] Anna Freud, "Adolescence," *Psychoanalytic Study of the Child* 13 (New Haven, Conn.: Yale University Press, 1958): 255–78.

The general acceptance of such views of adolescence affects the way many approach the thought of working with youth. Moms and dads often anticipate the teen-age years with anxiety and may draw back in their relationships with their children just when friendship and wise guidance is most needed. Couples in a local church may hesitate to work with teens, fearful that they will be unable to communicate with persons who are so "different." Churches may misinterpret the distinctive aspects of youth culture, seeing in hair styles, music, and fashion the "rebellion" they have been programmed to expect. All too often the uncertainty and fears of adult members of a congregation are experienced by youth as a judgmental or condemning attitude, tragically driving a wedge between youth and the adult Christians whom they need to emulate.

A BALANCED VIEW

A balanced view of adolescence must recognize it as a critical time in human development. Normal adolescence is marked by rapid growth. Puberty brings hormonal changes that are greater than at any other age period. Puberty also brings adult sexual capacity with a surge of emotions that are strange to young people. Research has shown that this is also a time of changing mental capabilities: adolescents are able to think differently and more deeply than when they were younger. And there are also social changes: the character of friendships with peers changes as well as increases in importance.

It is not surprising that such changes are associated with more depressive feelings and uncertainty about the future than are other periods.[2] But to acknowledge youth as a special time of life is not the same as characterizing it as unique, a time qualitatively different from that of childhood or adulthood.

In fact, the evidence suggests that most of us, with the normal measure of trauma, pass through adolescence without becoming delinquents. We pass our school examinations, suffer through our first love, find employment, and gradually develop independence from our family. Many of us do all this quite successfully, without rebellion or rejection of our parents' values.

---

[2]Michael Rutter, *Changing Youth in a Changing Society* (Cambridge, Mass.: Harvard University Press, 1980), 236–37.

Studies show that most young people even adopt the basic values and outlook of their parents.[3] Youth who have a history of delinquency are most likely to come from homes (whether broken or intact) in which parents show hostility to each other.[4] Youth from homes marked by a degree of parental harmony and concord tend to move through adolescence without great rebellion or unusual stress.

It is fascinating that even in the sixties and early seventies, when the "generation gap" was most widely accepted, scientific research indicated that

> adolescents are surprisingly close to their parents; they tend not to rebel against authority; they often share with parents goals and aspirations for their future role in society. . . . The findings of this study fail to support the notion of an extensive gap between parents and their adolescent children.[5]

A balanced view of youth recognizes and is sensitive to the special stress experienced by young persons. But the stereotype of adolescence as a unique period, a period when young people are somehow "different" from other human beings, must be rejected. If we approach ministry with young people with our vision distorted by stereotypes, we will respond to the false images we have of young persons and not to the young persons themselves. What youth need, as do all human beings, is to be met and accepted and loved as individuals of worth, and not treated as objects—mere members of a class of persons who are felt to be somehow different from the rest of humanity.

Once we are free from the constraint of the stereotype, we can act and respond to young people. Rejecting the stereotype relieves parents of some of their fears. It opens the door to wider participation by other members of their churches in youth ministry. It makes it possible for leaders to consider how young people might be brought into healthy relationships with the older members of the local congregation and be recognized as participating members in the body of Christ. But most impor-

[3] See Hill and Aldus, "Socialization and Parenthood" in D. A. Goslin, ed., *Handbook of Socialization Theory and Research* (Chicago: Rand McNally, 1969), 885–950; also Jennings and Niemi, "Continuity and Change in Political Orientations: A Longitudinal Study of Two Generations," *American Political Science Review* 69 (1975): 1316–75.

[4] See Rutter, *Changing Youth,* 149–50.

[5] See Denise Kandel and Gerald Lesser in M. B. Miles and W. W. Charters, eds., *Learning in Social Settings* (Boston: Allyn and Bacon, 1970), 305.

tant, a balanced perspective permits us to see the youth we work with as individuals, not members of some special class. It helps us realize that in youth ministry, as in every ministry, coming to know and love each young person for himself or herself is an essential concern of the one ministering.

A VIEW OF ADOLESCENCE

So far I have simply argued that the stereotypes we most commonly have of adolescents are faulty. Rather than seeing this time of life as somehow "different" and relating to young people as different, we need to see adolescence as a natural part of the developmental process. Although there are distinctive things about young people that we must know and will look at in future chapters, we must be aware that youth are *not* unique. Freed from stereotypes, we can approach ministry with youth as an exciting opportunity to build relationships with persons who are living through a special time of life in which our friendship can be vitally important.

There have been a number of ways of looking at adolescence as a special—but not unique and stormy—time of life. Most ways have tried to focus on what is happening to young people during this period. Researchers have looked at the special challenge of adolescence and attempted to describe them. Having some awareness of these challenges is helpful for us as we minister with youth, not because these are always true of every young person, but because they do describe issues you and I need to be sensitive to as we try to understand and help individuals.

Robert Havighurst has taken the approach of identifying tasks a young person must master to move successfully into adulthood. A young person's success or failure in the future seems to him to hinge on the following:

1. Accepting one's physique and using the body effectively
2. Preparing for marriage and family life
3. Achieving new and more mature relations with age-mates of both sexes
4. Achieving a masculine or feminine social role
5. Achieving emotional independence from parents and other adults

6. Desiring and achieving socially responsible behavior
7. Preparing for an economically fruitful career
8. Acquiring a set of values and an ethical system as a guide to behavior—developing an ideology.[6]

The following is a more extensive model of psychosocial maturity. It gives a careful description of the ideal goals toward which adolescents move.[7] This model, developed by Greenberger and Sorensen, focuses attention on the product of ideal growth. Its categories point up various issues that are critical concerns for anyone working with youth.

1. **Individual adequacy**
   - Self-reliance
     - Absence of excessive need for social validation
     - Sense of control
     - Initiative
   - Identity
     - Consideration of life goals
     - Self-esteem
     - Internalized Values
   - Work orientation
     - Standards of competence
     - Pleasure in work
     - General work skills
2. **Interpersonal adequacy**
   - Communication skills
     - Ability to encode messages
     - Ability to decode messages
     - Empathy
   - Enlightened trust
     - Rational dependence
     - Rejection of simplistic views of human nature
     - Awareness of constraints on trustworthiness
   - Knowledge of major roles
     - Role-appropriate behavior
     - Management of role conflict
3. **Social adequacy**
   - Social commitment
     - Feelings of community
     - Willingness to work for social goals

---

[6] Robert Havighurst, *Developmental Tasks and Education,* 3d ed. (New York: David McKay, 1972), 43–82.

[7] Greenberger and Sorensen, "Toward a Concept of Psychosocial Maturity" in *Journal of Youth and Adolescence* 3 (1974): 342.

Readiness to form alliances
Interest in long-term social goals
Openness to sociopolitical change
General openness to change
Recognition of costs of status quo
Recognition of costs of change
Tolerance of individual and cultural differences
Willingness to interact with people who differ from the norm
Sensitivity to rights of people who differ from the norm
Awareness of costs and benefits of tolerance

Havighurst, with Greenberger and Sorensen, may be taken as representative. Each sees adolescence as a vital period in human development: vital, because adult life is influenced by successful mastery of what must be learned in adolescence. Thus, many accept the notion that adolescence is essentially a time of transition, on multiple levels, from the dependence of childhood to the relative independence of the adult. This view is reflected well in Berzonsky's *Adolescent Development*.[8] Berzonsky conceptualizes adolescence as a time of transition toward what he calls "self-governance." By this he means ability to choose (will, decide) and to carry out decisions responsibly, without undue reliance on others. In other words, the goal of the adolescent period is to develop a *capable* person—or at least one with the foundational skills and attitudes needed to live as a capable person in our world.

CONCLUSIONS

This brief survey of adolescence has been provided for two purposes. First, as we approach youth ministry it is important to question our stereotypes of youth. We need to approach work with young people freed of presuppositions about what we will find so that we can get to know boys and girls as individuals. Second, it is also important to recognize adolescence as an important time of life. The young people we work with face some of the most crucial issues of life. Most will meet the challenges successfully and move on to a healthy adulthood. But even the most competent of our youth need mature Christian friends who can walk alongside them.

---

[8] Michael Berzonsky, *Adolescent Development* (New York: Macmillan, 1981).

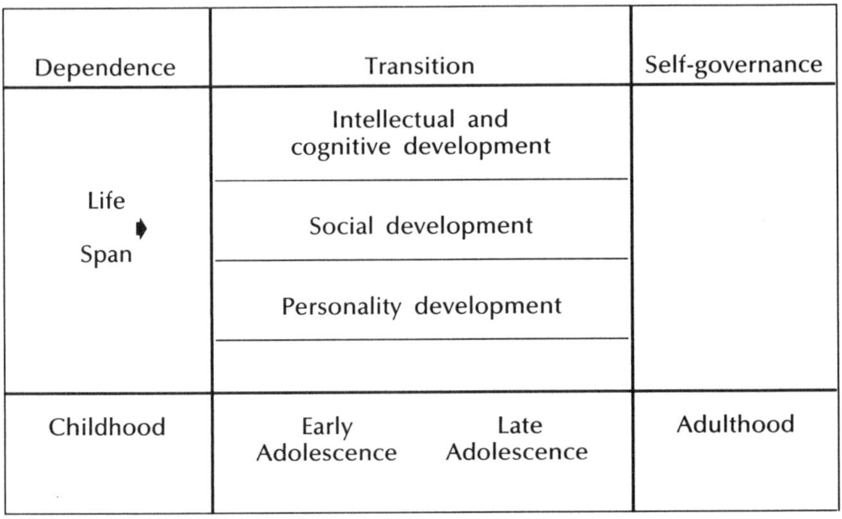

Dependence	Transition		Self-governance
Life ➧ Span	Intellectual and cognitive development		
	Social development		
	Personality development		
Childhood	Early Adolescence	Late Adolescence	Adulthood

Figure 1
Adolescence as a Time of Transition

Certainly your ministry with youth is an important one. You are touching lives during the transition years. And your touch is likely to be used by God to help young people choose—and reach out for—a truly Christian maturity.

PROBE

case histories
discussion questions
thought-provokers

1. Now is a good time to scan current material on adolescence. Why not brainstorm in your classroom or local church youth-ministry team a few of the common notions that people have about adolescence. Then assign different areas to individuals for research. See if you can find data that support or call into question the ideas about youth that you brainstormed.
2. Think about your own adolescence. Was it a time of trauma or a more comfortable time of transition? How would you characterize your relationship with your parents? What strong emotions do you remember? How much of your own experience do you feel you can generalize to other young people?

2

YOUTH CULTURE

In the sixties it was commonly accepted that there was a great gap between the generations. The adolescent world was thought of as a separate culture. Youth were believed to live in isolation from adults in a world marked by its own values and norms. As unrest on the campus disappeared and young people settled down to study and prepare for financial success, conventional wisdom noted a return to older values. Youth culture was thought to have drifted back again into closer harmony with the adult culture with which it coexists. This view of youth culture is understandable. The sixties did see a clash of generations and a challenge by youth of conventional values. But researchers increasingly question the view that there is a separate youth culture.

It is true, of course, that adolescence is an artificial time, the product of Western technological society. For most of human history the onset of puberty launched youth into the adult world. Young women were commonly married in their teens; young men worked in the adult world and when they were able, they took wives. Since puberty arrived later than it does today, there was little "gap" between childhood and days of adult responsibility.

Today, many years stretch between puberty and adult responsibilities. Those years are spent in education, with three times as many young people in colleges in the United States today as twenty years ago. Rutter notes that "adolescence is recognized and treated as a distinct stage of development because the coincidence of extended education and early sexual maturation have meant a prolonged phase of physical maturity associated with economic and psychosocial dependence."[1]

In our high schools and colleges, young people are thrown together in peer colonies, more involved with other youth than with persons in other age groups. It is not surprising that a special vocabulary and various shifting fads in dress, in fun activities, and in music develop in this colony situation, setting young people apart from others in the wider society. But the question remains: Is there a distinct youth culture, with values and norms different from those of the general culture?

SEPARATE VALUES

When we approach the question of whether youth culture has as a distinct and different view of reality from that held by adults in our society, we soon discover that no such separate outlook exists.

What is at issue, of course, is making a distinction between the basic, underlying values of Western culture and those more obvious but superficial ways in which young people's tastes and activities differ from the older generation's. Coleman notes:

> A fundamental distinction has been drawn between the influence of the peer group in such matters as dress and taste in music, and its influence upon antisocial behavior. In particularly it has been pointed out that . . . it is quite erroneous to assume that the adolescent peer group is normally a destructive force in society. We have also noted that the very concept of a "parent-peer issue" involves a false dichotomy, since for most young people the two reference groups reinforce rather than contradict each other. Where choices have to be made, however, the majority of adolescents, contrary to expectations, select parents rather than peers as final arbiters.[2]

Coleman's observations point up the fact that the basic values and norms of our culture infuse both youth and adults, and that where there is a conflict in basic values, the individual young person is most likely to follow the values of mom and dad.

The orientation of youth to adults and adult values is illustrated in many studies. A 1966 study showed that parents

[1] Michael Rutter, *Changing Youth in a Changing Society* (Cambridge, Mass.: Harvard University Press, 1980), 7.

[2] John C. Coleman, *The Nature of Adolescence* (New York: Methuen, 1980), 117.

were "most admired" by fourteen- to sixteen-year-olds. As far as moral or religious or political beliefs were concerned, youth tended to agree with their parents and looked to them for advice.[3] Rutter concludes that

> although young people's leisure activities with their peers increase during adolescence and although their shared activities with parents decrease, nevertheless in the great majority of cases parent-adolescent relationships remain generally harmonious, communication between the generations continues and young people tend both to share their parents' values on the major issues of life and also to turn to them for guidance in most major concerns.[4]

A study of the 1983 college graduating class also showed a close conformity of youth values with the values of the general society. Youth rated work, marriage, family life, strong friendships, and discovering meaning in life as their important goals, along with being financially well off.[5] While it is true that young people have a relaxed and relativistic view of sexual behavior, it is also true that this view of sex is reflected throughout our society and is not exclusive to youth culture.

Congruence between the cultural values of youths and those of adults both reassure and disturb us. We are reassured, for we realize there is no separate "world" of youth. They and we are part of the same world and share the same basic values. But we are disturbed, for American cultural values are not necessarily Christian values. At many points God's Word stands in judgment on our notions of what is important and calls us to build our lives on convictions that bring us into conflict with our culture.

YOUTH CULTURE DISTINCTIVES

While much research documents the harmony between the basic values of youth and adults, it is still true that youth culture does exist and in certain ways is set apart from the world of adults. Developmentally, young people face special challenges that are associated with adolescence, as we noted in chapter 1.

---

[3] Elizabeth Douvan and Joseph Adelson, *The Adolescent Experience* (London: Wiley, 1966), 35.

[4] Rutter, *Changing Youth*, 31.

[5] Reported in Charles M. Shelton, S. J., *Adolescent Spirituality* (Chicago: Loyola University Press, 1983), 6.

Culturally, young people create patterns that are distinctive to the peer group. We see these patterns in taste in music and clothes, in the ever-changing vocabulary of youth, in shifting fads in leisure activity. Most view these cultural creations as ways in which youth attempt to separate themselves from the world of their parents, not in rebellion but as part of the process of learning to function as persons who have grown beyond childlike dependence on adults.

It is important for anyone in youth ministry to understand and be sensitive to these symbolic expressions of separateness. We need not act like youth. But sensitivity to young people's ways will enrich our understanding and open many communication lines. How, then, do we become aware of the meaning of the things young people say and do? How do we understand the implications, well understood by youth, of those special things that set their culture apart from the adult culture?

The basic thing, of course, is to build sharing relationships with young people. As we come to know teens, to spend time with them, we will become more and more attuned to their ways. An accepting, nonjudgmental relationship with guys and gals is the best way to gain an introduction to youth's private world. But there are other things we can do to keep in tune with youth's ever-changing vocabulary, interests, and fads. Here are a few:

1. Meet your teens on neutral ground. Go to school events. Drop in on the current hangouts of young people. Ask questions and listen.

2. Listen to music's top forty. The issues and ideas imbedded in lyrics to popular songs are a vital clue to youth thoughts and concerns. Talking over current hits with teens, to grasp what those songs are saying to them, is a very important way to develop sensitivity.

3. Read the magazines and papers that your teens pore over. This may include good, ever-contemporary Christian magazines like *Campus Life* and *Group,* but will also include the wacky humor magazines popular with junior high students and the more sophisticated secular magazines for high schoolers. And be sure to include school newspapers on the list of required reading.

4. Read material about youth and their culture. Two good sources that will keep you up to date on youth's current concerns are the *Success With Youth Report* (Grafton Publications) and *Youth Letter* (Evangelical Ministries, Inc.).

To work effectively with youth, we need to enter their world and come to know them outside our church buildings and beyond our youth meetings. There is ultimately no other way than to step outside and socialize on their own ground, showing a willingness to listen and a desire to be friends.

CULTURE SHIFT

So far we have looked at two aspects of youth culture. We have suggested that the idea of separate cultural realities is not viable. The basic values of youth and adult are essentially the same. But we have also noted that in certain areas young people do create a superficially distinct culture. In the shifting areas of vocabulary, leisure-time activities, music, dress, etc., young people build what appears to be a separate culture. To communicate well with our youth, we need to be sensitive to and to understand this superficial culture, as well as recognize the basic needs shared by youth and adults as human beings.

But there is a third aspect of culture to which those in youth ministry need to be sensitive. We need sensitivity in this third area, because it affects the settings in which we conduct youth ministry. This area is subtle and shifting. It is an area of cultural fluctuation, in which shifts take place along several continuums. Changes here are more significant and yet more subtle than changes in the superficial or symbolic youth culture just described.

Perhaps the best way to introduce this area of shift and change is to look at four continuums along which culture, usually led by youth culture, may ebb and flow.

1. Orientation

present ______________________________ future

The first continuum calls attention to one's orientation. Are youth today oriented more toward the present or toward the future? The sixties were a time when the present and one's present experiences seemed very significant to young people.

Picking up on this orientation, sociologists dubbed young people then the "now" generation. Associated with this orientation were notions about validity and authority: what one experienced in the present was more important and more real than the distant possible consequences of one's acts. But a shift took place in the postsixties world. The future took on fresh significance. Young people set goals and realized that striving toward them called for a different kind of decision making. A strain of pragmatism emerged: How will what I do now help me achieve what is important to me in the future?

Of course, present and future orientations continue to exist in youth culture and among adults. Leisure-time decisions are often made for their present, experiential value—that is, especially, for fun. But other kinds of decisions are made more seriously, with a hard look at the future and with choices based on what one wants that future to hold.

2. Focus

questions ______________________ answers

Again in the sixties, few youth wanted answers. Rap sessions involved endless talk about issues, but when answers would be introduced, interest waned. The return of practicality saw a shift and an increasing desire for reliable information or ideas that would lead to solving the problems youth face. A series of books I wrote for young people in the mid-sixties (*Youth Asks*) followed the cultural bias—raising questions, developing a style that featured dialogue, and only gradually leading the reader to principles that provide answers. This series had to be revised in the 1980s, to become *Answers for Youth*. Not only was the title changed, but the thought process by which youth were guided to examine biblical principles and make personal choices also had to be revised.

Obviously, the way in which issues or biblical material is introduced to teens in youth meetings will be dramatically affected by whether the cultural focus of a particular generation has shifted toward one of the two extremes of this continuum.

3. Style

self-revealing ______________________ nonrevealing

It was impressive, sitting in on a group of a hundred teens, to listen as many opened up in very personal sharing. But that too was twenty years ago! The self-revealing style of youth has shifted, and with it the easy acceptance of others and of differences.

This doesn't mean that young people, like adults, do not need close relationships in which they are free to share feelings and problems with others. But the freedom with which sharing takes place, and the settings for it, do not remain the same.

Sensitivity to what it takes to build a sense of trust and community within a group, which will enable its members to share significantly, is important in youth ministry. Often approaches to ministry that involve different types of meetings for different purposes will work for a time—but suddenly they no longer seem to accomplish their purpose. What may have happened is that a shift occurred along the continuum of relational style, never noticed by youth leaders, but so significant that it alters the response of young people to our encouragements to share.

4. Shape

open groupings ____________________ closed groupings

This continuum is closely related to relational style. As we will see in a later chapter, every high school has subcultures. Membership in subcultures is indicated by clothing, language, attitudes, and activities. At times when youth culture is in an open stage, an individual can move freely from subculture to subculture. All it takes is a change of clothes and adopting the ways of the new group.

At times when youth culture is closed, the situation is very different. Then smaller "belonging groups" develop within subcultures. It is not enough to make a superficial change to win acceptance in the smaller groupings. Instead, a person must have a history of conformity to the subculture's expectations and build relationships with members of a belonging group. The sense of belonging and acceptance as "one of us" isn't a matter of loose "fitting in" with several hundred: it is a matter of close conformity to the expectations of a dozen or so.

The close conformity required during closed periods partly explains the hesitancy of individuals to share. Openness involves the risk of saying or doing something unacceptable to the belonging group and thus of being expelled from the group where a person feels he belongs.

These four continuums are not the only ones along which youth culture shifts. They simply illustrate the more subtle ways in which changes intrude to affect the outlook and patterns of adolescent life without their (and often our) awareness. The changes that the continuums represent are important to those in youth ministry, because the ways in which we go about building a youth ministry are affected by them.

An illustration of the impact of such shifts is seen in the development by one youth-ministry organization of a pattern for reaching teens—a pattern that depended on three different kinds of meetings. The pattern of these meetings had been carefully worked out over two or three years of ministry. Finally, confident that the pattern was valid, the organization printed manuals and thousands of dollars' worth of curricula. But after everything was distributed, *it didn't work*! The structure and activities of the larger group meeting, and even of smaller groups, simply failed to attract and involve teens. What had happened was simple. Youth culture had shifted along several relevant continuums, and what had worked earlier no longer fit the new generation of high schoolers.

The existence of a stable, underlying common culture for youth and adults assures us that the issues of life that we deal with in youth ministry will hardly be strange to us. The existence of superficial and yet symbolic differences between the adult and youth world reminds us that we need to enter youth's world to understand and minister to adolescents. And the existence of subtle, underlying shifts in outlook like those reflected in the four continuums reminds us that we must be constantly involved with youth, constantly sensitive to the often unnoticed shifts that take place in the orientation, focus, style, and shape of their culture.

PROBE

case histories
discussion questions
thought-provokers

1. Read Snyder's book *Young People and Their Culture*[6] (New York: Abingdon, 1969). It accurately describes the youth culture of the sixties. In what ways does youth culture, as expressed in the views

[6]Ross Snyder, *Young People and Their Culture* (New York: Abingdon, 1969).

and behavior of the young people you know, differ from the young people characterized by Snyder?

2. The author has provided four continuums along which he suggests youth culture (and adult culture too, actually) shifts subtly. These are not the only axes along which significant shifts take place. What other continuums might be constructed that show changes that are significant in describing young people and their perspectives, attitudes, or behaviors?

   If you cannot generate continuums in class by brainstorming, read one or two books on young people written from a sociological point of view and see what continuums your reading suggests.

3

CHRISTIAN "EDUCATION" OF YOUTH

In a book on the anthropology of education, John Middleton has a few cogent thoughts on the formal process by which we attempt to teach and train the next generations. He rejects the notion that education is schooling, and instead describes it as the "learning of culture." The really significant educational impact must be concerned with "the inculcation and understanding of cultural symbols, moral values, sanctions, cosmological beliefs. [But] in our society we separate out these parts from 'formal' education. . . .[1]

In our introduction to adolescence so far we have seen that it is a time of significant transition. In adolescence children, dependent on parents, develop the capacity and skills to move ultimately to self-governance. We have also seen that in our society this process takes place without the great jolt or rebellion conceived by those who emphasized a supposed "generation gap." Teens and collegians today, as in the past, share the essential values of their parents. The process of growing up in Western culture does in fact transmit the basic culture.

The transmission of culture is a complex thing. For youth, it involves the interaction of their expanding mental, social, and psychological capacities with the challenges they face in growing up. Here are shaped the beliefs they hold, the values they adopt, the patterns and attitudes they learn from social models. Although the classroom is involved in this process, it is

[1]John Middleton, ed., *From Child to Adult* (Garden City, N.Y.: Natural History Press, 1970), xiii.

only a part and not the whole of the process by which the adult outlook is formed.

The reason it is important for us to see growth through adolescence as socialization into a culture is simply this: *Communication of Christian faith also involves socialization into a culture*. Christians are citizens of Christ's kingdom, called to be disciples whose lives reflect Jesus Himself. Our goal in youth ministry is not to make sure that our young people know what the Bible teaches. Our goal is to help them grow through these vital transition years so that they adopt, and their lives express, distinctive Christian values.

The thing that we learn from research on youth culture, with the conclusion that young people in fact adopt adult culture as their own, is that we too must be concerned with those experiences of young people that shape values and commitment. We must look beyond the church building and the Sunday school classroom to understand more of those processes by which any value system is transmitted if we are to build a youth ministry that can transmit Christian faith and values.

We must begin to think of Christian education as the teaching and learning of Christian faith as culture—not merely as the communication of true information about life and the Bible.

In my writings I cannot break away from the first comments in Scripture on communicating the biblical faith. These comments declare that the communication of faith must be marked by several utterly basic characteristics. First is that the faith be experienced as a life commitment by adult models. Second is the expression of that faith-life in words. Third is communication of that faith-life in both concrete and abstract form, through adult modeling and verbal teaching in the context of shared experience. The biblical faith has always been meant to be communicated as a culture, as a total way of life, in the context of personal relationships and shared experiences. That passage is Deuteronomy 6:5–7:

> You shall love the LORD your God with all your heart, and with all your soul, and with all your might. And these words which I command you this day shall be upon your heart; and you shall teach them diligently to your children, and shall talk of them when you sit in your house, and when you walk by the way, and when you lie down, and when you rise (Deut. 6:5–7 RSV).

Strikingly, this is the way *any* culture is communicated. Persons who understand and are committed to experience life a certain way communicate their understandings to others by expressing their commitment verbally and through their lives, as they live together and share life's experiences.

To communicate as a life a faith that involves a distinctive way of understanding the world and ourselves through God's revelation, we dare not divorce words from experiences nor intellectualize truths that we must feel as whole persons.

Meyer Fortes points out the difference in psychological emphasis between an education that takes place naturally—through the ongoing experiences of life—and a training that takes place in classrooms rather than in "real" situations.

> The training situation demands atomic modes of response; the real situation requires organic modes of response. In constructing a training situation we envisage a skill or observance as an end-product at the perfection of which we aim and therefore we arrange it so as to evoke only motor or perceptual practice. Affective or motivational factors are eliminated or ignored. In the real situation behavior is compounded of affect, interest and motive, as well as perceptual and motor functions. Learning becomes purposive. Every advance in knowledge or skill is pragmatic, directed to achievement of a result then and there, as well as adding to a previous level of adequacy.[2]

Put simply, Fortes is saying that when we learn in the context of life, we learn as whole persons—with our motives and desires shaped in our learning as well as our understanding—but that training (whether in working arithmetic problems or mastering Bible doctrine) has little power to mold motives and, thus, little power to shape personalities.

But it is toward just this goal, the reshaping of personalities into the image of Jesus Christ, that Christian education must be directed! The child of God is not the person who can recite the Word of God for hours on end, but the one who lives the Word, motivated by a deepening love for Jesus Christ. So Paul writes to the young Timothy, "See that they look up to you because you are an example to them in your speech and behavior, in your love and faith and sincerity" (1 Tim. 4:12). So too John reminds us, "Obedience is the test of whether we really live 'in

[2]Meyer Fortes, "Education in Taleland," in *From Child to Adult,* ed. John Middleton (Garden City, N.Y.: Doubleday, 1970), 38.

God' or not. The life of a man who professes to be living in God must bear the stamp of Christ'' (1 John 2:5–6 PHILLIPS).

This, then, is the reason for this book, the conviction that youth ministry must be designed, not on the model of Western classroom "education," but on the model of culture communication, the communication of one life to another. And so too our task, as I will attempt to delineate it in this book, is to see *how* we can build a ministry with youth in the local church—a ministry that can lead a generation to "bear the stamp of Christ."

DESIGN FOR MINISTRY

I have suggested that the classroom model of education, which has been dominant in secular Western culture, is not a helpful model for the church. This is, however, a model on which most of church ministry has been developed. And so we need another model, one that is developed on a broader, culture-communication concept of education. Such a model must provide central roles for the three basic elements of culture communication outlined on page 32—(1) there must be those who model the faith-life, (2) there must be expression of faith-life's understanding in words, and (3) there must be communication of faith-life in "real life" situations.

The diagram on page 39 (Figure 2) shows the process through which these elements are blended into a plan for ministry with youth. And this diagram shows those elements of the youth ministry that I believe must be understood and lived by the youth worker.

Persons — The new model for youth ministry views youth and adults involved together in several processes. But a number of important questions and issues need to be settled before such involvement can take place. For instance, we need to explore what the young people we hope to so involve are like. By this I don't mean so much the marks of youth culture as the distinctive aspects of adolescence as a time of life.

Youth are moving in adolescence through a variety of developmental experiences. For example, they are gaining in intellectual powers, struggling with a growing yet uncertain self-image, reaching out toward emotional independence from parents, and learning new ways of relating to other youth of the same and of the opposite sex. These developmental characteris-

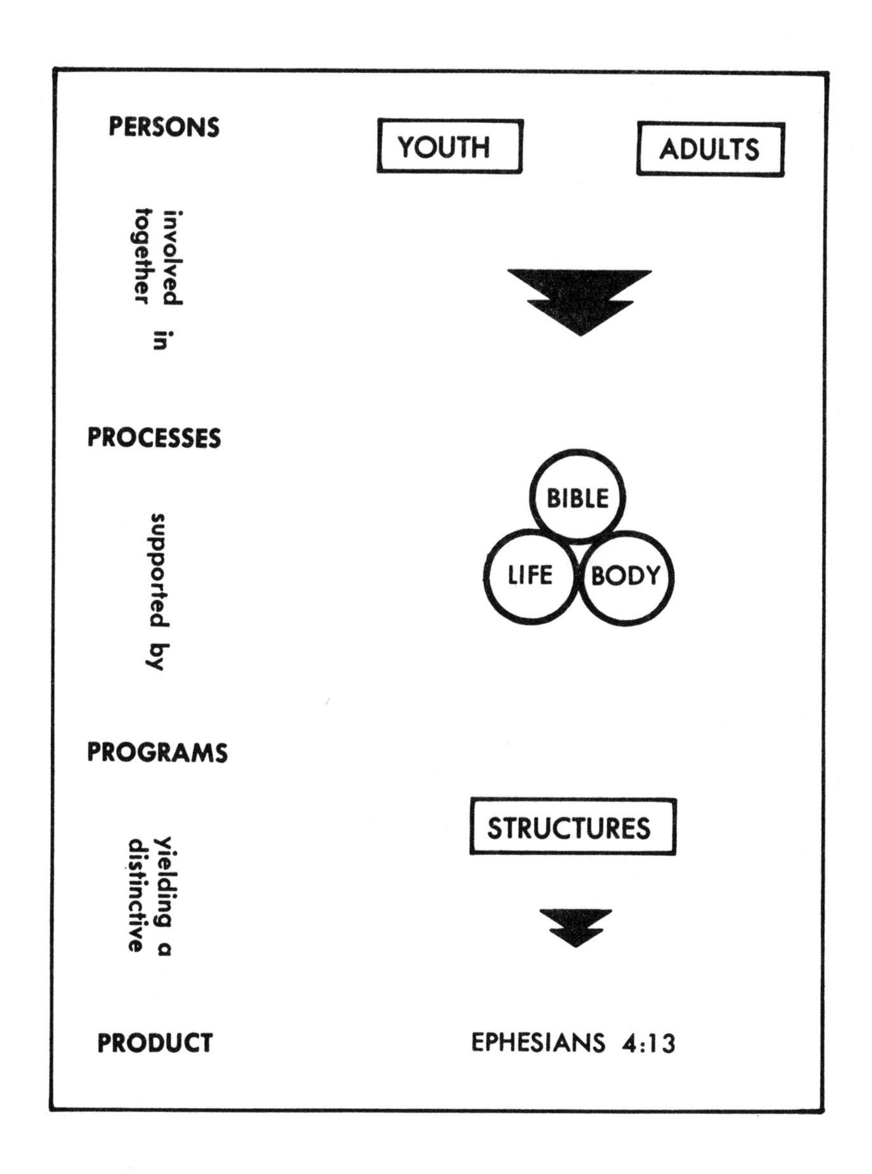

Figure 2
Model for Youth Ministry

tics mark adolescence as a special time of life and significantly distinguish youth from adulthood. The point is simply this: while the basic processes of Christian ministry with persons cuts across the generations, youth cannot be treated in the same way as adults. Young people need to be understood as they are: growing, learning, discovering, suffering—all in their special ways. So when we plan an educational ministry with youth, it is important to take time to understand *them;* individually, of course, but as individuals who share many common "growing up" characteristics.

So, in this book, chapters 4 through 6 examine youth as persons, sketching some of the special aspects of adolescence that one ministering with them needs to keep in mind.

At the same time, however, one who ministers with youth needs to understand his own role as "leader" and the relationships between himself and youth that facilitate ministry. Among the questions that must be answered here are those relating to the nature of the authority that youth recognize and to which they respond, the biblical concept of leadership, relationship with the group and individuals, the counseling relationship, and how to establish and maintain a relationship of mutual respect.

These issues are dealt with in chapters 7 through 9, and a portrait of the leader and his ways of leading is drawn. In the long run, the effectiveness of ministry with youth may depend more on understanding and accepting who youth are, on who the leader is, and on the relationship between them, than on any other factors.

Processes — Three primary concerns for ministry with youth are highlighted in the ministry model. They reflect my conviction that youth and adults must be involved together in Scripture, in building relationships as members of the body of Christ, and in living Christ's life in the world.

The chapters on Scripture (10–11) explore the meaning of the Bible as God's revelation of reality (which believers are invited to experience in Christ) and show how we can communicate the Bible as His fresh, life-pervading Word.

The chapters on body relationships (12–13) explore the biblical concept of the believer as joined with others and committed to others, in Christ's body. They show how the body functions to support the communication of Christian faith as life. The body of Christ, functioning as Scripture reveals, is an utterly essential means the Spirit of God uses to transform and to imprint on human personality the stamp of Christ.

The chapters on life (14–16) explore ways in which commitment to Christ and His way is expressed in the world, both in witness and in service. The Word and the body, when focused together on life, support the development of a distinctive Christian culture, a community of believers who find their citizenship in heaven and who, as ambassadors in a foreign world, live in joyful allegiance to a Lord whose ways are not the ways of the people around them.

Programming — Only when the persons and the processes involved in Christian education of youth are understood can we deal, in chapters 17 and 18, with programming for the local church. Thus, this topic, which typically has become the main concern of many books and most ministries, is reserved for the subordinate role it deserves. And the criterion by which programming for ministry in the church is to be evaluated is a simple one: "Does this support or does it inhibit the involvement of youth and adults in the central processes of ministry?" In these chapters, too, examples and principles for developing programs that will be means, not ends, are given, and the role of such normal features of church life as socials are critically examined.

Product — Finally, in chapter 19 the product of a restructured youth ministry is reviewed, and the whole approach is related to the biblical imperatives that must direct our thinking and give all our ministry its purpose.

CONCLUSIONS

There has been no real attempt in these first three chapters to take an exhaustive look at adolescence or at youth culture. There are dozens of books, filled with reports of research, that do this more than adequately. Instead I have tried simply to survey a few significant points. Adolescence is an important time of life; a time of change and transition. Young people can be met significantly in ministry at this stage of life and helped to make necessary transitions successfully. But adolescence is more than a time of growth and change. It is a time of orientation to culture, of defining what is important in life. Despite various radical views about "youth culture," our society has been successful in transmitting its basic cultural values. But it is the Christian's task to communicate something more than what is important to most Westerners. It is our challenge to communicate Christ's values, so that the emerging adult will face life with a commitment to be one of Jesus' disciples. Michael Warren reflects on this challenge when he observes:

> In some ways I am suggesting that youth ministry is partly about helping youth to pay attention to the right matters and encouraging in them an appropriate skeptical consciousness about the many con artists who seek to deceive them with junk and fakery. It is easy to run trips for youth, to schedule prayer groups, to sponsor socials. Much more difficult is the task of proposing in a compelling way human and Christian ideals by which to direct their energies for a lifetime.[3]

What *Youth Ministry* is about is an exploration of the "compelling way" to teach youth—an exploration of a process that takes account of all the relationships and settings in which we touch young people, as well as those traditional meetings on which we so often rely. Surely you and I can settle for no less a goal than to capture the imagination of young people and to help them direct their energies into a lifetime of Christian living and commitment.

PROBE

case histories
discussion questions
thought-provokers

1. Review the first three chapters and then evaluate the following statements of goals of youth work, taken from several different sources. Which goals are important in your view? Are any goals left out? Is there a better way to express directions for a youth ministry?

GOALS OF YOUTH WORK

1. Get into the Word and prayer
2. Get into Christian service for testimony
3. Relate to the body of Christ (including financial support)
4. Learn leadership
5. Learn how to establish a Christian home
6. Know how to find the will of God
7. Develop social and mental responsibility

---

[3]Michael Warren, *Youth and the Future of the Church* (New York: Seabury, 1982), 7.

8. Prepare for world-wide Christian service
9. Develop creativity
10. Provide activity in cooperation with home and school

Rev. Howard Hendricks[4]

1. Maintain personal relationship with teens
2. Develop respect for God's Word as relevant, contemporary
3. Develop devotional life
4. Encourage worship
5. Enhance self-discovery through moral living
6. Guide in doctrine and understanding of faith
7. Help growth in witnessing
8. Help them put God first in their lives

Rev. Donald Aultman[5]

1. Christian conversion
2. Christian knowledge and conviction
3. Christian living
4. Christian attitudes and appreciations (God, meaning of life, self, others, world)
5. Christian worship
6. Christian service

Rev. Elmer Towns[6]

2. A recent Catholic work on youth ministry—Charles M. Shelton's *Adolescent Spirituality: Pastoral Ministry for High School and College Youth.*[7] —makes a significant contribution. In this work, Fr. Shelton gives the following definition of adolescent spirituality and describes its characteristics. Essentially, spirituality is concerned with personal response to and growth in the Lord (p. 8). If his view were taken seriously, how do you think it would affect youth ministry as carried on in the typical protestant church? Why?

   A spirituality for adolescents is, then, first and above all *Christ centered.* It focuses on the personal, loving invitation given the adolescent to "come, follow me"—to walk the path of Jesus while increasingly realizing what journeying with Jesus really means. . . . A second characteristic of adolescent spirituality is its *relational* aspect. Human relationships also enter the adolescent's experience for

---

[4] Howard G. Hendricks, from class notes, "Christian Education of Youth," Dallas Theological Seminary, 1961.

[5] Donald S. Aultman, *Guiding Youth* (Cleveland, Tenn.: Pathway, 1965), 71–72.

[6] Elmer Towns, *Teaching Teens* (Grand Rapids: Baker, 1965).

[7] Chicago: Loyola University Press, 1983.

spiritual growth, incarnated in human encounters and circumstances. Relationships with family, peers, teachers, and others take on new meanings, as the young person attempts to integrate these others into a growing self-identity. A goal of adolescent spirituality, then, is the examination of these relationships, so that the adolescent's personal experience of Jesus might be realized more fully in family bonds, friendship ties, and relationships with the opposite sex. . . . As a third aspect of his or her spirituality, the adolescent adopts certain values, ideas, and strategies for future living. The adolescent begins to forge a mature identity that is made personally meaningful in the context of his or her current developmental level. Adolescent spirituality speaks to this present life in the context of the adolescent's future growth possibilities. In the adolescent's future plans, career goals, and deepening relationships, a spirituality for adolescents asks how these experiences encourage, in a yet-to-be future, the adolescent's response to Jesus' call (pp. 9–10).

Part Two

PERSONS IN MINISTRY

YOUTH AS PERSONS

ADULTS AS LEADERS

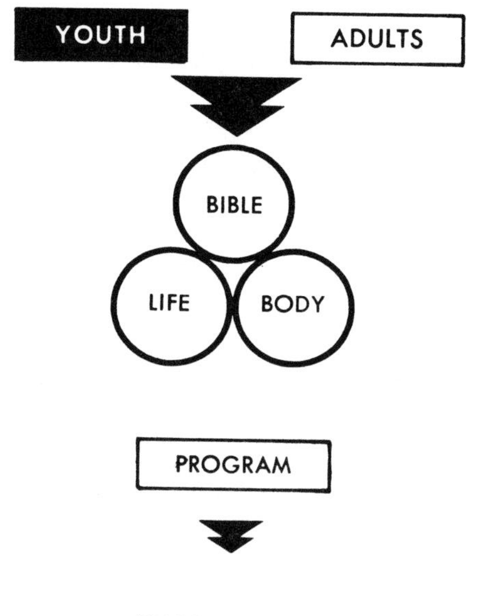

YOUTH AS PERSONS

CHAPTERS

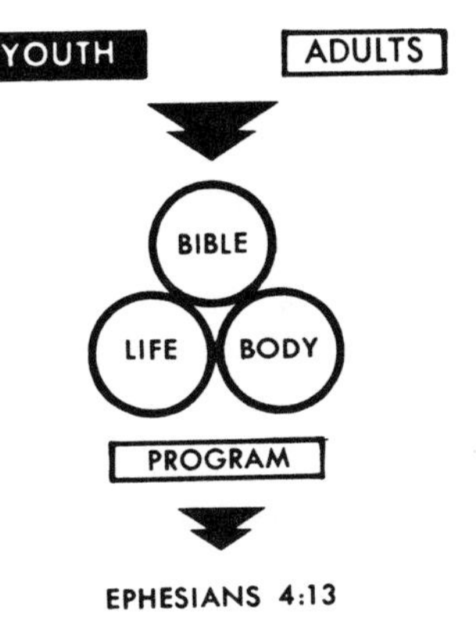

4

THE EMERGING SELF

I no longer know myself as a teenager. I remember some things. I remember a shyness that made me cross the street or look away if I met a girl I knew on the streets of our small town. I remember embarrassment when, all too regularly, a giant pimple would form on the tip of my nose, announcing its coming with hourly reddening until the whole pustule had formed. I remember the clumsiness that frustrated me in sports, for all my six-feet-two. And I remember quiet walks at night, moved by the pattern of warm and cool shadows to reverent wonder at the world, at being.

I remember, but I no longer feel these things. Somehow today I'm a different person, shaped by youth's experiences, of course, but no longer able to enter fully into the frustrations and the joys I knew.

And there's no way back.

All the texts and readings on adolescent development, all the theories of adolescence, all the empirical studies, can never recreate for me a world through which I—and most of you who read these words—have passed.

Yet this is what we need far more than grasp of theory and facility with psychological terms. We need a sympathy that grows from knowing deep within that youth is a special time of life. We need wisdom to see beneath behavior and quickly flying words and to understand, accept, and care about persons who are emerging from childhood, changing shape before us, and becoming adult.

So in these chapters on the young as persons I hope to avoid the clinical and the impersonal, to build a portrait we can feel together rather than produce an academic sketch that may well sharpen insight but all too often treats the teen as an object, stripped of humanness, stretched on a sterile slide for our examination.

To me this approach is important. Whatever else we say of ministry with youth, we must insist that every teen be valued, respected, and in every way related to as fully human, a person we have the privilege in Christ to love.

Framing our thinking about youth as persons around the concept of the "emerging self" has, of course, much precedent. David L. Lehman, summarizing sixty years of study by European and American psychologists, suggests agreement that "the fundamental task of adolescence is 'ego identity' or 'self-definition.'"[1] This, of course, does not mean that youth entering adolescence have no sense of "self." Various writers express their understanding of what happens in young people during the adolescent years in different ways. Together these writers sketch a picture we ought to have in focus before going on to see how this process feels to those going through it.

Friedenberg calls the process self-definition:

> Adolescence is the period during which a young person learns who he is, and what he really feels. It is the time during which he differentiates himself from his culture, though on the culture's terms. It is the age at which, by becoming a person in his own right, he becomes capable of deeply felt relationships to other individuals perceived clearly as such.[2]

Douvan and Adelson express the same understanding in these words:

> Identity does not begin in adolescence. The child has been formulating and reformulating identities throughout his life. . . . At adolescence, however, the *commitment to an identity* becomes critical. During this period, the youngster must synthesize earlier identifications with personal qualities and relate them to social opportunities and the social ideals. Who the child is to be will be influenced (and in some cases determined) by what the environment permits and encourages.[3]

Thus, identity building is not unique to the years of youth, but it is of vital, lifetime importance. Adolescence does not "mark the birth of a 'new self,' but it is true that the achievement of self-identity is not fully realized until the conflicts and problems of the adolescent period have been lived through."[4]

---

[1] David L. Lehman, "Current Thinking in Adolescent Psychology," in *Readings in Adolescent Development,* ed. Harold W. Bernard (Scranton, Pa.: International Textbook, 1969), 73.

[2] Edgar Friedenberg, *The Vanishing Adolescent* (Boston: Beacon, 1964), 9.

[3] Douvan and Adelson, *The Adolescent Experience, 14.*

[4] William C. Bier, *The Adolescent: His Search for Understanding* (New York: Fordham University Press, 1963), 140.

Although it would be wrong to picture the teen years as marked only by storm and stress, it should be clear that coming to terms with who one is and who one wants to be is hardly conducive to great calm and stability, particularly when all sorts of concerns exert pressures on the emerging personality. James Adams lists various types of problems that are felt by high school students as "the biggest personal problems which may be causing you some difficulty."[5] Grouped into fourteen categories of problems (in order of frequency of mention), along with explanatory comments as to the types of problems, the various problems that young people reported were these:

1. School—academic difficulties (extremely few negative comments about teachers)
2. Interpersonal problems—getting along with one's peer group and other people
3. Maturity—recognition by both others (mostly parents) and oneself
4. Emotions—lack of understanding of one's emotions, moodiness, fluctuation
5. Work—finding a job, deciding on a vocation
6. Sports and recreation—athletics, dancing, driving, use of leisure time
7. Health—skin blemishes, weight problems, mental and physical health of self and family
8. Ethical and moral problems—in dating behavior, religion
9. Family—parents, siblings
10. Habits—smoking, drinking
11. Finances—personal financial needs, family, college
12. Unclassifiable problems
13. No answer
14. No problem—often stated apologetically

---

[5]James F. Adams, ed., *Understanding Adolescence: Current Development in Adolescent Psychology* (New York: Allyn & Bacon, 1968), 5–7.

Strikingly, many of these are directly related to the question of the emerging self. What are my limits and abilities academically? Can I see myself as more advanced than others? Or a failure? Who am I in my relationships with others? Popular? A leader? Recognized as valuable and worthwhile? Am I ready now to take responsibility for myself? Or do mom and dad still see me as a child? Why do I feel so uncertain, so moody? Am I really an unstable person? Can I make up my own mind? Can I make my own way?

During adolescence, young people emerging into adulthood have to ask these questions and give at least tentative answers.

Whether the process is viewed as a reorganization of one's hierarchy of values[6] or as the achievement of self-identity, it is clear that this time is one of extreme importance to young persons and to Christian education. For if the years of youth truly are years of transition, of forming the person and personality, then these are crucial years for introducing youth to the fullness of life in Christ—crucial years to help teens discover who they are and can become in Him.

Those ministering with youth, then, desperately need to understand what is happening in the guys and gals they serve, not only in order to sympathize with them and feel with them as they know pressures we only dimly remember, but also to recognize the role Christian ministry can have in guiding youth to define themselves as Christ's persons, to help them crystallize, as their own, values and attitudes and personalities that bear His distinctive stamp.

THAT GUY IN THE MIRROR

It is striking how much impact a youth's physical characteristics and appearance have on his self-image. In fact, the first adolescent feelings for the self are probably rooted here. One writer notes that "it would appear from autobiographical material (submitted by both high school and college-age youth) that the adolescent not only is acutely aware of every physical variation from his concept of what is normal or beautiful or handsome, but that this is perhaps his most frequent frustration."[7]

---

[6]See a discussion of this theory of Spranger by K. Bruno Beller, "Theories of Adolescent Development," in *Understanding Adolescence,* ed. James F. Adams.

[7]D. Gottlieb and C. Ramsey, *The American Adolescent* (Homewood, Ill.: Dors, 1964), 113.

This shouldn't surprise us. Physical growth doesn't strike all youth with measured regularity. Jack may spurt up in height far beyond his age-mates at such a fast rate that his coordination and physical integration lag behind. Looking almost collegiate, he suffers burning embarrassment because of his clumsiness as he tries futilely to catch a football or execute a play. Ken, on the other hand, lags far behind; as a high school sophomore he is mistaken for a sixth-grader and retreats into quietness, hoping only to remain unseen in a society where delayed puberty makes him feel a helpless misfit. Growth comes unevenly to fellows and to girls during early and middle adolescence, and this alone leaves a definite mark on a teen's perception of who he is—a mark that often refuses to fade away. Thus, psychologist Harold W. Bernard points out that of ten early adolescents (ages twelve to fourteen) of low strength, six will show shyness and later adjustment problems.[8] So too, "the boy who is accelerated in physical development is socially advantaged in the peer culture; in adulthood the same success pattern continues: he is poised, responsible, achieving in conformity with society's expectations.[9] Also girls who develop faster tend to have greater prestige among their peers and, thus, generally greater self-confidence and assurance.[10] One's body gives early and powerful impressions of the self.

Physical deviation of any sort can cause anxiety and uncertainty and have a negative impact on youths' feelings about themselves. How prevalent this is is shown by the fact that of a number of adolescent girls (who characteristically enter puberty earlier and develop more rapidly than boys), over half have felt intensely that they were "too tall," while over half the boys of the same age group have been concerned that they are too short! Both are troubled by blackheads and pimples, and many girls become convinced that they are disfigured with a nose too large or some other feature that makes them homely.

The rapid, uneven growth of early adolescence creates many wide variances within the age group that, to teens suddenly sensitive about their bodies, seem to be terrible deviations from others and from the peer group's ideal of strong, athletic males and attractive, well-developed girls.

---

[8] Harold W. Bernard, *Psychology of Learning and Teaching,* 2d ed. (New York: McGraw, 1965).

[9] Mary Cover Jones, "Psychological Correlates of Somatic Development," in *Readings in Adolescent Development and Behavior,* ed. Hill and Shelton (Englewood Cliffs, N.J.: Prentice-Hall, 1971), 22.

[10] Margaret Siler Faust, "Developmental Maturity as a Determinant in Prestige of Adolescent Girls," in *Readings,* ed. Hill and Shelton, 50.

Of course, this time of wide variation is one that passes. Boys like Jack who spurt up too fast at last recover their coordination; the Kens who lag behind catch up and gain strength. And in time girls take the shape that God intended as they ripen toward womanhood.

Often, by the high school and college years, no sign of the earlier "distortions" that were so intensely felt remain. When we look at older teens, coming to the end of high school years and ready to step into the wider world of college or of a job and marriage, we may see a vibrant health of body and attractiveness that makes it hard for us to believe these youth could be anything but confident and proud. How wrong we often are! For all too often the shame that gripped the growing youth as he looked in his mirror and compared himself with others has been planted deep within. Often a teen does not see himself as you or I see ourselves, but he sees a self still warped by what he once felt himself to be.

This is one reason why we need to be sensitive to the physical makeup of youth. *It matters to them.* It matters intensely, for one of the first pictures of the emerging self is drawn from the way a person sees his body and the way he feels about what he sees. When a young person is ashamed of what he sees, his whole personality, his whole way of responding to life and other people, can be deeply affected.

So we must resist the temptation to look at a young person and relate to him on the basis of what *we* see, confident that the girl we find attractive will see herself that way, or that the young man we see as a leader, quick and intelligent, will have this same image of himself. We need to wait, to discover who each person believes himself to be, and meet him or her there with an invitation to become.

This is a lesson Lorraine, one of my students, learned from Jan, an attractive, busy fifteen-year-old. A "normal American girl," Jan worked hard at school, found summer and holiday jobs, played at tennis and in her school band, and found acceptance with a group of guys and girls at church. But appearances were somehow deceiving, as Lorraine learned in a relationship that grew and lasted over several years. In letters to Lorraine,[11] letters we will be looking at in this and other chapters, Jan showed her friend a personality that no casual

[11] Although the names in the letters have been changed, these are the actual letters written by the girl I have called Jan. The situations described are also actual situations.

observation would reveal—a "self" that did not match what Lorraine and others saw, but which was all too real to Jan.

Take a look at this first letter, reproduced here without comment, and jot down in the margin any words that seem to you to describe how Jan feels about herself.

October 7

Dear Lorraine

I'm sorry I didn't get these pictures and sketches to you sooner. Beth betrayed me, she wouldn't do them. So I decided to try once more and see what I could do. Well, not so hot. I just can't draw people. Lets face it I can't draw. I should of return the pictures sooner so you could decide what to do with them. I'm sorry. . . . You always helped me out on songs that I can't play, and not only that, put spiritual problems. So I figure I could repay you back, but I guess it didn't work out that way.

We won that football game last Saturday against Wilson North. I didn't see anyone from the other side that I thought I might know. Oh, well. . . .

We've to play for Northwestern this Saturday. That's going to be real nice. We have to live about 7:30 a.m. and we won't get home until 6 or 7:30 at night. We get to watch the football game free.

Then on Oct. 12, Columbus Day, the band was invited to attend in the Columbus Day parade. It's going to be televise and the band members get out of School. The other kids has to go to school. What ashame . . .

Don't forget about that staking date, Oct. 23 or 30. . . . So far Hellen, Jenny, Eve, and me, can go.

How's your tennis coming along? My gym teacher wants me to join the tennis team, but my mom says no. . . . I come home every night limping. My leg, that got tangle with the toboggan, gets weak so I can't hardly walk. I don't know whats the matter, it's been almost year now; it should of healed by now. When I'm on the trampoline and then when I get off; it seems like all the muscles in that leg tighten up, it aches. It's ridicules.

I joined the premet club at school again this year. That's about medicle stuff. We get some inventations from hospitals asking if we would like to take a tour of their hospitals and listen to lectures about medicle stuff. Last year we were invited to Hinsdale Hospital, it was real interesting and fun.

Well, I better sign off for now. I'm sorry about those sketches. I'll see you in church.

Love,

Jan

P.S. I hope you can
read my typing. My
fingers were numb.

AGE OF TURMOIL

This is what one writer calls early adolescence, those years when jolting bodily changes are accompanied by surging feelings that youth can hardly understand. Most of adolescence is marked by some inner turmoil, some sense of the grip of feelings and moods that lift to heights and suddenly drop to agonizing depths.

Lorraine was jolted one Sunday afternoon when Jan's emotions broke through her control as several girls were practicing a musical number. Jan burst into tears, then rushed from the church. That night Jan slipped a letter into Lorraine's hands; the letter showed her the turmoil inside—a turmoil that could sweep over Jan for no apparent reason. Here's that letter:

Dear Lorraine

I know this is the cowards way to say I'm sorry. I should tell it to you instead of writing it. But I wasted too much of your time this afternoon. I mean I could tell you after the Lord's supper, but I'd be here all night and all tomorrow.

I know the scene I put on this afternoon wouldn't prove to anyone that I was a Christian. I guess I still have that "old nature" in me. I don't know, I guess I was tired and too edgy (I think that's spelled right). I notice all this week I felt like harpen (I think that's spelled right) everybody—I just didn't feel like myself. I had so much to worry about. I mean my job, if I could do good, so they would keep me after the Christmas holidays, also. But then I have to go and make that charge account wrong—now I figure I would get fired and wouldn't get enough money for my Christians presents. And then keeping my grades up in school, handing in my homework, and also, keeping the title of 1st trombone in band and in school. And even thinking about the war over in Viet Nam, so many young men being killed, and the women and children, also, being killed over there. But my biggest worry is that my friends, some, will boing to the "Lost Eternity"—In seminar they talk about happiness and joyfulness, but they never realize that the Lord is coming soon, and they'd have to face hardness and deceitfulness instead of these lovely times so far. I ask myself, why should I think of other people of why should I think of the war over in Viet Nam, its not here, I'm still alive, I've got enough food to eat, a lot of clothes to wear, and shelter to keep warm and protected. But who else realizes this, who else cares, who else feels the same way I do. Nobody, and if there was, there's very few in this world.

But its really no excuse for this afternoon. All I can say is I'm sorry. But that's not enough, Lorraine, I'm jealous of Jenny. I have been ever since I've known her. I don't know why, she's always been a good friend to me, maybe too good. I don't know. It seems like every time when I like someone a lot she has to like that person a lot, also. And it seems like that person shows more affection and kindness, even love, toward her than me. Jenny can sing, play instruments, and get better grades in school than I do. Well, she deserves every talent she has, because she was willing to earn it. But it seems like I can't always realize this. And all I can say to her is, I'm sorry. So I try to stay away from Jenny and especially when shes around that special person. So I won't cause any commotion.

All I ask from you and Jenny is forgiveness. I'm sorry. If it still is possible. I would like to sing with you and Jenny this coming Sunday. We can still have a trio. You pick the song and I'll try my best to get every note right. I'm *tired* of giving up, I'm tired of putting it off, I know I can do anything and everything just as well as the next person. Please, Lorraine, forgive me.

Now you really know what kind of Christian I am. I *promise* to change and do anything you or anyone else ask of me the best of my knowledge and will power.

Please try to understand me. I don't know. I guess I'm a mixed up little kid. Yes, a kid. That *can't* grow up and realize what I have and what I can do, until I lose it.

I'm sorry. I want to show my life to the whole world as a Christian but I guess I'm going at it the wrong way. You want to know why I was crying Sunday. I was lonely. I didn't think anyone would care about me, I didn't think I deserve to be baptize with Diana, Jimmy, Carrie and Jenny. Because I didn't show my life, my attitude towards God, like they have.

Oh, there's a lot to say, but so hard to express. So hard to understand someone else.

Christmas is coming up. The season to be happy and to show forth love. I'm sorry.

Can we try that trio for next Sunday? Maybe even a quartet, Hellen can help out. I don't care, but *I* want to be in it, this coming Sunday.

Write when you have time.

Jan

PS If I can't get
every note, I'll
keep silent. Please.

To call youth a time of turmoil doesn't mean we must picture every moment as a time of agony, or every action irrational, controlled by feeling. Certainly not. But it does mean that we need to be deeply sensitive to youths' moods, and realize that many behaviors are symptomatic of inner struggles they, like Jan, feel deeply—struggles with forces they do not yet understand. Often youths' moodiness, criticalness, giggles, sulkiness, quarrelsomeness, brashness, daydreaming, argumentativeness—all behaviors that tend to irritate adults—signify not character but special needs.

Many factors can heighten insecurity, such as we see in Jan's letter: lack of harmony between parents, competition for their love, conflict of values between home and school and church, an inability to "keep up" in clothes and activity, major or minor physical difficulties. Insecurity grows with the awful fear that feelings may surge out of control, to cause a quarrel or sudden outburst, followed by agonizing guilt expressed in a pitiful "I'm sorry"—or by an angry feud as fear of oneself forces a bitter defense. In an age of turmoil teens need a constant example—adults who face life with quiet confidence in God and who feel and share their feelings, but who mirror a faith that carries a person beyond himself and his inadequate resources.

Youth need ministers who can live with youth without anxiety, with the ability to accept and love persons who have not yet grown to love or accept themselves.

PROBE

case histories
discussion questions
thought-provokers

1. I noted in this chapter that the physical can have a definite impact on self-image, often a very different impact than another might imagine. This is illustrated in the following conflict situation between Jack and Miss Giles, which I have described in my book *How I Can Be Real*.[12]

   As you read the sketch, note first of all how Miss Giles's image of Jack was formed—and how Jack's own image of himself reflects deeply felt physical inadequacies.

[12]Lawrence O. Richards, *How I Can Be Real*, rev. ed. (Grand Rapids: Zondervan, 1979).

Note also how each person's image of Jack affects behavior. Then after reading, think about the "questions for you" that follow.

Miss Giles was nervous. *If only Jack were more dependable,* she thought, glancing around the room all prepared now for her junior-high youth group's yearly parents' program.

She couldn't help liking Jack, a big, strapping fourteen-year-old. He had a ready grin, a wild sense of humor, an almost puppyish clumsiness. Besides, he was intelligent ("sloppy" his teachers called him, yet they always gave him high grades) and a natural leader.

But Jack was also something else: undependable. Miss Giles noticed it when she took over the youth group in January. Give him a part, and he always seemed to forget. Or he'd get stubborn and refuse to do it. Or he'd start clowning, and get the whole group roaring. Twice he hadn't even bothered to show up. *No wonder I feel a little nervous,* she thought. But then that magazine article had said, "The cure for irresponsibility is responsibility." And Jack had so much potential! So—out on a limb she went and gave Jack the major part for tonight's parents' program. *Oh dear.* She twisted uncomfortably in her chair. *I wonder where Jack is now.*

Jack, on his way to church, was feeling rotten. He hated it, and he hated his folks for making him go, and his thoughts bubbled in anger. Just for a moment, slip into Jack's mind and feel with him.

That stupid Miss Giles. I wish she'd drop dead! . . . Now, why did I think that! I wish I didn't slip into thinking bad things. Why can't I keep from doing things like that?

Really, I can't do anything right. He picks up a stone and throws it at a telephone pole. *Missed! I knew I would. Some kids are good at sports, but I'm not. I'm clumsy. Can't hit a baseball. Fall over my own feet at football. Can't do anything.*

Stomach is hurting more. With every step toward the church, he feels sicker. *Why didn't I look at my part this week? When that postcard came from Miss Giles to remind me, I tried . But it all looks so hard. And even if I did learn it, I'd just make a big fool of myself.*

Why do I always have to blurt out some stupid thing when I get in front of the kids? Then they all laugh at me, and I feel so stupid. And then I just can't seem to stop. I grin and laugh and act stupid and silly. . . .

There's the church.

How can Miss Giles do such an awful thing to me? She must know I can't do the part. She must hate me a lot. I can tell from the way she's been acting lately. She gets real sarcastic when I say anything in planning group on Tuesdays.

She must know I can't do the part. She's about as nasty as they come. It'll serve her right if I make a fool of myself and spoil her silly old program. It'll serve her right if I don't even stand up—not in front of all those people. And she'd better not try to make me!

QUESTIONS FOR YOU

a. How much of your expectations of the teens you minister with is based on your impression of their physical appearance?

b. How can you tell if you see each teen as he sees himself?

c. What clues might you expect in an individual's behavior to his view of himself?

d. Can you think of any individuals who have puzzled you, whose behaviors and attitudes might reflect a poor self-image?

e. How important for an effective youth ministry is getting to know teens so well that they share with you the same kind of things that Jan shared with Lorraine?

2. Youth need to work toward emotional stability. The following were suggested by one of my graduate classes as guidelines for promoting stability. What is your reaction to them? How would you change them? Or, more important, how might you implement them in your ministry?

   a. Set a good example of consistency.

   b. Help each youth build confidence by accepting him and giving him a sense of security. Be liberal in praise, sparing in criticism, and avoid all ridicule. Create an atmosphere of security, love, and valuing of each individual.

   c. Give each a standard to live by. Every youth is working toward a philosophy of life—something to give life meaning and make it worth living. Show your teens that the Christian life centers in Jesus Christ. It is His life in us, not an imposing and unreasonable set of "don'ts."

   d. Impress each teen with his personal importance to God, and demonstrate his importance to you. Each teen needs to know that someone cares about him as a person. He needs to realize that you, and God through you, value him as a unique, one-of-a-kind person.

3. Even in ministries where the atmosphere facilitates the growth of emotional stability, outbursts will occur. One such is reported in the following experience of another of my students, who handled it creatively and well.

Read her report, and see what principles of dealing with emotional outbreaks you can draw from her description of the situation.

The place is a church during Sunday evening youth group. Tom, a fairly large boy for his age (fourteen), and Bill, small for his age (also fourteen), often have spiffs. As I walked in this evening, Tom and Bill were at it as usual and Tom looked quite angry.

"OK, fellas! Break it up!"

"But Miss Lind! Tom. . . ."

"What's the problem?"

Bill was always the first to say something and I thought that Tom was just a big bully.

"I'd like to see you after the meeting, Tom, . . . and you, too, Bill."

Later, in the pastor's office, alone with Tom: "Tom, what was the real problem tonight when you and Bill were cuffing one another?"

"Aw . . . he's a fink."

"Why? What does he do that makes him a fink?"

After talking awhile, I ferreted out that Bill was the source of the problem. Unbeknownst to me, Bill had goaded Tom for a long time, teasing him constantly about being a big bully and calling him a fumbling moose. Tonight he had cruelly told Tom that his dad was dumb—that even though he had grown up, he hadn't grown out of his awkwardness—and Tom would be a social misfit, too.

When I learned about that, Tom and I talked about why Bill would say this (because he was so small), and then we talked about patience and how Tom might avoid Bill's attacks.

Then, after church, I had a chance to discuss the outburst with Bill. He told me that Tom was so big and always bullying him. I asked specifically what had been said, and he said he couldn't remember. From there I started talking with Bill about school and his activities. He told me all about it, relieved that I had left off talking about the fight; he told me about the school play he had tried out for, and that another fellow had got the part because he was bigger, even though the teacher had told him that his expression was better.

From there I asked Bill if he would like to direct the play that we were going to put on for the Passion Week services. Eagerly he took it up.

I made it a point to find how to involve Tom in something he felt confident in, too. In his case it was making props for the stage.

4. I noted in this chapter that Lorraine's association with Jan continued over a period of years. The following is her evaluation of Jan and her growth in those years and an account of the ways Lorraine tried to minister to Jan as a person.

AN EMOTIONAL PROBLEM IN A CHURCH CONTEXT

Jan and Jenny were both in my Sunday school class of twelve- and thirteen-year-olds and were very close chums. They sat together, shared a locker at school, confided in each other, played softball, and rode bicycles together. They frequently talked nervously and excitedly about going to high school.

Following graduation from eighth grade both girls entered high school as freshmen. Within two months Jan refused to speak to Jenny. If Jenny joined a group where Jan was present, Jan would promptly separate herself or, ignoring Jenny completely, become very sulky and silent. When Jenny made attempts to reach her in any way, Jan would jerk away. The growing feud between the two made its presence felt in the class and among the young people in general, since one was almost forced to be on one side or the other.

I know both girls quite well and something of their background. Here I will speak for Jan, expressing what I think her feelings were—anger toward Jenny, who suddenly seemed to overshadow her in every way. The result was that Jan felt she had lost status in the group.

"I hate Jenny. She thinks she is so smart and can do anything. She thinks she's better than I am. Just because she gets mostly *A*s in school and I get mostly *C*s. And she plays the piano, flute, and violin and owns her own instruments, while I only play the trombone and have to rent it from school. She takes private lessons, too.

"She has a lot of pretty clothes because her grandmother sews for her. And her clothes always look good on her. I have only a third of the clothes she does and besides, they're old and some don't fit right. My mother doesn't know anything about sewing and I don't have any money to buy new clothes. I tried to get a job at the Tastee Freeze last summer, but they said I wasn't old enough. It just isn't fair.

"Last summer we were good friends; but since we started high school, Jenny is so stuck up! She's always talking so nobody else can get a word in edgewise. She always has her hair fixed nice, too—mine just sticks out all over. I wish I knew how to fix it.

"She's always asking me what the matter is and why I'm so touchy. Why should I have to talk to her if I don't want to? I've got other friends besides her.

"She thinks her family is better too because they live in a nice brick house, and her father works in an office, and her mother visits and plays bridge. My mother works six days a week in a factory and my dad runs a gas station—when he's sober, that is. Our house is little and old and ugly and the street isn't even paved out front—it's full of holes. I'm embarrassed to have anyone else come along when Lorraine drives me home.

"I'll never speak to Jenny again!"

HOW LORRAINE TRIED TO HANDLE THE SITUATION

a. Made efforts to maintain friendship with both—generally felt this was successful.

b. Didn't try to push the two together by force or convincing.

c. Tried to take every opportunity to compliment Jan on changes of her hair style, dress, etc.

d. Encouraged her to talk about current hair and dress styles in school.

e. At times was able to offer specific suggestions, which she experimented with.

f. Suggested she work up a song on her trombone to play for the Sunday school.

g. Spent time accompanying her on the piano as she practiced her trombone.

h. Occasionally wrote her brief letters during the week.

i. Invited her with a friend to the *Messiah* at college last Christmas—they accepted.

j. Tried to find opportunities for her to use her budding drawing skill.

RESULTS APPARENT THIS FALL

a. Jan and Jenny friendly with each other and a larger group.

b. Marked improvement in Jan's grooming.

c. General improvement in social skills.

d. Regular attendance at church twice each Sunday.

e. Active participation in Bible study—attends older girls' club from church.

f. Talks freely of friends and activities at school.

g. Grades in school now mostly *B*s.

h. Relatives gave her a used trombone.

i. She invited me to have Sunday dinner with her and her mother in their home.

j. I don't pretend to have brought about these changes, but I do feel I was able in some measure to be used by the Lord in helping Jan.

Jan was growing through the age of turmoil.
How are the youth you minister with growing?

5

THE SOCIAL SELF

Teenagers move out of early adolescence into a time of relatively steady physical growth. Usually adjustment to and acceptance of their bodies has come, though often, as I noted in chapter 4, real scarring of the self-image may remain. Still, with movement into the high-school years, the focus of youths' growth in personhood shifts to the social and interpersonal.

In shaping youth ministry it is vital to understand the impact of the social environment on the emerging person, to be sensitive to the pressures and needs of youth, and to develop a Christian community in which a distinctive Christian understanding of persons and a distinctive pattern of Christian relationships exist.

The area of personal relationships deserves a whole chapter in this book, not only because this is an area that deeply concerns the young people with whom we minister but also because in and through relationships with others a person's set of values, his very sense of who he is, takes shape.

If we were to put it academically, we might say it as Anderson does: "The psychological self-image is formed early in life as a result of the succession of experiences of the child with significant people in his environment. It is built out of interpersonal experiences for survival."[1] This point of view has been expressed most strongly by Sullivan, who is explained by Jersild:

[1] Camilla M. Anderson, "The Self-Image; a Theory of the Dynamics of Behavior," in *The Self in Growth, Teaching, and Learning,* ed. Don E. Hamachek (Englewood Cliffs, N.J.: Prentice-Hall, 1968), 6.

> The "self-system" has its origins in interpersonal relationships and it is influenced by "reflected appraisals." If a child is accepted, approved, respected, and liked for what he is, he will be helped to acquire an attitude of self-acceptance and respect for himself. But if the significant people in his life—at first his parents and later his teachers, peers, and other persons who wield an influence—belittle him, blame him, and reject him, the growing child's attitudes toward himself are likely to become unfavorable. As he is judged by others, he will tend to judge himself. Further, according to this position, the attitudes concerning himself which he has thus acquired will, in turn, color the attitudes he has toward other persons.[2]

Although this is an *inter*personal process (none of us is merely wax on which others press infallible imprints), it is easy to see why personal relationships are so significant for teenagers. During adolescence teens are struggling toward a fresh, yet lasting understanding of themselves. How others respond is particularly important to youth; often one's sense of worth as a person is tied to the acceptance and approval of others. As "the work of Cooley, Mead, and James makes clear, the individual's self-appraisal is to an important extent derived from reflected appraisals—his interpretations of others' reactions to him."[3]

The importance of others to teens helps explain why so many of the symbols of youth culture that irritate adults, the fads in hair styles, in clothing, in music, are of much concern to the young. To be a part, to be approved of by the group with which most of life is lived, reflects directly on a youth's sense of worth and personhood.

PARENTS AND THE EMERGING SELF

It is obvious that during the earliest, the so-called formative, years of a child's life mom and dad have the greatest influence on the developing personality. Many studies show a relationship between parental attitudes and behaviors and the characteristics of their children. Even though during the adolescent years there is a distinct shift toward the peer group as a reference for many values and decisions, we should not get the

---

[2] Arthur T. Jersild, *Child Psychology*, 5th ed. (Englewood Cliffs, N.J.: Prentice-Hall, 1960), 116–26.

[3] Morris Rosenberg, *Society and the Adolescent Self-Image* (Princeton: Princeton University Press, 1965).

impression that high school and college years are marked by a total rejection of the parental way of life. One recent study by a Chicago psychiatrist leads him to believe that most middle-class American teens grow up with a desire to become part of the suburban culture into which they were born. In a longitudinal study of "average" teens, those not disturbed or suffering economic or emotional deprivation, Dr. Daniel Offer found that "the boys admired their parents and shared and reflected their values; success in school was of utmost importance to them, and more than 90 percent wanted to marry and have families like the ones in which they were raised."[4]

Other studies show a similar impact of the parents on attitudes held by teens toward love,[5] and they show that certain kinds of choices teens make during adolescence persist in being parent-conforming even while other kinds of choices are peer-conforming.[6] An interesting (unpublished) study of college students by Dr. James M. Lower, Professor of Education at Wheaton College, showed that in the sophomore year young people still tended to see themselves as having the same personality traits as the parent (or parents) they designated as an *influential other*. Only later did self-descriptions tend to become less related to the student's perception of their parents and more distinctively their own.

It is not possible here to work toward a definition of the parents' role in helping their teenagers move from dependence and toward a healthy independence (actually an interdependence) that marks maturity. But it is important to note the impact that relationships with parents can have on how young people feel about themselves. This is illustrated by the following experience of one of my former students. She had extremely good relationships with her parents but felt deeply the impact of a particular experience on her sense of worth as a person. Her evaluation of the overall relationship shows a sensitive awareness of the issue we are discussing.

---

[4]Reported in *Science News*, 96 (27 September 1969).

[5]David H. Know, Jr., "Attitudes Toward Love of High School Seniors," *Adolescence*, vol. 5, no. 17 (Spring 1970): 89–98.

[6]Clay V. Brittain, "Adolescent Choices and Parent-Peer Cross-pressures," in *Readings in Adolescent Development and Behavior*, ed. Hill and Shelton (Englewood Cliffs, N.J.: Prentice-Hall, n.d.), 201–9. Brittain concludes that peer-conformity dominates in making choices in areas in which social values are changing rapidly, as opposed to areas in which social values remain relatively stable and in areas where immediate consequences are anticipated in contrast to those where the emphasis is on long-term effects.

Accepting the adult authority of my parents was always one area of development I thought I had under control. Of course, my parents made it easy for me, since most of their rules were reasonable and helped instill in me a sense of right and wrong. The rules were never really spelled out, but were understood nonetheless. My parents never found it necessary to inflict punishment by taking away the car or any other privileges like dating or school activities. They never had to because, quite frankly, I never did anything "bad" and I shared with them everything I did. Actually, I was afraid to do anything bad, not because of the punishment I might receive, but because of what it would do to my parents' image of me.

Some people said I lived a "sheltered life"—they thought I was a "white knight." Such comments never really bothered me because I didn't want to be the way everyone else was—so self-concerned, boy-crazy, manipulated, insecure, and unstable. Perhaps my "sheltered" life and high standards kept me from doing a lot of things with the crowd, but they were things I would have felt out of place doing.

Then came an experience that I will never forget. It has made things a little different ever since. During my junior year in high school I became interested in dramatics. Kenyon College, a men's school nearby, always relied on "home talent" for its female roles. They needed a May Queen: just a young girl to look pretty and say two lines. I tried out and was given the part. Being in a college play was just what I needed at the time. I loved dramatics and felt much more at home in the college-age group. My parents sensed that I was more mature than most of my peers and were glad that I had the chance to develop my interest. However, for the first time they spelled out a rule: "You can be in college plays, but you can't date college men." Their rule never pleased me. I was excited about Kenyon men as *people* with so many different personalities and goals. They made me feel like a queen on stage and off. I continued to share my good times with my parents; they knew almost as much about the different boys I met as I did. *And* they knew that I especially liked Rory Rogers.

And so it seemed perfectly natural and right for me to accept Rory's offer to "drop in" for a little while on a fraternity dance one Friday night after rehearsal. Rory said he could take me home, so I told the lady I came with to go on, and then I decided I'd better call my parents and let them know that I'd be home an hour late. In my mind, I wasn't having a date with Rory. I'd never been to a fraternity dance before and considered the evening more of an adventure with a good friend.

I called home.

"Hello, Dad? This is Rhoda. Rehearsal was over early and Rory asked me if I'd like to go over to his fraternity party for about an hour. He has a car, so he'll bring me home. Okay?"

"No! Stay where you are. I'll be right there."

"But, Dad!"

"I said no. Stay where you are. I'll be right there."

Click.

I was numb, completely confused, and so very frustrated and humiliated. As I explained what had happened to Rory, I found myself getting madder and madder at Dad. Why? Why was Dad all of a sudden saying NO? It didn't make sense. I thought they *trusted* me—they had no reason not to!

Rory waited with me until Dad came. I didn't say a word on the way home—I just sat there feeling very much like the defeated foe submitting to his conqueror. I was bitter and spent the whole night and following day in tears up in my room. My room. For the first time they were forcing me to voluntarily ostracize myself up in my room. I just didn't want to ever see either of them again. They had humiliated me in front of Rory, a member of the one peer group I wanted acceptance from. They had as much as said, "We don't trust you. You can't make wise decisions." And worst of all, they had made me feel *immoral*—as if my intentions had been dishonest and sexual!

I was beginning to feel a real communication barrier between my parents and me. I recognized and even *welcomed* their authority over me as long as their demands were understandable and explainable. But just a cold NO?

I never quite overcame that experience. Of course, time took away my humiliation, but it never really gave me back my former self-confidence or sense of self-worth. I know now that it was best that my parents ended my relationship with Rory before it ever had a chance to begin. But the way in which they went about it caused a resentment to grow within me that probably did more harm than dating Rory ever could have caused. Suddenly I felt that if my parents couldn't trust me, why should I continue to trust them? Should I even trust them with my thoughts?

I can look back now on the experience more objectively. I now know that it wasn't me they mistrusted, but

> Rory. How much it would have helped heal my injured self-image to have known that then! My parents' authority over me guided me through adolescence—but such unquestioned obedience on my part has left me a little less sure of myself now and capable of unbearable and quite unnecessary guilt complexes when I do act independently.

HELPING HANDS

One factor that reinforces the importance of age-mates for the high schooler is his need for support in the struggle to understand himself as an individual apart from his family. The Smarts see "one of the basic functions of the crowd" as providing "a group identity which separates adolescent from parent, a 'we' feeling apart from the family. Thus the adolescent strengthens his own sense of identity by being a member of a group that defines his difference from his parents."[7] The same point, that being a member of the peer group is felt by youth as an important hand up toward independence, is made by others. Coleman sees adolescence as a unique transitional period when a boy or girl "is no longer fully in the parental family, but has not yet formed a family of his own, and close ties with friends replace the family ties that are so strong during most of the rest of life. He is moving out of the family he was part of in childhood, not yet within the family he will be part of as an adult."[8]

The sense of not belonging in the adult world (at least not as a person in one's own right) makes it extremely important for the young person to belong in the world of youth. For many teens, belonging and acceptance in the peer world is felt as an intense need. I remember clearly one student explaining how in high school he let his grades drop from As and Bs to Ds because he felt he must conform to his friends to be one of them. That this is not unusual is illustrated by another student, a girl, who shares this story of her conflict:

> In junior high, wow, how I yearned and tried and struggled to be one of the "in crowd." I tended to do anything, say anything, go anywhere, so that I might be accepted and thought highly of. An incident that caused me

[7]R. C. Smart and N. Smart, *Children: Development and Relationships* (New York: Macmillan, 1967).

[8]James S. Coleman, *The Adolescent Society* (New York: Free Press of Glencoe, 1961), 174.

> difficulty related to school. I liked school. I did most of my work and more. Kids in my class were not as academically inclined as I. They liked to goof off and didn't care what their grades were. One of my friends directly tore me down because I didn't do as they did. I remember even physically fighting with her! I went home in tears. What should I do?

The need to belong with one's age-mates is so strong in our culture that when churched teens in one study expressed their values and goals, the goal ranked number one was "Being a person well-liked by everyone."[9] Other social values (such as making a happy marriage and enjoying good times with others) were also high in priority.

The adolescent attempting to "disengage"[10] from dependence on his family is far from being able to stand on his own. Still involved in the process of self-discovery, still dependent on others to confirm and support his emerging perceptions of himself, the teen is driven by deep need to seek identity with the peer group. And in the world of youth, identity with the group is normally gained through conformity.

Bell points out that

> the adolescent often sees himself as deviating from adult society. He often thinks of himself as an individualist. But he is not. There are probably few subcultures more demanding of conformity than that of the adolescent. What he fails to see is that the subgroup deviates from the adult world, but that the value of conformity within the subgroup is extremely strong.[11]

When we understand the need felt by teens for identification with other youth and for social support in their struggles toward maturity, we can see several warnings and directions for Christian education.

A Christian education that seeks to force young people to reject, "for Christ's sake," identification with other teens (as we Evangelicals have been known to do!) puts unknown pressures on the forming personality (and distorts Christianity itself, for our faith calls for a redemptive *involvement* with

---

[9]Merton P. Strommer, *Profiles of Church Youth* (St. Louis: Concordia, 1963), 71–72.

[10]This term is used in an excellent discussion of the family in E. Douvan and J. B. Adelson, *The Adolescent Experience* (New York: Wiley, 1966).

[11]Robert R. Bell. *The Sociology of Education* (Homewood, Ill.: Dorsey, 1962), 108.

others—not withdrawal). And certainly a Christian education of youth which fails to build toward a strong Christian peer group will never achieve maximum impact. Once we realize the vital importance of interpersonal relationships to teens, we will make it a definite emphasis of our ministry to help them build the kind of relationships with each other that will support growth toward Christian maturity and provide that sense of security[12] so important to healthy feelings about oneself. It also goes without saying that if the values of the individual reflect the values of the group to which he belongs, the development of a peer group in which Christian values are expressed and transmitted is one of the most important ministries we can perform for individuals.

In Christian education of youth, helping teens develop the kind of personal relationships with other teens and with parents that facilitate the formulation of Christian personalities is of central concern. Not only can Christ's own values be best transmitted in a context of close personal relationships, but definition of oneself as a maturing Christian person demands just this context. Rather than fighting the natural dependence of teens on age-mates, struggling to break up cliques and other natural groupings, we must recognize these phenomena as evidence of personal needs, and as opportunities for creative ministry.

Yet, while youth need each other in their search for identity, many factors in adolescent relationships hinder rather than facilitate growth. I have just mentioned *conformity* to peer expectations as the unadvertised price of belonging. For many, this means a painful struggle to appear to be something they are not, a struggle to maintain a façade of what they may eventually become. My own research with high school and college-age youth has revealed how terribly hesitant they are to say what they think and feel. Uncertain about how they will be received, fearing the pain of rejection or ridicule, most adolescents cut themselves off from the very support they cluster together to find! Even more significantly, establishing relationships on the basis of one's performance (and this is exactly what conformity involves—the buying of acceptance through expected behavior)

---

[12] Morh and Despres, in *Adolescence: The Stormy Decade* (New York: Random House, 1958), point out that high status in the peer group is not necessarily the key to security, but that security comes with a warm, close friendship. "Individuals who had no status in their peer group, but did have one or two close friends, came through the adolescent years well. Status belonging and friendship belonging are not necessarily the same things" (p. 121).

is completely contrary to the Christian approach to relationships and to the Christian understanding of persons. Although this topic has been discussed in depth in my book *How I Can Fit In* and demands more extensive development than I can give it here, a brief orientation is important because a particular concept of the Christian interpersonal relationships underlies the approach to ministry this book suggests.

SELF-ACCEPTANCE

Scripture portrays one class of people Jesus' ministry of love was unable to win to discipleship. These were the Pharisees, who, the Bible tells us, considered themselves righteous. They conformed to all the outward standards. As Jesus put it, "Alas for you, you hypocritical scribes and Pharisees! You are like whitewashed tombs, which look fine on the outside but inside are full of dead men's bones and all kinds of rottenness. For you appear like good men on the outside—but inside you are a mass of pretense and wickedness" (Matt. 23:27–28). These were men who had made careers of constructing façades, forcing themselves to pretend with each other and the general populace until they were unable to be honest even with themselves. And so we see the Pharisee in the temple thanking God that he was "not like other men—especially that sinner over there"—and going away more alienated from God and from himself than ever. The sinner, seeing himself as he was and realizing his need, cast himself on God's mercy and went away forgiven and restored.

Surprisingly, the first step toward a truly healthy self-image and the kind of self-love that Jesus commanded[13] is to reject, as a measure of worth, all performance (whether outward conformity to divine law and human tradition or conformity to whatever standards one's society and peer group establishes) and to face the surging forces of sin within. For sin mars with pride and selfishness and envy the best that we do and makes us aware of our guilt and shame.

The Bible stridently insists that each of us recognize himself as a sinner and recognize that both God's generous dealings with us and His judgments are meant to lead us to the confession of sin and repentance. Thus, God's way to a healthy

---

[13] This is, of course, implicit in the command "Love your neighbor *as yourself*."

and mature Christian personality requires honest awareness and evaluation of all that is bad within us.

But the Gospel goes far beyond the demand that we recognize ourselves as sinners. It asserts that though we have fallen short of what we ought to be when measured by God's law, God *still loves us*. God asserts that we are valuable as persons—incalculably valuable. And "the proof of God's amazing love is this: that it was *while we were sinners* that Christ died for us" (Rom. 5:8).

Our sense of worth is not to be anchored in performance, but in the gospel's assertion that we are loved and valued by God for ourselves.

When we take this divine point of view, we are freed to love and accept ourselves as God does—and to have this same attitude toward others.

Thus, youth culture's pattern of demanding conformity as the price of acceptance, though utterly human, is tragically unchristian. Young people, like all of us, are to accept and love one another freely, because of Christ's love, valuing and appreciating each other as persons because God asserts each person's infinite value and worth.

Strikingly, the Bible presents this kind of self-acceptance and acceptance of others as the key to growth toward Christian maturity. When all the self's energy is stimulated to maintain the façades behind which shame impels us to hide, we close ourselves off from God and his Spirit. But when Christians, in an atmosphere of mutual love and acceptance, step out from behind the façades, personalities are open to the healing ministry of the Spirit as He works through the prayers and support of others as each seeks to bear his brother's burden. Grasping the fact that, as the Bible says, we *have* peace with God through our Lord Jesus Christ frees us to enter confidently into a new kind of relationship, one of *grace*, and to take our stand here in happy certainty that God has glorious things for us in the future as He remolds us to be more and more like His Son (Rom. 5:1–2).

This theme will be developed further in the chapters on body ministry, but it is important to point out here that a major thrust of youth ministry must be to help teens break out of performance-based, conformity-producing relationship patterns, to help them learn to be and express themselves with others in an atmosphere of acceptance and love. Helping young people accept themselves and others freely, to assert their worth as persons apart from what they do or at the moment are, and to express this conviction of the worth of persons in a community of love and care is utterly basic to meaningful ministry with youth.

PROBE

case histories
discussion questions
thought-provokers
resources

1. Developing a biblical understanding of persons and acceptance-based relationships and experiencing this as self-acceptance and a way of living with others are vital to ministry with youth. You might want to look at my book *How I Can Fit In* (Zondervan, 1979), which addresses youth for this purpose. The book can be used in a variety of group situations as well as for individual reading.

2. I noted in this chapter the importance of the parent in the adolescent's growth toward maturity. Because parents do play a vital role in the development of youth, our ministry with youth definitely needs to include a ministry to parents.

   Look over the following goals. These are goals that might be set for this aspect of ministry with youth. Which seem most important to you? Which are you actually working toward now? How might each be implemented?

GOALS IN WORKING WITH TEENS/PARENTS

1. Education

a. Equip parents for the responsibilities in Christian nurture.

b. Help parents understand adolescence and their own teenager(s).

c. Work toward agreement on a community of standards (hours, participation, etc.).

d. Help parents understand the nature and approach of the church's ministry to teens.

2. Involvement

a. Involve parents in the ministry of the church to teens.

b. Involve teens in the overall ministry and goals of the church.

3. Communication

a. Help parents and teens keep open lines of communication on feeling as well as idea levels.

b. Keep parents informed of church-sponsored activities and the involvement of their teens.

c. Keep communication lines open between church workers, parents, and teens.

3. I have held several parent/teen seminars in which we worked toward several of the above goals, particularly that of helping parents understand adolescence and their own teenager(s) and that of opening the lines of communication between adults and teens.

   I am including an outline of a six-session seminar that has been developed for these purposes. This seminar is best conducted in a retreat setting or on a single weekend at home. While much of the material is given only in outline, it may be helpful as an illustration of the kind of thing you may want to try in your own ministry.

PARENT/TEEN SEMINARS

It is the purpose of these seminars to promote the development of relationships between parents and teens that will support youth in their transition from childhood's dependence to a mature Christian interdependence. Several factors seem important for the existence of such support: (1) an atmosphere and experience of *intelligent* love; (2) an effective guidance role for the parent, as perceived by both parent and teen; (3) an open communication situation, which facilitates honesty and trust.

For the purposes of the seminar, these factors may be defined as:

Intelligent love — a desire for the benefit of the one loved—a desire that issues in behavior that actually is beneficial (rather than harmful).

Guidance role — an awareness by both parents and teens that the directiveness of parental authority has been replaced in most situations by a guidance that extends freedom to make choices within limits set by parents and is extended as the teen exhibits a developing maturity.

Open communication — the sense of freedom within the home that permits all members to express themselves freely to others, assured of acceptance if not agreement, without threat to self. This does not imply that each member of the family must communicate everything to the others: it implies rather an atmosphere of confidence.

The approach of the seminars is to work toward these goals by involving adults and teens in meaningful interaction, not by preaching at or lecturing to them. Although content is introduced in the sessions, it is so introduced as to make more meaningful the interaction between the parents and teens involved.

MECHANICS

Parents/teens come to seminars together.

Before the seminars begin, each family is given a copy of *How I Can Be Real* (Zondervan, 1979) and is asked to read it individually.

Interaction is stimulated in a variety of ways on a variety of levels, with content input used primarily to stimulate interaction and build understanding.

Time: Two-hour sessions are desirable.

Situation: A retreat or weekend setting is best so that there will be attendance by the group members at all sessions.

The leader is expected to "play by ear" in guiding the interaction and discussions that develop.

SESSIONS OUTLINE

Communication

1. Who, me?
2. What, listen?

Intelligent Love

3. White pedal pushers? Never!
4. Here's how I felt about . . . .
5. Product and process.

Guidance

6. Freedom now! (?)

Session 1

To help participants begin to share themselves significantly with each other.

Process

1. Seminar goals (pp. 75–76) are shared with the group. Time is given for questions and expression.

2. Show filmstrip "Members One of Another" and briefly discuss what it is saying. The filmstrip is produced by Christian Education Press, 1505 Race Street, Philadelphia, PA. It is also available at 1720 Chouteau Ave., St. Louis, MO.

3. Give each participant large sheets of paper and crayons and ask him to use the colors and shapes to draw his real "self"—to creatively express his personality as he sees himself.

4. Divide the group into teams of six or eight, mixing adults and teens as evenly as possible but not placing any teens with their own parents. Then ask each group to explore in depth the "self portrait" each has drawn—beginning with each person's explanation of his drawing and continuing discussion until each feels he is beginning to understand the others.

These teams of six or eight should be retained whenever the larger group is asked to break down into working units.

Session 2

To help participants see how their responses to each other can open up or cut off communication.

Process

1. Point out in an introductory statement the need for listening to one another and "hearing" what is said. This session will help participants listen and respond so as to keep communication lines open.
2. Pair an adult with a teen to listen to typical youth statements and practice the following kinds of response.

   Advice-giving
   Reassuring
   Understanding
   Self-revealing

   Discuss the implications of each type (see pp. 121–24).
3. Have a panel of teens discuss which kinds of responses they prefer in various circumstances.
4. Break into family groupings to discuss what kinds of response seem to each member to characterize their lives together, and their daily communication.

Session 3

To help parents and teens distinguish areas in which high schoolers can make good decisions and areas in which both believe parents ought to exercise guidance or control.

1. As participants come in, give each the appropriate one of these two questionnaires to be filled out. (Results should be collated as the session continues.) Leave plenty of space for answers, of course.

FOR PARENTS

a. List those things you do in your relationship with your high schooler because you love him or her.

b. List things about your teen that you particularly appreciate.

c. List things about your teen that particularly bother or upset you.

d. Complete the following sentence:
"I attempt to guide my teen by ______."

FOR TEENS

a. List those things in your relationship with your parents that indicate to you that they really love you.

b. List things about your parents that you particularly appreciate.

c. List things about your parents that particularly bother or upset you.

d. Complete the following sentence:
"My parents could help me most by ______."

2. Introduce the session by stating that although in the last session the group talked about relating to one another, it is important to remember that they are persons in a particular relationship: a parent-teen relationship.

   This session will help define that relationship more clearly and work toward a spelling out of the responsibilities of a parent to a teen, and a teen to parents.

3. Discuss adolescence as a transition from dependency to independence; the teenager's task of becoming a real person in his own right. (You can use material from these chapters, particularly the next, and from the book *How I Can Be Real.*)

4. In the process of working toward maturity, it is vital for parents to know what they can do that will help, and what will hurt. Lead the group to discuss together the following true story:

   "My daughter has always been responsive; I can't understand what's happening!" the distraught mother blurted out.

   Of course, she had been shocked when her sixteen-year-old had come home and announced that she wanted to buy white cord pedal pushers. "They look so . . . hoody!" her mother had protested ("hood" being the then-current term for the socially undesirable kids). The girl had reacted violently. "No, they aren't! My friends all have them. Besides, I know what's hoody at my school."

   Both were hurt and upset at the other's reactions, and neither would give in.

   Ask the group to discuss two questions First, What would intelligent love do in this situation? Second, who really knows what is hoody?

5. Divide into small groups (established at the first session) to discuss how both adults and teens feel about the following ten items that research has shown to be a cause of conflict in the home. Remind them that in the groups they are to treat and listen to each other as equals—no authoritarianism allowed.

PARENT/TEEN CONFLICTS

(showing percentage of boys who checked each item as seriously disturbing their relationship with their mothers)

a.	Won't let me use the car	85.7%
b.	Insists that I eat foods I dislike	82.4%
c.	Scolds if my school marks aren't as high as others'	82.4%
d.	Insists that I tell her what I spend money for	80.0%
e.	Pesters me about table manners	74.8%
f.	Pesters me about personal habits and manners	68.5%
g.	Holds my sister or brother up as example	66.9%
h.	Objects to my riding around in my car at night	65.7%
i.	Won't let me follow the vocation of my interest	64.5%
j.	Complains about neck or fingernails being dirty	55.7%

6. Reassemble for briefing on results of initial questionnaire. Leader comments on any significant results, such as adult/teen difference in perception of what shows love, relationship of "things that bother" to "things parents do to their children because they love them."

Session 4

To help parents and teens better understand the pressures that motivate actions.

1. Session three pointed out conflict areas between parents and teens. Introduce this session by saying something about the need for insights into how teens and parents feel in conflict situations—even where the points at issue are relatively inconsequential.
2. Pass out the sheet "When Teens Talk Back" (information gathered in a survey of Christian teens). Discuss: "What does this suggest about teens' feelings and needs?" Also, give teens in the group the opportunity to say which advice seems most significant to them.

"WHEN TEENS TALK BACK"

Recently I asked a group of several hundred teenagers to complete an open-ended statement. The statement (below) encouraged high schoolers to give advice to parents, expressing anonymously and honestly what they would like to say in person.

Here is the statement, and some of the most common completions.

"I'd like to tell all teenagers' parents to ______"

make sure they remember what they did when they were kids before they pass judgment

don't be overprotective; get to know their teenagers; discuss things concerning the family with teenagers; give their teenager some responsibility in the home.

realize kids are not living in the same day and age they did—really try to understand.

not let their kids do everything they want to.

not be too strict, but to care what their child is doing.

try harder to understand that we are living in another generation than they did. I wish they would practice what they preach.

try to understand their teens. Little by little they should see their teens wanting to become independent, but they should make sure the teens still depend on God.

stop nagging their kids.

talk to their teenagers as they do to adults, and not forget that they are still teenagers.

talk to their kids instead of telling them what to do—don't give kids straight no for an answer when they don't want kids to do something—discuss it with them instead, explain why they don't want them to and let the kids make their own decision. In other words, cut the apron strings.

not be so sheltering but not too lenient.

talk to their teenagers and try to understand their viewpoint, but also explain to them how they feel about the situation.

try to understand their teenagers, help them whenever they need the parents' guidance, and try to always show them love.

try to understand teens' problems and set down adequate standards (rules) that they must obey to avoid misunderstanding.

let the teens make some decisions and mistakes of their own.

love their teenagers and be something they can respect.

3. Suggest that the following skit may give insight into why the teens gave the kind of advice they did—and why parents may at times need that advice! Ask that while watching the skit, the teens listen to see how Karen (K) feels; the adults listen to see how mom (M) feels. In the discussion following, let the members of each group share their insights. But keep the interaction focused on the feelings of each—not on the rightness or wrongness of the actions.

KAREN CONFLICT

M. Karen, I thought you were doing your homework. You certainly don't have your reports ready, do you?

K. Mmm, no. I'll do it in a minute, though. I'm still working on this party.

M. Oh, yes, I meant to tell you. I got a new recipe from Hazel Carrelson. It's for a delicious pineapple and chocolate cake. So I thought we could make that up for the kids. Her family is crazy about it.

K. O mother, I told the kids we'd have pizza. They go for that more than cake.

M. Pizza! Karen, do you realize what pizza for that crowd would cost! Plus all the pop they drink! You'll just have to tell them you changed your mind. We can't afford it.

I'll make up that recipe and it will do just fine. If I know your friends, they'll eat anything.

K. Mother—.

M. You know they'll eat anything.

K. But mother, I want this to be a nice party.

M. Well, we can't afford it, Karen, and that's that.

By the way, I saw Mrs. Dawson at the beauty shop the other day, and I mentioned you were having some kids over and that it might be a good chance for her daughter to get to know some of them. I thought you could call and invite her.

K. Marilyn Dawson! Oh, mother! How could you? You don't know what the kids think of her. I couldn't ask her. The girls would just hate me.

M. Well, what's wrong with her? Mrs. Dawson says none of the girls pay any attention to her.

K. No, but the boys do! You should see the way she throws herself at them. It's sickening!

Mother, I just can't ask her to come. The girls would never forgive me. We can't stand her. She'll wreck the whole party.

M. Well, I told Mrs. Dawson that you'd contact her. She even gave me her phone number. I don't think it would hurt your reputation to ask her to one party. Besides, she's probably a very nice girl. She just needs some friends.

By the way, just who are you asking?

K. Oh—well, if you have to see it—.

M. Roger Darby. Karen, you know what your father and I think of this boy. I don't think he's the kind of boy you should be hanging around with. He's no good influence. And he so often sways the crowd.

K. Mother, please stop interfering. I can take care of myself. Roger's the life of the party.

M. Karen, it's only because we care about you that we feel this way. Your father and I try to do so much for you. I think the least you can do ______.

K. Mother, I'm not a baby anymore. You and Daddy don't understand teenagers. Why can't I plan my own party? Why don't you just leave me alone?

M. Oh, Karen, we're only trying to help you! It seems that you don't even want your own parents around anymore. We love you and want to have a part in your life.

4. When both points of view have been discussed and appreciated through the reports of adults and teens, ask the whole group (adults and teens) to try to identify with Karen's mother's feelings and to give some advice for teens.

   Ask parents to meet together in small groups to develop responses to this statement: "I'd like to advise all teenagers to—." Ask teens to meet to develop responses they believe the adults will give. Come together to compare.

5. Conclude with a Bible study of Ephesians 6:1–4. In view of the seminar studies so far, what seems to them to be involved in "honoring parents" and "not provoking children to wrath"?

Session 5

To help participants understand factors that contribute to growth toward Christian maturity.

1. Have the group discuss together how best to describe the mature Christian person. What is he or she like? Follow this with a brief review of adolescence as a transitional period and a discussion of what the goal of adult/teen relationships should be to aid in this transition.

2. Develop a lecture covering material indicated on the following chart of personality types. This chart comes from Robert J. Havighurst and Hilda Taba, *Adolescent Character and Personality* (New York: Wiley, 1949).

PECK & HAVIGHURST

Factors & Focus
in Character Development

CONFORMER	EXPEDIENT
"consistent authoritarian" makes . . .	"parents support without demanding obedience or love"
+ Regularity, Rules + Trust, approval – Autocratic control – Severe discipline	+ general support – no clear cut right-wrong pattern – laissez fasire
R—ALTRUISTIC	**AMORAL**
"well-integrated, mature, internalized moral principles on which he acts, rather than on 'rules'"	"typically a rejected child"
+ Consistency + Mutual participation + let make decisions + trust & approval + consistent (lenient) discipline	– distrust – inconsistency – rejection – harsh discipline

3. Break into family units for an evaluation of home atmosphere. All participants at this time should, without necessarily agreeing, be able to accept each other's evaluations and feelings. Discuss the presence or absence, strength or weakness, of factors listed on the chart.

4. Have an open question-and-answer time, with the leader answering the questions or reflecting them back to the group for discussion.

Session 6

To help parents and teens define areas within which they sense a need for parental rules and guidance.

1. Read from *How I Can Be Real* the story of Jan (pp. 61–62) and discuss her ambivalent feelings.

   Point out that youth are asking for *complete* freedom and that parents should not feel free to give it. But teens need freedom, and parents need to fulfill their parental responsibilities. The goal this session is to seek a balance and provide guidelines for both adults and teens.

2. Parents and teens divide into separate groups to discuss: "What areas should be controlled by clear rules and standards set by parents?"

   The points of view of each should be shared in the whole group.

3. Break into mixed groups (established at the first session) to attempt to work out guidelines for expectations in each area that either parents or teens have indicated as calling for parental involvement.

4. Conclude with a general discussion of the guidelines worked out in the small groups.

5. Ask each family to discuss the seminar at home and to set goals for their life together according to the insights they gained in the seminar.

6

THE RESPONSIBLE SELF

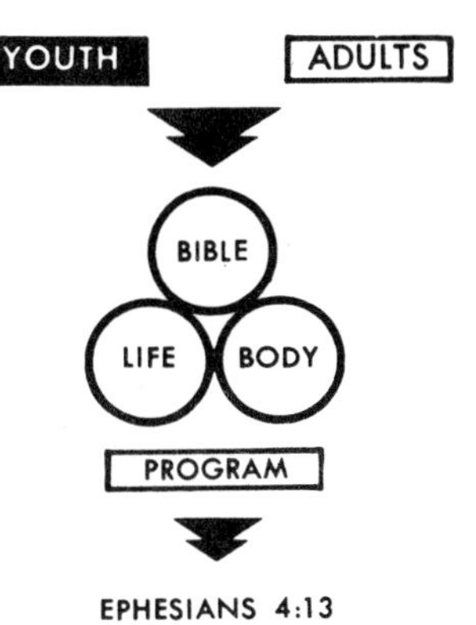

Growth toward maturity is marked in adolescence by the increasing capacity of the young person to function as an adult. Ability to think and understand shifts from childhood patterns to those that mark adulthood. But seldom is a teenager given the opportunity in church or society to develop his capacity into ability. Instead, in most areas of life, adults withhold responsibility from young people. Loukes, in discussing youth's passage to maturity, comments:

> Today we make our children economically dependent long after the age when we can call them "children." Our complex society demands a long period of initiation, when we dare not trust the young with the power of decision. And so the process of initiation becomes a long exclusion from initiative. The young must learn how to do, but they must never do. For us, therefore, the grant of "freedom" becomes a kind of game. We deny the young real responsibility, and try to compensate then by giving them "free time," in which they can "do what they like." But human beings, curiously enough, do not want to "do what they like." They want to exercise responsibility, to make real choices, to engage in real human relations. We deny them real relationships with adults, and insist on their being content with the pupil-teacher relationship. So they respond by making their peer-group relationships which are, in a limited way, "real," with real risks and real choices, and so digging of the ground of human existence.[1]

[1] Harold Loukes, "Passport to Maturity," in Bernard, *Readings,* p. 167.

While there is certainly reason to withhold some kinds of responsibility in a culture as complex as ours, there is little excuse for our practice in the church of withholding from youth the opportunity to live responsibly as Christians. And there is no excuse for our failure to concentrate on helping youth move toward a responsible living of their faith.

There are many ways we withhold—or seek to withhold—the power of decision from youth. One of the clearest examples is often found in classes where the Bible is studied. Look, for instance, at these descriptions of the Sunday school given by Christian teens:

> Week after week, we would go to the class, sit down, and listen to the teacher talk. The teacher would give the lesson, using little variety in the presentation, and without challenging us to think. There was little practical and personal application with which we could identify or practice during the week.
>
> Teacher talked *to* not *with* the class . . . teacher was more interested in giving his ideas than letting students develop their own . . . . Class topics were not relevant to the needs of the class . . . . Students had no interest, and attendance was a problem.
>
> Inevitably, after he had read the Scripture portion, he used this text as a sounding board for all his pet peeves against young people. And he would talk on in this fashion for about forty minutes. There was never any discussion. I do not remember anyone asking a question. Occasionally he would ask us a question, but it was like pulling teeth to get us to answer.

And from a visitor to a youth class:

> When I saw the teacher take out a little book and proceed to read from it, I saw each of the others there simultaneously settle back and tune out. When one of the guys raised his hand to make a comment, the teacher ignored him and droned on. Finally the boy interrupted, made a fairly perceptive statement, and got some interaction going, but this was soon squelched by the teacher who had to make it through the whole lesson before the time was up. I felt cheated.

Although of course it would be wrong to characterize *every* teen class by these descriptions, it is important to note that in none of the classes described (in fact, not in most classes in our churches) are teens treated as *responsible* persons—persons with the ability, and right, to think through issues for themselves.

Yet adolescence marks a definite growth in ability to consider issues; it marks also the development of a special need to do so. Garrison describes both the impact of youth's growing ability to think critically and the consequent generation of doubts in this way:

> Many adolescents, especially those whose early training has been dogmatic in nature, become very skeptical of all problems not concrete and not specific in nature. As the growing, developing youth increases his realm of knowledge and develops better habits of thinking, he is led to question many of the things he had formerly accepted uncritically. The youth coming into contact with more of life's realities assumes more mental and moral independence. He is thrown upon his own initiative and required to make decisions for himself. He comes to learn that many of the things he had been taught earlier and uncritically accepted are not in harmony with facts as presented at school or in his everyday readings. Early faith, so firmly entrenched, thus receives a serious setback when the child learns that the answers to many of his questions are not based upon almost obvious fact.[2]

So doubts come naturally to the adolescent. Sensing their growing ability to think, skeptical and demanding the right to test all things in order to know what is genuine, desiring reasons for their faith and better able to judge the validity of their own and others' reasonings, teenagers need a special kind of guidance—guidance that grants the right to think responsibly about faith and life.

The experience of a former student shows how deeply youth may feel about taking responsibility for their own actions.

> It has been in the church where I have had conflict over accepting adult authority. I don't have trouble accepting someone's authority over me; it's with the authority of the adult rules that I have had the conflicts.
>
> Ever since I can remember, as I was growing up in the church, we have always been told the many "don'ts." When I was in primary and junior high days, I never gave a second thought about them. Now that I am a teenager, I am

[2]Karl C. Garrison, *Psychology of Adolescence* (Englewood Cliffs, N.J.: Prentice-Hall, 1965), 179.

reacting differently. I am thinking about these "don'ts" and making my own convictions about them. I believe it's between you and God to set your guidelines.

When I began to question these many "don'ts," the attitude I got from adults was, "Don't question them, just accept them." Yet I couldn't do this. I wanted to know *why* I had to stay away from these sinful things.

One conflict stands out in my mind. In our Youth Group at home, I was vice president. Our youth director did not care for rock and roll. As a group we had had many discussions on the issue, but he seemed so narrow-minded. He wouldn't realize that there is a wide variety of rock and roll—from folk rock to hard rock. We knew not all the songs were clean, and we felt you should do your own distinguishing in listening.

One Sunday our youth director decided anyone who wanted to hold a top position as leader or committee head had to give up rock and roll. Of course, I was upset. But I prayed about it. In all honesty, I felt nothing was wrong with rock and roll, so I decided to resign rather than be a hypocrite.

Our whole youth group seemed on the verge of breaking up. Our pastor became aware of the situation, and after he talked with our youth director, the restriction was lifted. It took several weeks before our group united once more.

To me, it seems as if the church is putting more emphasis on the "don'ts" of Christianity. I feel they should concentrate on God's love and how He can become real in your life. Once a teenager reaches this plateau, many of his activities may just go.

As I am growing, I am seeking God's will in my life. I am trying to live as I feel He would want me to live. At the same time, I try to understand why adults have set up these "don'ts." Only by realizing why, can I evaluate why I believe differently and see if I may need to make some revisions.

Ministry with youth demands not only that we recognize the young person's capacity to accept such responsibility for his own actions *but also that we actively encourage it*. The Bible exhorts believers to "live life . . . with a due sense of responsibility, not as men who do not know the meaning and purpose of life but as *those who do*" (Eph. 5:15, italics mine). Abdicating responsibility in our life with God, acting uncritically on what others say we need to do to please Him, is completely unscriptural. And ministering with youth in such a way as to encourage such irresponsibility fits neither youth's characteristics nor Scripture's portrait of that maturity into which we want to guide them.

The following letter written to teachers, parents, and sponsors by a man who served as youth department superintendent in a large evangelical church describes something of what is involved in treating youth responsibly. And it describes ways in which adults seek to withhold that responsibility for which teens' growing capacities fit them.

> Dear friends,
>
> *The situation among some young people in our church is serious.* Many of them are dissatisfied. A few have begun attending another church. Others are starting an organization through which they hope to find something they are not getting here.
>
> Those involved are upperclassmen, primarily seniors. They are, as a rule, our *best thinkers and leaders.* They are doing a good job of spreading discontent among *all* our young people.
>
> There are many reasons for today's youth problems, which are by no means limited to our church. But one, which is very relevant to an evangelical church, has to do with the *inability of some parents, teachers, and sponsors to tolerate disagreement on the part of young people.* We often do not give our kids an opportunity, in a climate of acceptance and understanding, to say what they really think and to ask the questions that really trouble them.
>
> It is essential that we grant young people, without reservation, *the right to reach their own conclusions*—even when these conclusions are wrong. No matter how much we want to, *we CANNOT think for our young people,* nor can we compel them to accept our convictions. Only God can do that—and the sooner we accept this fact, the better. All *we* can do is to encourage them and *provide a climate that will be conducive to right conclusions.*
>
> When young people don't accept our views, we must *encourage them to talk about their differences of opinion.* You don't change a person's mind by closing his mouth. If our kids don't talk in our hearing, they'll talk elsewhere—often without the presence of understanding adults who could help them think through to the logical conclusions of their ideas. *By being unwilling to listen, we are driving our kids underground.*

> Our young people need our love. It will not do merely to act as though we love them, while we are annoyed and upset. They are highly allergic to phony love, which includes only those of whom we approve. God can give us a genuine love—and ability to communicate it in words, actions, and attitudes. Our young people need our understanding and our acceptance *as they are*—not as we want them to be.
>
> Otherwise, we'll soon be wondering where our young people have gone.

It would, of course, be wrong to suggest that youth have no need for adults in their reexamination of faith. Judgment comes with experience and involvement in life, which they usually lack. As a result, youths' examination of faith often breaks down at points where all critical thinking may go astray: failure to comprehend the problem, failure to gather enough information to draw meaningful conclusions, and failure to organize information and insights appropriately. In all these processes, adult guidance is often needed. But it must be, as my friend points out, the kind of guidance that treats youth as responsible persons, grants them "the right to reach their own conclusions—even when these conclusions are wrong," and maintains a relationship of genuine love.

COMPETENCE

So far in this chapter we have looked at youths' expanding intellectual powers—their ability to think and question. Growth in ability to function on the "idea level" marks an increasing capacity to function as a whole person, not only to think about issues, but also to express conclusions by living them out in experience. As William Kvaraceus notes in *Dynamics of Delinquency:*

> Too often and too long American youth have been limited in their participation in important and worthwhile adult-like activities by law, by sentiment, and by overzealous adult-planning for youth. As a result, youth are too often relegated to passive participation roles or to the role of recipients of services rendered by adults in such areas as recreation, social and civic activity, religion, and schooling. . . . Locked out of meaningful and worthwhile adult-like tasks and activities, youth will try to fill in this waiting period with some kinds of maturing activities even though

> these may be along disapproved and delinquent routes. The emerging independence-seeking concerns of youth would tend to indicate that high school students are more ready to accept responsibility for adult-like tasks than the grown-ups are ready to provide opportunities for such experience.[3]

Two general approaches to solving problems created by failure to develop competence have been suggested. One is to stop isolating youth from the problems and challenges adults face. Arguing from this approach in the *Journal of Marriage and the Family,* Ethel Venables notes that

> one of the worst aspects of any alienation of young people from the adult world is that they are cut off from discussion of adult problems. To live through these is an essential preliminary to making responsible decisions when these are faced on one's own. . . . Young people must not be "protected" from the troublesome aspects of civilized living—they need to be prepared to face them; and in this writer's experience, they are ready to respond to any overture which welcomes them into the adult community and indicates a genuine desire to hear their opinions.[4]

Certainly a similar approach is open to us in Christian education of youth. We need not protect young people from the challenges of Christian life and ministry to the world. Rather, we need to let them share involvement with and concern for others. We need to let them participate with us in all that being Christ's disciples means. Far too often, the image of "irresponsible" teens (who in one church I served were so characterized because they didn't fulfill assignments to bring potato chips and dip to one of our too-frequent socials!) is one we ourselves have fostered by cutting them off from activities that all but the youngest must view as childish.

What I am suggesting, then, and will develop in later chapters, is that we structure youth ministry to involve our youth in real life, not to *protect* them from it; and that youth be guided toward maturity by helping them accept responsibility for their own growth and activities under a distinctive adult leadership that at all times treats teens as responsible persons.

---

[3]William C. Kvaraceus, *Dynamics of Delinquency* (Columbus, Ohio: Merrill, 1966), p. 237.

[4]Ethel Venables, "Proposed Affinities in British and American Perspectives on Adolescence," *Journal of Marriage and Family* 13 (May 1965), 25.

TOWARD INTERDEPENDENCE

In thinking of the emergence of youth as responsible and disciplined persons, it is important to see adolescence as *the* time of transition—the time when each young person is working toward a new and lasting definition of who he is as a person. When we see our youth in this framework, our ministry goals shift from those that involve external conformity to those that involve character formation. We want young people whose values are distinctively Christian, who live responsibly with others in the church and the world, and who in dependence on God make wise and mature choices.

During the adolescent years, those years of physical, emotional, social, and intellectual transformation, children grow out of their childhood toward the kind of men and women they will become. Since adolescence is the time of the emerging self, the time of becoming, *the way we understand and guide our young people has the greatest of impacts on the kind of Christian persons they become*. Understanding their feelings and needs, the pressures that operate within their personalities and their culture, we can better relate to youth as persons and better provide the distinctive kind of ministry they need.

Perhaps the sharpest impression that I have from my study of and experience with youth is that they need *facilitating relationships*. These include (1) relationships with their parents, marked by openness of communication and willingness to explore one another's feelings and viewpoints without condemning or demanding change; (2) relationships with other adults, marked by the adult's growing respect for the young person as a responsible person, and certainly in the later high school years marked by treatment of teens as fully responsible persons, extending to each the right of decision making and involving each in discipleship; and (3) relationships with other teens in which needs and feelings and perceptions are honestly shared, and in which support, love, and (where needed) forgiveness are extended.

The context of supporting, helping relationships permits a growth toward maturity that is *growth into interdependence*—not independence, for none of us is truly independent. We need others. As Christians we stand in particular need of other believers, who with us form Christ's body. For it is in and through the body that Christ's Spirit works our individual transformation and guides us corporately into the will of Christ, our Head. The mature Christian is an interdependent person, who ministers to others and is ministered to and who, through lifelong involvement in such supportive relationships, increasingly truly reflects and represents his Lord.

But along with facilitating relationships, young people need an honest experience of life. Christian interdependence is not designed to protect the individual from the challenges of life, but to equip him to meet them. The Christian is far better represented by the figure of the soldier than of the sheep, and by terms like "disciple" and "witness" and "servant" than by "child." For the Christian is called to live vigorously in the world that *is*. Equipment for such active involvement for Christ demands the opportunity for the young Christian to develop competence. How foolish to withhold from youth the chance to function as Christ's disciple during the growing years—and then expect on the arrival of a birthday or on graduation from a school some sudden appearance of traits of character we never permitted to develop! If the "self" that develops during adolescence is to be the competent, responsible Christian self we see portrayed in Scripture, then our ministry during the transition years needs to be geared to developing just that competence with which adulthood is to be marked.

PROBE

case histories
discussion questions
thought-provokers
resources

1. Much work has been done on cognitive and, especially, moral reasoning development in childhood and youth. The best-known name in the field is that of Lawrence J. Kohlberg, and an extensive literature has developed around his work. It may be valuable to pause here and explore some of this literature, which can be found in all college and many public libraries.

   While reading, keep in mind the comment of Michael Berzonsky:

   Research reveals that a number of factors may influence or be related to the development and utilization of formal-reasoning strategies: verbal skill, personal characteristics, cultural influences, educational demands, and specific training experiences. It is suggested that a comprehensive theory of adolescent reasoning will have to go beyond an assessment of spontaneously produced reasoning strategies. A comprehensive theory will have to consider also the degree to which a youth can evaluate problems, choose and enjoy appropriate problem-solving strategies, and monitor activities in terms of feedback from ongoing problem-solving.[5]

Also, ask yourself how important such things as moral content (a knowledge of right and wrong), social support, and situational factors are in youths' responsible decision making.

2. In his book on pastoral ministry with youth, *Adolescent Spirituality,* Shelton gives examples of "spirituality direction," a ministry format much in favor in Roman Catholic circles. Included below are two examples of the process, closely associated with youth's movement toward responsible selfhood. Study the pattern used. What are its strengths? Are there parallels in Protestant youth ministry? How closely can the pattern seen here be followed by youth ministers and youth sponsors in local churches?

The Dilemma of Decision Making

Adolescent Behavior — In making decisions about life and relationships, young people sometimes act out of what might be called the fallacy of perfect choice. Because adolescence is a stage of new-found freedom, the adolescent grows to realize that he or she is presented with many choices in life, and when one choice is made, other choices are effectively eliminated. Or, as is often the case in adolescence, when no choice is made—for example, putting off writing a term paper, or applying to a college or dealing with a troubled relationship—a choice is, in effect, often made for the adolescent.

Choosing requires decision making that is clear and insightful. However, inasmuch as adolescents often lack experience and frequently worry over the choices that must be made, making decisions can sometimes be difficult and frustrating for them. Thus, in order to simplify the ambiguity and anxiety that is present in these choices, many adolescents engage in the fallacy of perfect choice. Adolescents (and many adults, too) will sometimes picture one choice as totally good, offering "everything that I am looking for." In making a decision about college, for example, the adolescent might rate one school as *the* school to attend and no other will do. Or, in a relationship, an adolescent might be attempting to either find the *perfect friend* or construct an ideal of how a friend must act. Frustration often develops out of these unmet ideals. The adolescent needs to perceive the limitations inherent in any choice that he or she makes. Additionally, the adult might help the adolescent realize there are other choices which might combine the original choices that the adolescent thought were the only ones available.

---

[5] Michael Berzonsky, *Adolescent Development (New York: Macmillan, 1981), 340.*

Clarifier approach — When the adult confronts circumstances such as those described in this example, the role for the adult is that of "clarifier." The adult aids the adolescent in clarifying the issues and dynamics of everyday life decisions. The adult also helps the adolescent to see beyond the narrowing perceptions that are inherent in the fallacy of perfect choice. A sequence of stages can be used in helping the adolescent to clarify the important elements in various decisions. The adult might use guidelines such as the following:

Information stage — Explore with the adolescent the intent behind and the purposes of selecting this choice. What were the antecedent factors that influenced the adolescent? Reflect on these with the adolescent. It is important for the adolescent to realize that other influences in his or her life might favor one choice over another or might cloud the decision-making process. Do certain past experiences bias the choices that are made? Can the adolescent recognize these influences?

Option stage — What viable alternatives are available to this adolescent? Sometimes it is good to have the adolescent write down his or her various options, listing the advantages and disadvantages of each alternative. Does the adolescent perceive the difference between the various choices that are available?

Consequence stage — Does the adolescent understand the consequences of each stage? Can he or she admit the limitations of the choice he or she is making? In other words, the adolescent needs to realize that no choice is perfect and that there will no doubt be times when the choice that is made is less attractive and/or beneficial than another.

Spiritual direction focus — We can explore with the adolescent various values that exist in making a choice. If the adolescent chooses one college, for example, what are the values that are influencing him or her to attend this school? What do these values say about the adolescent? If the adolescent faces the choice of a job or career decision, what values underlie the choice of this type of work? Especially when adults are directing college undergraduates, time may be profitably spent exploring the values that are involved in deciding on a particular college major. What value does this particular major reflect? What does it say to the adolescent about himself or herself? If the adolescent is unsure about college, work, career, or the like, the adult can present hypothetical situations that invite the adolescent to imagine various choices and their attending values. The adult might wish to suggest that the adolescent examine how a particular Gospel value, such as compassion, peace, or care for the poor, meshes with the choices that are under consideration.[6]

---

[6]Charles M. Shelton, *Adolescent Spirituality: Pastoral Ministry for High School and College Youth,* rev. ed. (Chicago: Loyola University Press, 1983), 184–85.

The Dilemma of Goal Striving

Adolescent behavior — Much of our behavior can be better understood by examining the goals we have developed for ourselves. Our goals often underlie much of our behavior; that is, when we desire something, we strive for it. This very human reaction can lead to problems if we do not fully understand these goals and the effects the goals and our goal-attaining behaviors have on both ourselves and others. It is important for us to keep this goal-striving in mind when we are working with adolescents. The demands of adolescence, including the needs for independence, separation from parents, self-understanding, and one's growing identity often lead the young person to pursue various goals that facilitate development tasks and give potentially stressful situations a sense of stability. In striving for goals, adolescents often engage in a variety of "typical faulty goals." These faulty goals include superiority, popularity, conformity, defiance, sexual promiscuity, inadequacy, charm, beauty and/or strength, sexism, intellectualizing, and religiosity. In one way or another, these goals represent the adolescent's attempt to obtain self-esteem and a sense of relatedness to others.

Goal probing approach — Ask the adolescent what goal is underlying a particular behavior. Then, attempt to identify what goal the adolescent or young adult is seeking to fulfill. When doing this, ask inquiry questions concerning these various behaviors, such as, *Why* are you doing this? It is helpful to summarize past concrete situations and experiences in the adolescent's life that portray these behaviors, and then challenge the adolescent to consider more deeply what is *really* going on when these behaviors are manifested. If a high school adolescent relates various incidents that imply difficulty with parents, for example, present a summary of these experiences based on previous statements or discussions with the adolescent, and then, to explore the adolescent's behavior, raise inquiry questions such as the following: What do you think you were trying to accomplish when that happened? What are you really looking for when this happens? Gather insights from these questions so that you can have some understanding of what is behind the adolescent's behavior. But, always remember that when you are working with the adolescent's mistaken goals, it is important that you do not reinforce goals by praise and encouragement. If an adolescent is overintellectualizing, for example, it is important that you offer alternative ways to behave without overly stressing the intellectual endeavors. Thus, it is important for the adult to reflect with the adolescent on possible alternative behaviors.

Spiritual direction focus — An adult who is ministering to adolescents might want to explore ways in which Christian values might mesh with adolescent goals. Discuss with the adolescent some concrete instances from Scripture, for example, in which Jesus' actions benefited others. Then, suggest that the adolescent reflect on these passages and discover for himself or herself what specific goals Jesus had. Also, pose questions such as, What values or qualities of being a Christian do you find most appealing? Then, ask the adolescent to reflect on his or her own behavior and what steps the adolescent has taken to obtain and demonstrate these qualities in his or her own life. A direct relationship of means to end is then established for the adolescent. In other words, the adolescent must determine to what extent his or her actions, behaviors, and attitudes have really led this adolescent to portray the Christian values he or she admires. The adult can then reflect with the adolescent on acceptable and appropriate behaviors that truly mirror these values.

Another positive behavior technique that can be used is the "best-self-forward" technique. With this technique, the adolescent is asked to imagine his or her "best self." The Christian values that are present in this self are then explicitly explored and discussed with the adolescent. In this discussion, the adolescent is encouraged to both think of his or her own values and explore ways to express these values in his or her life. Incremental behaviors (ways to act, various types of reflection) to achieve Christian values (patience, understanding, charity) can be suggested. Be cautious, however, in suggesting incremental behaviors; do not instill unrealistic goals in the adolescent; encourage the adolescent to set *obtainable* goals.[7]

[7] Ibid., 191-92.

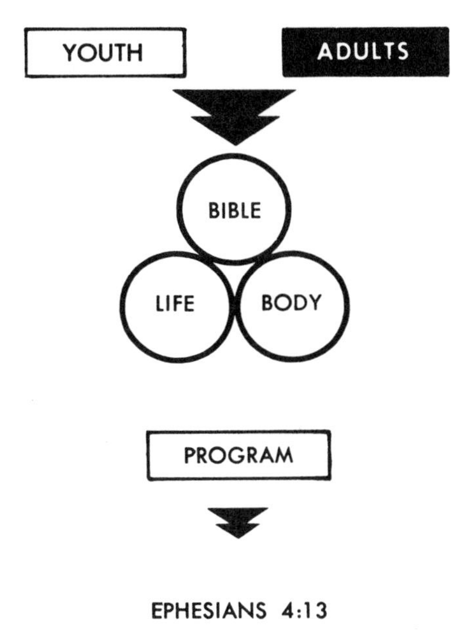

ADULTS AS LEADERS

CHAPTERS

7

BEING A LEADER

Earlier I suggested that we need to think of youth ministry as "the involvement together of youth and adults in three processes that are basic to maturing in the Christian faith." In the preceding three chapters we looked at youth, trying to see them as persons, distinct individuals certainly, but at the same time as individuals who share developmental experiences common to all. In the next three chapters we will consider the adults who minister with youth. We want to see them as leaders—to understand what, according to the Bible, Christian leaders are and how they minister. We want to see them in relationship with youth—to understand the nature and quality of the person-to-person contact leaders must develop to be effective ministers. And we want to look at adults as counselors—an often-misunderstood role, which requires redefinition.

Strikingly, leadership in the church of Jesus Christ differs dramatically from what the world thinks of as leadership. As Christ pointedly reminded His disciples, "You know that the rulers of the heathen lord it over them and that their great ones have absolute power? But it must not be so among you. No, whoever among you wants to be great must become the servant of you all, and if he wants to be first among you he must be your slave—just as the Son of Man has not come to be served but to serve, and to give his life to set many others free" (Matt. 20:25–28). The implication of this active, servant style of leadership has seldom been understood in the church. Rather than become the servant and *do*, church leaders, like secular leaders, have tended to grasp at authority and *tell* others to do. But "it must not be so among you." Christian leadership—and especially leadership with youth—finds its distinctive pattern in the servant.

I noted in the preceding chapter that one of the ways youth feel adults differ from them is in their *competence*—their ability to function effectively.

It is clear that even within youth culture, competence is highly regarded. The athlete is respected for his competence on the sports field; the friendly, well-liked boy or girl is admired for social competence. Because both physical and social skills are highly valued by youth, admiration is shown in imitation. The admired person, the competent person, is imitated.

The role of imitation and the importance of the social model in learning and character development has been stressed in the social sciences. Roger Brown, in discussing the acquisition of morality, points out that "observation of adults" produces much more change in behavior than "direct reward."[1] It is more important to see attitudes and values expressed in life than to be "told" what to do and be rewarded for specific behavior.[2]

This concept is one definitely tied into the Bible's teaching on leadership, not only as implied in the concept of the servant (one who acts and *himself* performs necessary tasks rather than telling others what to do), but also as shown in the example of Christ and Paul and in exhortations to young leaders. We are all familiar with Christ's method of leading: He took His disciples with Him as He taught and healed; He explained His actions and teachings when they were alone together; He sent them out to act as He had, listening to their reports and correcting them; after His resurrection and return to the Father He gave them the responsibility of acting as He had acted in this world.

The apostle Paul also put much stress on living in such close relationship with his converts that they could see the Christian life made concrete and practical in him. He did not hesitate to put himself forward as a model. He told the Corinthians, "In Christ Jesus I am your spiritual father through the gospel; that is why I implore you to follow the footsteps of me your father" (1 Cor. 4:15–16). He exhorted but when he called for a particular attitude marking spiritual maturity, he said, "Let me be your example here, my brothers; let my example be the standard by which you can tell who are the genuine Christians among those about you" (Phil. 3:17). And he called on other converts to imitate him, as he himself imitated Christ (1 Cor. 11:1).

When we understand the need all learners have of a model to imitate, we can grasp the significance of Paul's advice to young ministers: "Keep a critical eye both upon your own life

---

[1] Roger Brown, *Social Psychology* (New York: Free Press, 1965), 387.

[2] See also the discussion by A. Bandura and R. H. Walter in *Social Learning and Personality Development* (New York: Holt, Rinehart & Winston, 1963).

and on the teaching you give" (1 Tim. 4:16). The *life* is mentioned before the teaching! For the reality, the truth of the words of the gospel are to be incarnated in the person—the character, the behavior—of the Christian leader. Thus, something of the meaning of Paul's statement that links words, life, and spiritual power becomes more clear. "The Kingdom of God," he says, "is not a matter of a spate of words but of the power of Christian living" (1 Cor. 4:20). And Christian living, incarnating in the person and behavior of the leader all those realities God's Word calls us to experience, is utterly basic to leadership with youth.

Young people have been shown to overvalue and to idealize adults—to have a much higher opinion of them than is realistic. Particularly liked and appreciated are adults who have some leadership relationship with youth and who are perceived by them as considerate, fair, and reasonably capable.[3] Simply put, young people respond to adults who minister with them, and if they are not turned off by a leader's personality or incompetence, *will* model themselves after him.

To a large extent, the impression young people have of the nature of the Christian life will be gained not from our words but from our example.

Thus, the first criterion for selecting persons to minister with youth is *competence as Christians.* Youth sponsors and leaders must, in fact, model the attitudes, the feelings, the values, the enthusiasm, and the dedication that they seek to develop in youth. The concern for who the leader is overrides any other concern in youth ministry.

The place of the example and the servant nature of leadership in Christian ministry specifies those situations in which adults are to be involved with youth. Too often in the contemporary church youth and adults come together only within church walls, or on occasions where they *talk about* the Christian life—not *live* it. And for this reason we often develop young people who can talk a good faith but have no capacity to express faith through their life in the world. All too often they have not seen adults live their faith in the real world.

So the processes in which youth and adults need to be involved together *must* include "real situations"—situations in which adults serve as models of Christ's love and Christ's

---

[3]Ethel Lawin, *Later Childhood and Adolescence* (New York: Macmillan, 1963), 200ff.

concern for others in those very arenas where the ground of our existence is probed. So, too, no adult who ministers with youth dares to relate to teens only in the formal situation of class or meeting. *He has to go out into the arenas where their lives are lived, to be with them on their "home turf" and there demonstrate the power of Christian living.*

LEADERSHIP AND AUTHORITY

Probably there is little that irritates and concerns adults more about young people these days than youth's apparent rejection of authority. While much of this reflects youth's struggle for independence, other reasons are rooted in their view of authority itself. In the church very often our conflict with young people is caused by our own failure to come to grips with the implications both of Christ's warning about the wrong kind of leadership and of His parallel presentation of the servant as a leadership model.

One thing is sure about a servant: he does not *command* the obedience of those he serves!

Yet there is in Scripture a definite authority invested in leaders. Paul writes to the Thessalonians, "Get to know those who work so hard among you. They are your spiritual leaders to keep you on the right path. Because of this high task of theirs, hold them in highest honor" (1 Thess. 5:12–13). Other passages give insight into the fact that helping others stay on the right path involves a variety of ministries—including rebuking, exhorting, and opposing a person who has strayed, even bringing a believer before the church for the whole group to discipline by withdrawal of fellowship. Scripture gives a distinct impression of vital and aggressive leadership in the church. There is no wishy-washy withdrawal from conflict or from contact when things within the church need to be set straight.

Yet the central place of leaders in the life of the church gives, in itself, no indication of *how* their authority is exercised—of *how* the leader leads and "keeps others on the right path."

We see more of the "how" in Peter's words as an elder to other elders:

> Now may I who am an elder say a word to you my fellow elders? I speak as one who actually saw Christ suffer, and as one who will share with you the glories that

> are to be unfolded to us. I urge you then to see that your "flock of God" is properly fed and cared for. Accept the responsibility of looking after them willingly and not because you feel you can't get out of it, doing your work not for what you can make, but because you are really concerned for their well-being. You should aim not at being "little tin gods" but . . . examples of Christian living in the eyes of the flock committed to your charge (1 Peter 5:1–3).

And to this leader, who acts out of concern for his flock and who serves as an example of all that being a Christian means, believers are to "submit" (see 1 Peter 5:5).

It is important to note that in his word to leaders Peter gives no hint of pulling rank or insisting that others do as leaders say. These things are simply not within the leadership style of the church. Leaders are servants. They do not command or demand. But as servants Christian leaders have the most compelling of all authorities: the authority of example, the imperative of competence.

The confusion that is generated in the church between the generations about leadership and authority isn't really too surprising. The idea of "authority" is a complex one, one capable of encompassing contradictory ideas. But the confusion may be reduced by clarifying different dimensions of authority.

The base of authority — There are several possible bases for the exercise of authority. Among them are open coercive power, the institutional role, and ability.

A person or organization can command obedience and regulate obedience because it has the power to punish those who disobey. We see this in government, which can fine, imprison, or, in the last extremity, execute those who break its laws. Through its coercive powers, governmental authority is *enforced.*

Another base for authority is seen in the institutional role. Here persons are organized together for the accomplishment of some purpose, and to better achieve that goal different functions are assigned to specific offices. We see this in a business, with its president, comptroller, personnel manager, department heads, foremen, etc. Each of these *offices* has certain powers to reward or punish behaviors that aid or inhibit the reaching of organizational goals. A person who is late for work may be docked an hour of pay; a person who fails to perform well may be given low efficiency ratings or fewer raises, or he may be fired. The right of an individual to so reward or punish resides in the office he holds, in the functions that that office is assigned within the organization. The authority resides in the job, not the man.

A third type of authority base is provided by ability. Because others recognize a person as having a special degree of competence, they follow his lead. Sometimes this competence is recognized by giving the person a particular job (in this way organizational and ability bases of authority may coincide). But the response to his leadership and direction is still one that rests essentially on others' recognition of his competence. Some years ago I saw an example of this among youth. A group of teens working in a grocery store disregarded the directions of an adult supervisor in planning and carrying out their work in the stock room. Instead, they followed the informally given suggestions of another teen. He clearly knew more about the operation and had better ideas than the supervisor did. His companions recognized his authority, one of competence, and rejected the organizational authority of the adult.

Authority context — The context in which authority based on open coercive power is exercised is essentially an impersonal one. Laws, rules, and regulations are stated, and the person under authority is to respond *to them*. When laws and rules are broken, power to punish or enforce behavior is exercised, again in an essentially impersonal way.

The context in which authority derived from the organizational roles is exercised is also impersonal. For one thing, a boss doesn't become too friendly with his employees. There may be much more interaction between persons in the organizational context, and loyalty to a good leader may develop. But the leaders still have an overriding concern for the goals of the organization and will, when the need arises, use impersonal sanctions to produce conformity.

The authority that I have described as ability-based, however, exists *only* in the context of relatively close interpersonal relationships. Only when ability and competence are demonstrated and the evidence of competence is maintained through continued contact, will an ability-based authority produce response.

Authority impact — It is interesting to look at the impact of various kinds of authority. Open coercive authority, resting on power and expressed in rules and laws, may be obeyed and even appreciated. But at the same time there is always a tendency to reject and to rebel on the basis of situational and personal variables. For instance, we all generally agree that it is best as well as legally demanded that we stop our cars at a red light. But in every situation? What about at night, when there is no car in sight for miles? What about when we are really rushed—we just *have* to be somewhere? As long as there is a basic trust in the rightness and helpfulness of the laws, there is conformity. But when, as with many youth today, there is a *distrust* of laws and of those who administer them, the kind of authority that rests on open coercive power is more likely to stimulate rebellion than obedience.

The inability of the authority that relies on the organizational role to produce conformity has also been clearly demonstrated in classic sociological studies of bureaucracy. In every office and branch and bureau, people find ways to circumvent directives they do not *want* to obey. The indirect coercive power of the employer is wholly unable to produce the desire for total obedience.

Ability-based authority is distinctively different. *It relies totally on recognition of its validity by others, and it rejects all coercion; thus, ability-based authority produces a conformity that is characterized by an inner desire to respond.*

I think it should be clear by now just what I'm driving at. When Christ presents the servant as the model of Christian leadership, He removes all possibility of direct or indirect coercive power. A servant has no power to enforce. The servant can only *do*. When Paul speaks of the "power of Christian living" and when Peter urges leaders to "be examples of Christian living," both are pointing to the most exciting authority that can ever be exercised: an authority of ability, an authority gained by the quality of one's life as a Christian and freely granted by others who, knowing the leader well, *want* to be like them.

Here, too, the importance of the model is reinforced. Young people will not *want* to grow in Christ only because of what they read about the Christian life or because of what we *say* about Christian experience. Their motivation to grow toward maturity will be created and maintained by what they see of the reality of Christ in us.

Among today's youth there is a distinct decrease in responsiveness to authority based on coercive or organizational powers—a distinct shift toward response to ability-based authority. Young people are searching for models. Young people want to know and grow close to those whom they can respect as competent and real. The adult in the church or society who stands off in the distance and insists that youth obey his rules and his lists of do's and don'ts earns only contempt and produces rebellion. The adult who steps out from behind the protection of rules to demonstrate in living with youth the reality of Jesus Christ, the power of His love, and the excitement of total obedience to Him, finds youth eager to respond to him and to his authority.

One of the primary way functions of church leaders, then, is to provide an example of Christian character and living. Such an example awakens in other believers responsive desire to follow the leaders. The dynamics of this kind of leadership is interpersonal, and it is self-authenticating. It does not rely on any coercive power to cause response; it relies entirely on the working of the Holy Spirit through the power of example in Christian living, including a hardy, self-sacrificing love of others. The servant life is the key to servant leadership.

SELECTING LEADERSHIP

Understanding the nature of spiritual leadership helps us avoid common mistakes in selecting adults to minister with youth. Too often selection is based on verbal skills ("He sure can preach a good sermon," or ". . . lead songs enthusiastically") or on skills in fulfilling organizational roles ("She's a good administrator, knows how to function on a committee, and can really 'get things done'"). The leaders youth need are not primarily talkers or organizers. They are models, persons who by the power of their own Christian example motivate dedication to Jesus Christ. Youth leaders—like all Christian leaders—are to be selected on the basis of Christian growth and character.

Understanding the nature of spiritual leadership also helps us in "organizing" the youth group. Probably the most common approach in youth ministry today is to appoint youth officers, group leaders, or committee heads, and to divide up among them the tasks of planning and carrying out activities of the youth group. I will have more to say about this later under programming (chapters 16 and 17), and will in fact suggest an "organic" concept of organization very unlike the structures the church seems determined to adopt from the business world. But for now it is important to note simply that leadership in youth ministry is *never the exclusive role of the adult.*

Youth have among them peers who are leaders and who function in exactly the same way adult leaders are supposed to function—by serving as models.

In an interesting study of adolescent social structure, Dexter C. Dunphy examines the stages of group development in adolescence (Figure 3, below) and notes the emergence of crowd and clique leaders who do not "boss the others around" but who often rather lead "simply by virtue of superior social skills" and the fact that they "embody personality traits admired in the group."[4] These natural leaders are normally *not* the highly visible, well-liked, "life-of-the-party" persons adults often assume to be the leaders! The true leaders are most easily marked out by being overchosen on sociometric instruments,[5] being advanced in boy-girl relationships, and often by having a number of others designated by their name: "Rod's group," and "Julia's crowd."

Because this crowd leader is often not visible to adults and often will lead in nondirective ways, he may be overlooked when attempts are made to develop "leadership" within the youth group. And because the natural leader's approach to leadership is through modeling and example, he may not be suited for the kind of leadership adults who work with youth often expect! Too often in the church young people are forced into leadership through the organizational role. And as group after group has found, even those capable of providing effective informal leadership by their example may be rejected when they are forced by their "office" to urge, cajole, push, pressure, and command other teens to help keep a youth program going.

The solution for adults is to turn again to the biblical teaching on spiritual leadership. For leaders are not called by God to stand behind a program and push; they are called by God to go before their brothers and *lead.* They move others by example, not by the power of their office.

---

[4]Dexter C. Dunphy, "The Social Structure of Urban Adolescent Groups," *Readings in Adolescent Development and Behavior,* ed. Hill and Shelton (Englewood Cliffs, N.J.: Prentice-Hall, 1971), 214–25.

[5]Sociometry in its simplest form is the pattern of selection by individuals of other individuals when asked such questions as "Who do you like best?" "Who likes you best?" "Who would you choose if you could have only three friends?" The interrelationships between choices made by members of groups has been found to give valuable insights into a number of group dynamics and relationships.

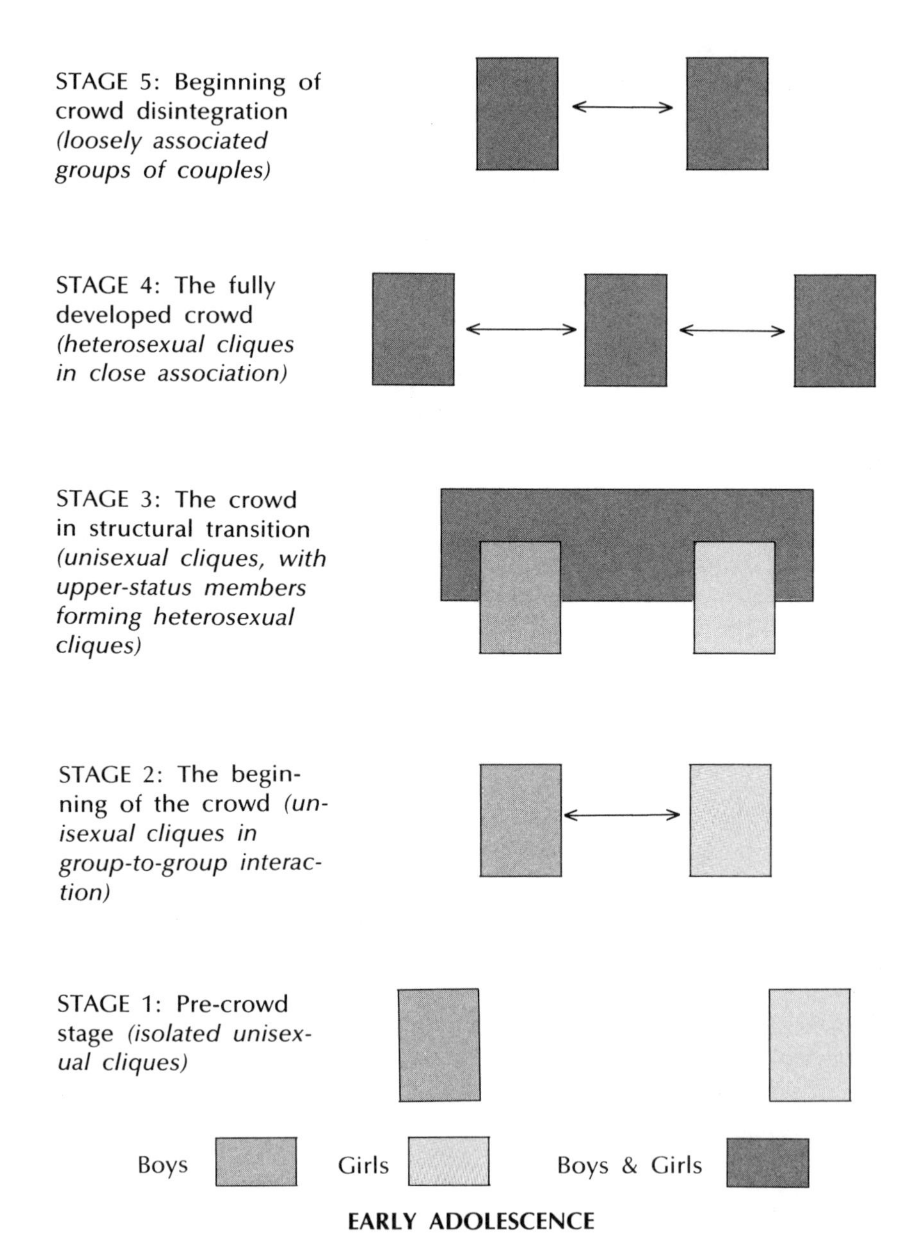

Figure 3
Stages of Group Development in Adolescence

Many working with youth in extrachurch agencies have recognized the significance of locating natural leaders among groups of youth and building personal relationships with them. It is important for those *within* the church to develop ministry on this same principle and to realize that leadership in youth culture is very often far closer to the biblical concept than the church's own approach! While the *how* of organization must be developed later, it is vitally important to realize that the distinctive style of leadership on which adult ministry must be built is the same style of leadership that we must develop among the youth. Far too often our "president" and our "committee chairman" and our "program leader" roles hinder rather than aid in this important task.

PROBE

case histories
discussion questions
thought-provokers
resources

1. If my emphasis in this chapter on the modeling task of leadership and the centrality of example in fulfilling it seems overstated, consider these three passages of Scripture (taken from the translation by J. B. Phillips). How much of what is said deals with who the leaders are, and how much with particular skills or abilities? What does the emphasis you note suggest to you about the leader?

   It is quite true to say that a man who sets his heart on holding office has laudable ambition. Well, for the office of bishop a man must be of blameless reputation, he must be married to one wife only, and be a man of self-control and discretion. He must be a man of disciplined life; he must be hospitable and have the gift of teaching. He must be neither intemperate nor violent, but gentle. He must not be a controversialist nor must he be fond of money-grabbing. He must have proper authority in his own household, and be able to control and command the respect of his children. (For if a man cannot rule in his own household, how can be look after the Church of God?) He must not be a beginner in the faith, for fear of his becoming conceited and sharing the devil's downfall. He should, in addition to the above qualifications, have a good reputation with the outside world, in case his good name is attacked and he is caught by the devil that way.

   Deacons, similarly, should be men of serious outlook and sincere conviction.They too should be temperate and not greedy for money. They should hold the mystery of the faith with complete sincerity (1 Tim. 3:1–9).

[Elders are] to be men of unquestioned integrity with only one wife, and with children brought up as Christians and not likely to be accused of loose living or lawbreaking. To exercise spiritual oversight a man must be of unimpeachable virtue, for he is God's agent in the affairs of his household. He must not be aggressive or hot-tempered or overfond of wine; nor must he be violent or greedy for financial gain. On the contrary, he must be hospitable, a genuine lover of what is good, and a man who is discreet, fair-minded, holy and self-controlled: a man who takes his stand on the orthodox faith, so that he can by sound teaching both stimulate faith and confute opposition (Titus 1:6–9).

Paul's own style of leadership is described in this significant passage:

Our message to you is true, our motives are pure, our conduct is absolutely aboveboard. We speak under the solemn sense of being entrusted by God with the gospel. We do not aim to please men, but to please God who knows us through and through. No one could ever say, as again you know, that we used flattery to conceal greedy motives, and God himself is witness to our honesty. We made no attempt to win honor from men, either from you or from anybody else, though I suppose as Christ's own messengers we might have done so. Our attitude among you was one of tenderness, rather like that of a devoted nurse among her babies. Because we loved you, it was a joy to us to give you not only the gospel of God but our very hearts—so dear did you become to us. Our struggles and hard work, my brothers, must still be fresh in your minds. Day and night we worked so that our preaching of the gospel to you might not cost you a penny. You are witnesses, as is God himself, that our life among you believers was honest, straightforward, and above criticism. You will remember how we dealt with each one of you personally, like a father with his own children, stimulating your faith and courage and giving you instruction. Our only object was to help you to live lives worthy of the God who has called you to share the splendor of his own kingdom (1 Thess. 2:3–12).

2. Leadership by example involves an entirely different approach to ministry than is common in our churches. Chuck Miller is one exciting young youth minister who has just this kind of ministry. His simple description of the role of the leader, a role he has himself fulfilled with great blessing from God, is this:

First, the leader does it *for* the youth.
Next, the leader does it *with* the youth.
Then, the youth do it *with* the leader.
Finally, the youth do it *without* the leader.

What Chuck is expressing is the simple fact that young people need to experience through an adult's ministry to them the reality he is trying to communicate. They need his example to make God's truth and way of life real. Then the young people need to become involved with the leader to see how he ministers to others. After that they need the opportunity to begin to minister as they have seen their leader minister to them and others, with his support expressed through his presence, encouragement, and additional instruction. Through this personally involved example-leadership, young people grow into the ability to minister on their own.

There is a great difference between the leadership tasks and approaches appropriate to example-leadership and those used by program-leadership. Let's suppose there are two leaders, one who adopts the philosophy expressed by Chuck Miller and the other an "old school" leader who organizes programs and studies and people. In general, one *shows,* the other *tells.*

Now, how will each leader attempt to reach each of the following goals? Spell out as clearly as possible the steps each will take, and why.

> *Goal one:* to have our kids really love each other.
> *Goal two:* to have our kids pray for and support each other.
> *Goal three:* to have our kids take an interest in and show love for non-Christian friends.

3. The following are lists of responsibilities of various "youth leadership" offices suggested for youth-group organizational structure by several Christian educators. Look them over and compare the responsibilities of office and the kinds of leadership needed to fulfill them with the responsibilities and leadership behaviors that I have suggested in this chapter as appropriate to Christian leadership.

   What conclusions do you think might be validly drawn from your comparisons?

The *president* of your youth group holds a place of honor, because his election indicates a trust placed in him by the members of the youth group. The president should be a person of integrity and high Christian standards.

The president should be one of the older senior high students who will be looked up to by other members. He should have some leadership ability, though he can learn this as you work with him behind the scenes.

The president should:

1. Preside at all business meetings for the youth group.
2. Serve as ex-officio member of all committees. He should attend as many committee meetings as possible or have each committee chairman report to him at the cabinet meeting.
3. Know the activities of the planning group at all times. Work with the sponsor and the planning-group leaders in making assignments to these groups.

4. Work with the sponsor in steering the entire youth group, implanting enthusiasm and inspiration in the other members.
5. Plan projects for the Training Hour, together with the sponsor, and work out these plans through his planning-group leaders and committee chairpersons.

The *vice-president* works as an assistant to the president. He is responsible for membership and enlistment and may have a committee to work with him, if your group is large enough. The vice-president should be a person who is interested in people and is not afraid to speak to newcomers and visitors.

The vice-president should:

1. Preside at business meetings in the absence of the president.
2. Greet visitors and make them feel at home in the group.
3. Know when members are absent and let them know that they were missed. This may be done by mail or by personal contact.
4. Keep an up-to-date record of all regular and active members of the youth group. Take attendance each week.
5. Work with the sponsor in contacting prospects through phone and home calls.

The *secretary* should be a person who is faithful in attendance and diligent in keeping records.

The secretary should:

1. Take minutes at all official meetings of the officers.
2. Keep accurate records of activities of the youth Training Hour for the church's annual report. This should include records of programs presented by planning groups, names of committee members, missionary activities, projects, socials, and attendance at meetings.
3. Take care of all official correspondence of the youth group, sending for materials and books needed, writing to missionaries, and sending thank-you notes to speakers and others who do special favors for your group, such as parents who help in programs.
4. Order materials and equipment at the direction of the president and planning-group leaders.
5. Keep a yearbook containing snapshots and a history of youth activities.

The *treasurer* should be a person who is vitally interested in stewardship and capable of keeping accurate records of the finances of the youth group.

The treasurer should:

1. Keep an accurate record of all incoming and outgoing money and prepare a monthly report for the youth-officers cabinet.
2. Open a bank account and deposit all money of the youth group in the bank.
3. Pay all authorized bills promptly by check. Bills paid in cash should be receipted.
4. Plan special projects for promotion of stewardship. Keep the group informed of expenses and missionary giving. Remind them of their financial responsibilities.
5. Prepare charts to show amounts given for special projects.[6]

---

[6]Roy B. Zuck and Fern Robertson, *How to Be a Youth Sponsor* (Wheaton, Ill.: Scripture Press, 1960), 19–20.

YOUTH ADULTS

BIBLE
LIFE BODY
PROGRAM

EPHESIANS 4:13

8

DEVELOPING FACILITATING RELATIONSHIPS

Few youth have significant personal relationships with adults who are not their parents.

Yet the nature and quality of personal relationships between youth and the adults who are involved with them in the three processes (in Scripture, in church-body relationship, in life) leading to spiritual maturity are vitally important. The Bible demands, as we saw in the preceding chapter, that the leader be with his "flock" and demonstrate in the real world the power of Christian living. Only here is the imperative authority of example truly communicated. But the nature of the interpersonal relationships in which such leadership is exercised is just as distinctive as the leadership itself.

Perhaps the central element of the context of personal relationships that facilitates growth and ministry is that all enter and maintain the relationship as equals. Adults who minister must minister as persons, both respecting and being respected as individuals. The lack of this attitude toward youth is perhaps the greatest hindrance to effective ministry in our churches.

Understanding which relationships are facilitating, the adult attitudes and behaviors that underlie them, and how they are developed is vital for all of us.

Why does communication between youth and adults so often break down? It is easier to understand this problem when we look at some common conversational response patterns and see their impact on communication.

Before we look at the response patterns, however, we need to sketch the setting in which we are going to see them. That setting is *not* a "counseling" setting where a young person has come to an adult for help. The setting is informal and conversational. It is talk between a young person and an adult that may take place in a living room or while they are leaning against a car in the church parking lot or drinking a coke at the corner hangout. The setting is one in which two people are simply trying to communicate.

In this informal setting we are going to suppose that the teenager makes some self-revealing statement. This itself needs some explanation. One time when I was in Scottsdale, Arizona—where my family and I were summering—I had an exciting time of sharing with a half-dozen kids in a small group; we were examining together some pretty basic thoughts about life. One of the guys had shared his concern about perfectionism, feeling that this was something about which Christ might ask him, "Do you want to be healed?" (cf. John 5:1–9). As a musician, he felt constantly driven to be better but was always falling short. When he and his pastor had sung together in church the week before, their failure to be as good as he felt they should have been made him angry and frustrated. Another teen expressed his sense of need for closer relationships with more kids—the kind of relationship in which he would feel free to say and be what he was. In the group, these young people had honestly and trustingly revealed something of themselves, expecting trust and concern in return. But now, as I was leaning against the car with a boy who had not been in our group, something else was happening. This boy was talking to me in a constant stream of words. He was telling about the scout camps in Arizona he had been to, the way it had rained and the size of the raindrops, a recent float trip down the Salt River, how far they had gone that compared to the distance they had covered the week before at the same time, and so on. And in all this spate of words there was nothing *personal;* nothing that revealed anything of who he was as a person, how he felt, what he valued. Even when I asked simple questions like, "I guess you enjoy your scouting, huh?" he could only nod and hurry on with his description of circumstances.

When at the beginning of the preceding paragraph I said that in the informal setting the teen "makes some self-revealing statement," I was specifying something important. In conversation he says something about *himself.*

How we respond to communication on this personal level is the key to facilitating relationships.

Many of us have learned to talk endlessly about nothing, using words that may be full of sound and even fury but signify nothing. Drawing close to another person, trying to understand and appreciate him or her—this is significant.

We have our setting, then. It is informal (not "counseling"), and in the talking together self-revelation occurs. The young person makes a statement, communicates something that reveals a little about himself. The critical issue now is, *How do adults respond?*

Over the past three years, in dozens of meetings with youth and adults, I have presented four patterns of possible response for analysis. *In every case* the evaluation of the teens has been the same. The four patterns of response[1] that I have suggested the group think of are *advice giving, reassuring, understanding,* and *self-revealing*. To get the feel of the relational impact of each and to clarify the way I'm using these terms, let's suppose that an adult is talking to one of the fellows I just wrote of (we will call him Mark) and hears him say,

> What bothers me is this feeling that everything's got to be perfect. I mean, I can play with my band or sing with the pastor as I did last Sunday, and when it doesn't go just right, I go off, and when somebody says, "What's wrong?" I snap at him. I get mad at myself and other people, too.

The adult might respond to this personal sharing in any of the four ways.

Advice giving — This, according to the teens, is the most common adult response to such personal communication of sharing. An advice-giving response to Mark might go something like this:

> Mark, when you feel that way, you've just got to remind yourself that nobody is perfect. Keep saying, "Nobody's perfect" over and over again and see if that doesn't help.

or

> Mark, the thing you ought to do when you feel down isn't to go off by yourself—it's to get right in there with the others. Chances are they won't have noticed the things you thought were poor in your singing, and they will start telling you how good it was. Try that next time, and just see if I'm not right.

[1]The four keys to response patterns that I am using in this chapter come from Ross Snyder, who has used them in an interesting approach to training youth workers. I have used and tested these concepts with dozens of groups of youth in the way described in this chapter and invariably find the results that are cataloged here.

Both of these responses illustrate an attitude that underlies all advice giving: "I've got the answer. I can help you. Do what I say." The one giving gratuitous advice presents himself as strong and represents the other as weak and inadequate.

Reassuring — Reassurance is quite similar to advice giving. It also implies that the reassurer has greater insight into the problem than the one who is living it. Reassurance seems to imply that the feelings and problems revealed are unimportant, but are best shoved aside as unworthy of concern.

For example, let's look again at Mark's statement and then at a couple of pressuring responses.

> What bothers me is this feeling that everything's got to be perfect. I mean, I can play with my band or sing, as I did with the pastor last Sunday, and when it doesn't go just right, I go off, and when somebody says, "What's wrong?" I snap at him. I get mad at myself and other people, too.

We might try to reassure him in this way:

> Why Mark, you're so much better than anyone else around here! It's wonderful. You don't need to feel bad—you're just great.

Or we might say:

> Don't worry so much about it, Mark. You're young yet. You can't expect to be as good as you're going to be in a few years. So take it easy. With more practice you'll be right up there.

Whatever else the reassuring response implies, it says loud and clear that the thing that bothers *you* isn't very important to *me*.

Understanding — A third kind of response is one that expresses a desire to understand. It is not condescending but questioning. It is one way a person tries to say, "If something is important to you, it is important to me, and I want to understand."

This kind of response is an invitation for further communication. In some ways it is an inadequate invitation, because it invites the other person to come closer while you stand still and wait for him. But it does show concern.

What might an understanding response to Mark be like? We might say:

> You really feel frustrated when you're not as good as you want to be.

Or we might search out his feelings a little more carefully:

> You mean you feel you fall short all the time, or just when you really mess it up?

Again, whatever may be said about this type of response, if it is spoken sincerely, it shows an interest in Mark and a willingness to accept his perception of his problem.

Self-revealing — While the understanding response invites the other person to come nearer, the person who gives a self-revealing response himself takes the first step closer. What Mark has said reveals something of himself: he is reaching out as a person for acceptance and care. In making a self-revealing response, the adult identifies with Mark's feelings and perceptions, and says in effect, "Yes, I think I understand. I'm human, too—I share your experiences and feelings about life." The self-revealing response is an attempt to meet the other individual *person-to-person,* to identify with him as bound up together with you in the common bundle of life. The self-revealing response says, "I am willing to meet you where you meet me."

What might a self-revealing response to Mark be when he says:

> What bothers me is this feeling that everything's got to be perfect. I mean, I can play with my band or sing with the pastor as I did last Sunday, and when it doesn't go just right, I go off, and when somebody says, "What's wrong?" I snap at him. I get mad at myself and other people, too.

Perhaps this:

> You know, even now in my job I feel like that sometimes—sort of driven to keep at it till it's done perfectly. And I get really upset when I don't have time or something goes wrong.

Self-revealing, then, involves searching your own experience of life to find a common ground, an area in which you share as a human being the other's feelings and needs. When you find that common ground, rather than hiding your humanness, you take a step closer to the other person by revealing yourself to him just as he has revealed himself to you.[2]

THE IMPACT OF RESPONSE

I mentioned that in thinking about these patterns of response with groups of young people, each group has agreed to their evaluation of them.

For one thing, young people agree on the frequency with which they get each type of response. When they were asked, "From your experience, which response are you most likely to get from adults you know when you make a personal or revealing statement? The overwhelming answer was: *advice giving*. The most common way adults respond when youth express their feelings or perceptions in a conversational setting is by giving advice. In descending order, the frequency of other responses, according to the youth, is *reassuring, understanding,* and, finally and least frequently, *self-revealing*.

I don't suggest that any of these patterns of response is appropriate to *every* situation. There are times when advice giving will be the best response. *But it is serious when youth hear adults trying to relate to them primarily through advice and reassurance*. When we picture the relationships implied in each response, we can see why this is so serious. I have asked young people to show, diagrammatically, *where* the adult who gives each response *places himself* in relationship to the one who makes the personal statement. They have consistently come up with a uniform analysis. (See Figure 4, p. 125.) Advice-giving places the adult above and far away from the teen. Reassurance still places him above, but perhaps a little closer. Understanding responses are felt by the kids as an attempt to be on their level, but as still a little above. And self-

[2] "Common ground" does not necessarily imply that one has experienced feelings and perceptions of life that are *exactly* like the other person's. The Bible says of Jesus: "He was tempted in all points like as we are, yet without sin." This does not assert that *every* human experience was His. For example, He never experienced the pain that a husband feels when he is rejected by his wife, nor did He undergo the dragging agony of years spent as an invalid. But He *was* tempted and tested in every area of human experience. He knew rejection by His own people and the physical exhaustion of constant, wearing travel and of emotion-laden situations. Common ground for us does not require that we be in the exact situation of another, but that we have in our unique experience of life known an experience *like* his or hers. It means that in our humanness and vulnerability to people, to physical and emotional and spiritual strain, we truly *are* like them.

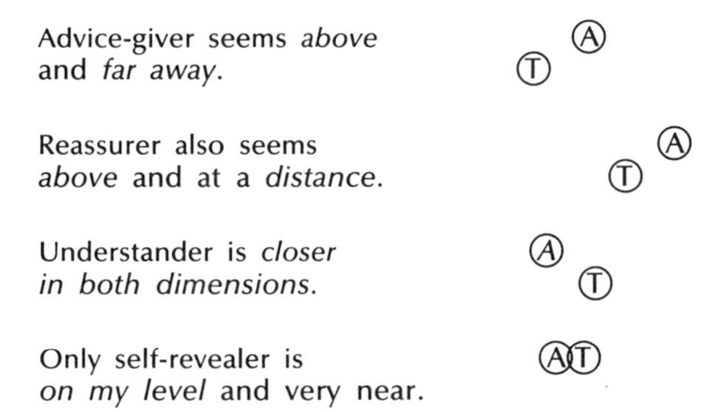

What distance and position does each type of response indicate?

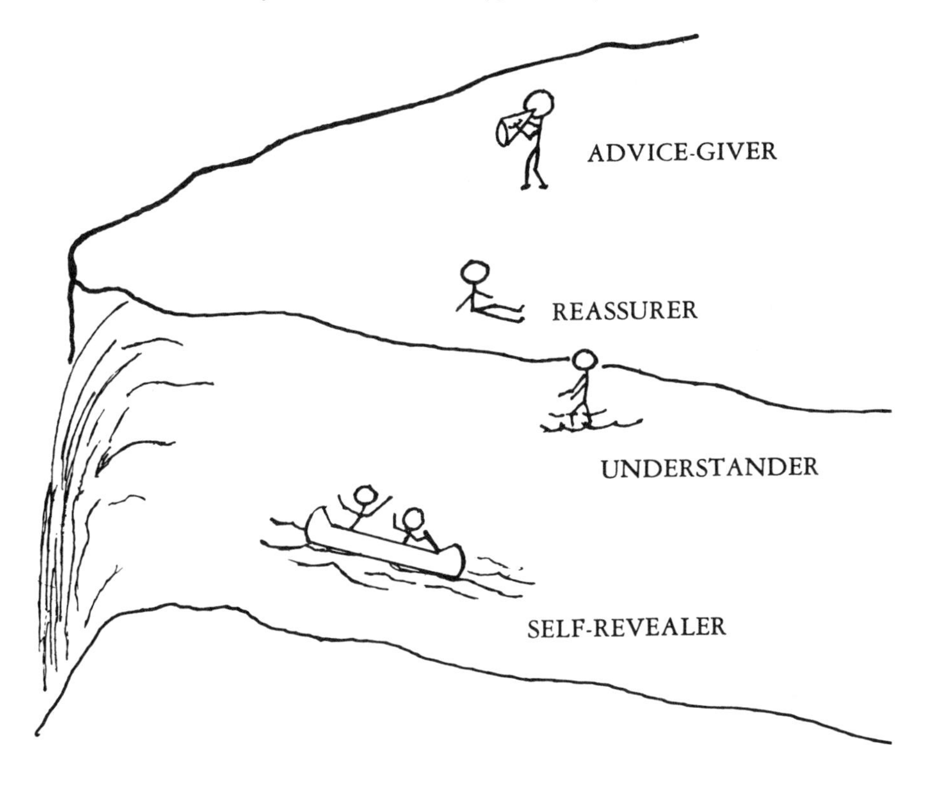

Where is each in relationship to the person in the canoe heading for the falls?

Two Representations of the Relational Implications of Adult Responses to Youths' Personal Communications.

Figure 4

revealing responses are felt as being on the same level (and very close or overlapping).

Shifting the analogy to picture the person who makes the initial statement as being in a canoe, drifting toward the falls without a paddle, the advice giver is seen by youth as standing way up on shore, shouting through a megaphone. The reassurer is on the beach, seated and relaxed, looking over his shoulder. The one attempting to understand has begun to wade out into the water, usually with a rope that is too short. And the self-revealer has swum out and is sitting *in the canoe* with the person who desperately called for help.

Leaving aside for the moment the question of which position is best for ministry (an important question, certainly, as many are afraid that to be in the same canoe necessarily means you're without a paddle, too!), we need to ask which of these relationships facilitates communication. That is, which response is most likely to free the young person to keep on sharing—to make him want to move closer to you as a person? Here, too, the response of the young people has been clear. *When youth are talked down to, as in advice giving and reassurance, they have no desire to keep on sharing.* There is little motivation to develop a relationship in which you do not feel yourself an equal.

Anyone who has served as an enlisted person in one of the armed services knows what I mean. Your buddies are those from the ranks, like you. You don't seek out and develop friendships with officers. When you are with them, no matter how fine they may be as persons, you always feel your subordinate position. Friendships demand give and take between equals and, thus, are reserved for those who view and treat you as an equal.

A relationship with young people in which adults characteristically *relate down* to them, responding to their self-revelation with advice and reassurance as a superior to a subordinate, is a *relationship that will not support or permit a truly biblical spiritual ministry.* The context of relationships that permits spiritual ministry and makes it effective is one in which each person is perceived and treated as a responsible, valuable, and equal person.

Strikingly, the *characteristic* response pattern that communicates such equality and plainly says, "I respect and value you as a person like me" is the self-revealing pattern—the response that communicates willingness to speak with youth "on the same level"—to admit that we sit with them in the same boat.

WITH A PADDLE

I have suggested that a ministry-facilitating relationship is one in which the adult admits and expresses his equality with youth as persons by encouraging mutual self-revelation and in which youth and adult each learn to trust the other with his thoughts and feelings and experiences, knowing that he is valued and respected.

This approach, this seeking to identify on a personal level with youth, bothers many adults—and some young people, too. Perhaps the most common objection is this: "But how can I help a person unless he thinks I have answers?" The thought seems to be that self-revelation necessarily involves admission of weakness (and it does) and that this admission destroys confidence in the leader (which it does *not!*). To answer this common objection, we need to go back to our understanding of the gospel and of who we are as Christians. Lutheran theologian Merton Strommen says it well in a 1966 *Eternity* article. He suggests we live with youth as those experiencing *simul justus et peccator.*

> That Latin phrase, "at the same time justified and a sinner," is a key one. It refers to a truth basic to the Christian life, but one that is difficult to teach conceptually. It must be experienced.
>
> The experience is one that comes when a youth hears his pastor admit to his struggles as well as releases; his rebellions as well as realizations of God's guidance. It is the experience of having a parent apologize or ask forgiveness. It is the frank realization that we, young or old, must live in the forgiveness of God.[3]

Living constantly in God's forgiveness is central to the reality presented in the gospel. God has not accepted us and called us His children because of our accomplishments. In fact, Scripture is very blunt in insisting that the person who says "I have no sin" is actually lying. Walking in the light necessarily involves honest recognition of who we are. Only when we are honest with God and confess rather than hide our sins is He free

[3]Merton P. Strommen, "I Can't Get Close to My Young People," *Eternity* 17, no. 10 (October 1966): 22.

to "forgive us our sins and cleanse us from all unrighteousness" (1 John 1:5–10 KJV).

We are then *both* saint and sinner; actually participants in Christ in the divine heredity, falling short of Him, yet in the process of becoming like Him. As Paul puts it, Jesus was "raised from the dead by that splendid revelation of the Father's power so that we too might rise to life on a new plane altogether. If we have, as it were, shared his death, let us rise and live our new lives with him!" (Rom. 6:4).

Our lives, then, are lived in a tension between who we are and who we are becoming. We are saints, yet sinners. And the wonderful truth is that, while we are still burdened by aspects of our old life that cling to us, we are different from what we were! We are in the process of becoming.

When we understand this and are assured of God's love, we do not have to hide either the sinner or the saint. Confidence in His love and acceptance frees us from fear, and we know that, whatever we may be like now, God is at work, forming Christ within our personalities. As the Bible says, "Love contains no fear—indeed fully developed love expels every particle of fear, for fear always contains some of the torture of feeling guilty" (1 John 4:18). Because we love God and know His forgiving love, we can accept even our imperfections. In spite of them, God loves and values us, and in fact He is working in us to remove all that blocks His free expression of Christ through us.

The Christian who accepts himself as *simul justus et peccator* is free to be honest with God. No false fronts are necessary. And because this *is* the gospel, this good news of Christ's forgiving and transforming love, *it should be clear too that we need to be ourselves with others. Only as they see us as we are, human and needy, yet becoming through the power of God's Spirit new and different persons, will others understand the gospel and the great gift God has given us in Christ.*

I personally become very disturbed by those who say, "You mustn't get too close to people you minister to," or "Don't reveal your weakness, or people will lose confidence in you." The Christian who ministers with others is not trying to lead them to confidence in *him*. He is instead seeking to lead them to confidence in *God*—by his example. Only by living with others as one who is in need, yet who constantly finds that Christ meets need, can trust and confidence and dependence be shifted from the human leader to the Lord.

Self-revealing, as I have presented it in this chapter, means that the leader exposes his humanness and identifies with the youth. He seeks to meet young people person-to-person and to step into the same canoe. *But he does not come "without a paddle."* He comes instead with a confident awareness that Christ, living in the human personality, is our glorious hope for everything that is to come in this life and eternity. He comes with the willingness to expose his weaknesses so that all can see that the power, the love, and the discipline that also mark his life are found through Christ.

In reality, the leader who presents himself as strong is never able to minister to others. As he stands before them wrapped in his own strength and hiding his weaknesses, he appears different from those who are burdened with a consciousness of needs and failures. And by his difference he stimulates despair. He is what the others can never hope to be, for he is strong, and they are weak.

The leader who presents himself authentically, willing to reveal his weaknesses and needs and willing as well to reveal what Christ has done to transform him does not burden, but inspires. He is a living testimony that God can take the weak things and the despised of this world and miraculously reshape them for His glory. Like Paul, who saw himself as chief of sinners and who never hesitated to reveal his sense of need or his times of discouragement, the authentic person is a leader whom others can trust and model themselves after. Only the authentic person, the self-revealing person, can serve as a living demonstration of the grace and power of God.

And so we see something of the relationship pattern that must exist in ministry. It is a relationship that may be characterized by saying that the leader always takes his place as a *person with* the others.

The adult who has discovered that the gospel gives freedom to be authentic with others creates, by who he is, the relational context for spiritual ministry. When we are freed, as Paul was, to express ourselves in utter honesty ("We should like you, our brothers, to know something of what we went through in Asia. We were completely overwhelmed; the burden was more than we could bear; in fact we told ourselves that this was the end"), we are freed to present Christ as He is for us ("Yet we now believe that we had this experience of coming to the end of our tether that we might learn to trust, not in ourselves, but in God who can raise the dead," 2 Cor. 1:8–9).

The adult who sees youth as brothers and sisters, who speaks to them and listens to them as responsible and free human beings, expecting and giving acceptance, is the leader youth need. The adult who opens up his life to youth, extending and receiving forgiveness, granting and accepting the love that "covers a multitude of sins," can serve with youth as an example of the authentic Christian. Such personal involvement is the context in which spiritual ministry takes place.

BUILDING RELATIONSHIPS

It should be clear from what I have said about the relational context in which spiritual leadership can function that this context does not exist in most churches. Too often youth and their leaders get together in formal situations, where the leader is cast as a teacher or program director. In these roles the adult is placed in a *superior-to-subordinate* position. And too often on these occasions the group involved is large—too large for interactive self-revelation to take place.

Other contexts in which leaders and youth commonly come together also fail to permit building the *"person with"* relationship. Socials and recreational activities, while they do let kids see the adult leaders out of their authority roles, are hardly conducive to self-revealing conversations. Committee meetings and officers' business meetings deal with business—not persons. *All too often formal and informal-superficial contact situations make up 90 percent of teen/leader interaction!*

This says much about our programming of youth ministry. It says that we need to restructure, to give priority to contact situations where mutual self-revelation is encouraged and can take place—situations in which teens can come to know adult leaders as persons, and where the adult can stand with youth as equally human, meeting on the common ground of shared need for experience of God's grace and His transforming power.

PROBE

case histories
discussion questions
thought-provokers
resources

1. The following statements are typical of those made to me at various times by teens. To develop sensitivity to the several responses you might make to teens who share something with you, jot down a

couple of responses of each type (advice giving, reassuring, understanding, self-revealing).

I prefer not to talk to my parents, because they are very intolerant of ideas they feel are wrong, and I like to avoid fights.

I have got more conflicts right now over religion than ever. I know I must accept many teachings by faith. But I still have many doubts.

The biggest problem for me has been my parents and my church forcing a Christianity on me that just doesn't agree with what Christ advocated. Why is everyone so sure dancing and movies are wrong, while judging and gossiping aren't? It's no wonder Christianity has a bad sound to the world, when all they see is negative—don't smoke, don't drink, don't play cards, don't dance, don't go to movies. Negatives are no good without love.

2. One concern of persons who object to adopting a self-revealing relationship pattern with youth is that no helpful or corrective ideas will be introduced. It seems to me that there are two important considerations in responding to this viewpoint.

   The first is this: Which relationship/response pattern creates a willingness to listen? . . . a desire to continue communicating? Look back over the different responses you made to the teen quotes above. Which responses if given to you would have made you want to keep talking? Which would have killed motivation for future expression on your part?

   A second consideration is this: Which relationship/response pattern is most likely to give a young person the feeling that the adult really understands his situation and perhaps has something to contribute? Look back over your hypothetical responses to the three quotes again, and ask yourself which response if given to you would give you some confidence that the adult who made them might actually be able to help you?

3. In the concluding thoughts of this chapter I pointed out that most "ministry" situations in which youth and adults come together inhibit rather than encourage the development of a personal relationship. Although implications of this fact will be developed later, it is important to note now that even the formal ministry situation is *not necessarily characterized by a teacher/student, superior/subordinate relationship.*

   I mentioned earlier in the chapter my conversation with Mark. To describe the setting a little more fully, Mark, five other teens, and I were sitting or lying on the floor of the preschool classroom of their church, studying the Bible together. In this situation I was not "the teacher." I was a person with the teens, submitting myself as they submitted themselves to the Word of God, and together we revealed what its searching light disclosed. The following is the "lesson" we studied together. Taken from Lyman Coleman's *Serendipity* (Waco: Word, n.d.), it illustrates how we can be involved in the Word interpersonally, without being forced into the format pattern so common in our churches.

I believe that there are ways to personalize nearly all ministry settings, and that we must begin to personalize immediately! The church of Jesus Christ must once again develop the relational context in which spiritual leadership can be exercised.

AN EXERCISE IN SHARING (ONE HOUR)

Preliminary Exercise (15 minutes) (in small groups)

1. Read John 5:1–9 silently, pausing after each sentence to let your imagination recreate the situation for you.

2. Imagine yourself a psychiatrist who has been studying the behavior of the crippled man with a view to helping him and read over the passage a second time. Take special note of the dialogue between Jesus and the crippled man, beginning with the question of Jesus, "Do you want to recover?"

   Then on the basis of your own examination of the evidence write out a "case history" report on this man.

   The easiest way to get started is to imagine yourself a psychiatrist who interviews this man before his encounter with Jesus to get his basic history and interviews him again after his encounter with Jesus at the end of the passage.

   Simply start out your report with the words "This man is—" and proceed to describe what you feel was wrong him and what happened to him in his encounter with Jesus Christ. For instance, you might say, "This man appears to be afflicted with a terrible sense of self-worthlessness and self-pity, stemming back to his childhood . . . .

3. In the remaining moments of silence, think back over your own life and ask yourself this question: If Jesus came to me in the same way that he came to the crippled man at the pool of Bethesda and asked me the same question that He asked the crippled man, what would He be referring to in my life? Or, to put it simply, Where do I need to experience the release of Jesus Christ from the hurts and pain in my life?

   For instance, for one of you, it might be a childhood memory that is keeping you from opening up in your small group; for another, it might be a sense of bitterness.

   Whatever you say, be honest.

Small Group Interaction (30 minutes)

1. Gather together in small groups and move your chairs in close.

2. Ask the group to share one by one what they wrote as the psychiatric report for the crippled man and ask them to explain why they feel as they do about their analyses.

3. Again, ask each person to share, if possible, what came to mind when he faced his own life with the same question; that is, that area of hurt or distress in his own life that needs to know the healing of Jesus

Christ—whether physical, emotional, or spiritual. In particular, face with each other the question, *Do you want to recover?* (Some of us would prefer to lick our wounds and soak up the pity [especially the self-pity?] that comes with sickness, rather than seek the Great Physician for His release and healing.)

Some of the small groups will have difficulty with this kind of sharing until they have reached the point of trust and acceptance that is really deep.

Celebration (15 minutes)

1. In each group, ask each person to think in silence of a gift that he would like to give in the name of Jesus to the other members of his small group—something for each person who has opened up his life and shared any hurt or pain in his past.

   For instance, if someone in a group has opened up his feelings of hurt at the sudden death of his dad when he was a boy, one of the others in his group may want to give him a gift of *understanding* of God's ways; and another may want to give him the gift of *tears* or the ability to cry; and the third may want to give him the gift of *love* . . . and accompany the words with a big bear hug.

   After a minute to collect your thoughts, break the silence and give out your gifts.

2. In each small group, move up close together and join hands or put your arms around the shoulders of one another as in a football huddle, and in this posture look each other in the eyes and thank each other for the gifts that have been given to you. If you wish, close your session in song and prayer.

3. When your small group is through, slip out quietly without disturbing the other small groups that are finishing up.

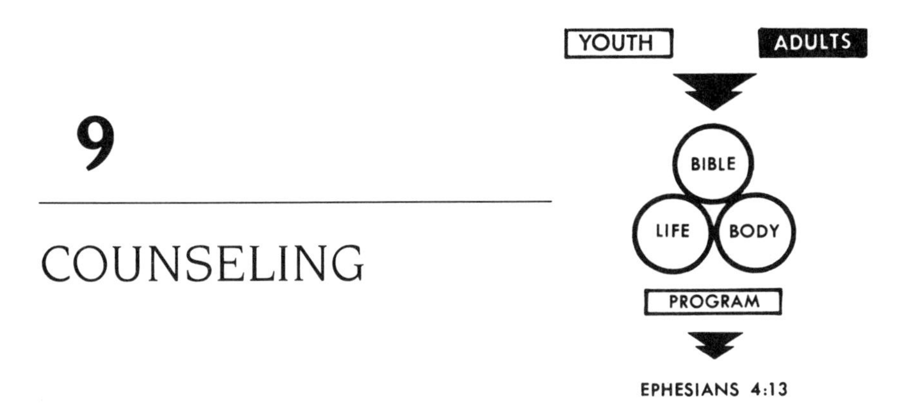

9

COUNSELING

There is often a great emphasis on counseling in many schools training young people for ministry. This disturbs me, because counseling can never be the heart of an effective ministry. Growth toward maturity, and the healing that often must take place in persons before they are free to grow, comes essentially through involvement with others in the processes of ministry—particularly through body relationships and Scripture. The church of the New Testament is a transforming *community*, and transformation is a community transaction, not primarily a transaction between two persons—especially when they are cast as counselor and counselee.

This point of view is not distinctively mine. Many behavioral scientists believe that under conditions of rapid social change, it is more important to pay attention to social structures and processes than to individual therapy in guiding individual persons through the changes. And this is true whether they speak of increasing motivation in school or of reducing discrimination or of any other value or personality-rooted concern—or, I would add, of guiding young people toward Christian maturity.

None of this is to suggest that there is no place for the Christian psychologist or psychiatrist. Obviously there are individuals in the church who need professional help. But in the normal situations of ministry, "counseling training" is not as important as an understanding of the interpersonal dynamics that free people to grow. And often "counseling training" is harmful. For the spiritual dynamics of change cut directly across the grain of many counseling theories and methods, and these dynamics, like other aspects of the Christian leader's ministry, rest on the impact of the "person with," the person whose personality is stamped by the authority of example.

The pictures that the term "counseling" can conjure up in people's minds are interesting and varied. Some see it almost as "consoling." Here is a young person overwhelmed by troubles who sits, pouring out his heart to a sympathetic adult. The adult reflects his feelings, and nods his head encouragingly, until the youth, relieved by the chance to express his emotions, says with surprise: "Why, I feel better now!" With warmest thanks he leaves the office, while the grateful adult, glad to have been of help, sits back in his easy chair to stare contemplatively at the wall until the next troubled teen appears.

Too often counseling does operate something like this, with the emphasis on the expression of feeling, and with the greatest value for the counselee being the release of emotions. Then he goes into the real world again and finds himself faced with the same situations that tied him in knots in the first place. He discovers that the same feelings and frustrations are building up again—building up until the comforting adult is sought out once more.

Another picture, much like the first, is that of an adult gently questioning and probing, helping the young person understand why he feels so inadequate. Perhaps his mother rejected him when a new baby appeared. Has his failure to get the grades his older brother was able to get left a psychic scar? When he understands himself, this wise adult counselor nods; now the young person will be able to accept himself and perhaps the intensity of his unhappy feelings will be reduced.

Neither of these pictures of counseling is particularly helpful in youth ministry—or Christian ministry as a whole. For each approach treats the counselee as a truly inadequate person—one who actually cannot help himself or herself. So each develops, not personal responsibility, but personal irresponsibility. Rather than responding to life, persons treated in these ways find ready excuses for their failure.

The Bible makes some amazing demands on Christians—demands that would be totally unreasonable if God Himself did not infuse us with His power to change. Paul speaks of the dynamics of release and power when he writes:

> You *belong* to the power which you choose to obey, whether you choose sin, whose reward is death, or God, obedience to whom means the reward of righteousness. Thank God you, who were at one time the servants of sin, honestly responded to the impact of Christ's teachings when you came under its influence. Then released from the service of sin, you entered the service of righteousness.

So now, Paul goes on to say:

> Give yourselves to the service of righteousness—for the purpose of becoming really good (Rom. 6:16ff.).

The Christian is *not* an inadequate person. The Christian is released from the control of sin, which expresses itself in every aspect of the human personality, and *can* give himself or herself to the service of righteousness.

So Christian counseling demands far more than the release of feelings and an accommodation to circumstances. *Christian counseling seeks to free persons to choose the freedom that is ours through obedience to God.* Christian counseling focuses not on emotions, but on the will.

A pastor friend of mine made a perceptive comment recently. Speaking of classroom training for the ministry, he noted that it is essentially "intellectual-spiritual." That is, the biblical view of life is studied to be presented primarily in an intellectual framework in sermons and teaching. But the ministry itself, he said, is essentially "emotional-spiritual." The biblical portrait of reality has to be communicated and grasped where people live; communicated as life to life so that it can be felt as well as understood.

In saying, as I did a moment ago, that Christian counseling focuses on the will rather than the emotions, I am not suggesting that the intellect is the basic avenue of approach in counseling. Instead, as this chapter will show, I am convinced that the emotions provide a better avenue of approach to the will than the intellect does. People do not live "rational" lives; we are not merely minds. Emotional and intellectual components are complexly blended in the human personality, and that personality must be touched and motivated as a whole.

Focus on the whole person eliminates one other portrait of the youth counselor that commonly comes to mind. This is the picture of the answer man, who sits behind his desk with files full of psychological tests and vocational preference tests, helping kids decide their future. "Which college shall I go to?" "Who has the best journalism program?" "Is a Christian or a secular college best for me?" "What kinds of jobs are open these days?"

Such contacts are information-seeking and information-providing. Although in conversation more personal concerns may surface—as, for example, in the question "How can I tell God's will for my life?"—the contacts still usually remain oriented to information. In effect, the young person is asking the adult to supply or point out facts that he needs in order to make a decision. Certainly there is a place for such vocational or educational counseling. But this is not our primary concern or orientation in this chapter.

When I speak of "counseling" in this chapter, I want to focus on our primary concern and suggest an approach that will enable the adult who ministers with teens in the local church (normally without counseling training) to understand what his counseling role is and how he can best fulfill it.

WHEN WE COUNSEL

I have sketched several portraits of what counseling is not. Let me sketch one or two portraits of what it is in the context of youth ministry.

Rich drops into your office. He is slow in talking, but soon his feelings and his story come pouring out. For one thing, he is afraid—afraid that God is going to push him into the one way of life he doesn't want: being a missionary. And there is this girl he is interested in. He is afraid God isn't going to let him marry her. In fact, he feels as though he is in a box, squeezed together, tighter all the time. What difference does it make what he wants or doesn't want? Isn't God going to make him do what *He* wants?

And Rich keeps talking, to tell you about the Sunday school class of boys he has just quit teaching. Somehow, suddenly, all the words about God he has been brought up on and all the words he has been telling the kids seem unreal. He doesn't believe them anymore. They're empty—and so he had to stop teaching. He couldn't be a hypocrite.

There are others.

Debby's mother drops in, all upset. Her daughter has been such a good girl, and now, suddenly, they seem to be strangers. It all happened with those white cords. Debby wanted them, but mom is sure they look like what the hoods wear. Debby strikes back: "All the girls have them. I *know* what's hoody!" But mom won't give in. Debby, usually so open and relaxed with mom, feels terribly hurt and cuts her out of her life.

So now mom tells you she wants to make an appointment to bring Debby to you at 2:30.

At 2:30 you go outside, and there's Debby, angry at being forced to keep an appointment she never wanted to make, looking at you defiantly.

And there's Jan, a girl you have noticed losing interest in meetings recently, growing distant from her Christian friends. Jan drops in, talks small talk, and at first seems unable to say what troubles her. Here is her story:

It was tough to decide to talk to Mr. Jack. But there wasn't anyone else to talk to now. It had been tough, all that past semester. At first Bob was just a nice fellow, someone to chat with in the halls, maybe even get to young people's meetings or talk with about the Lord. That was the motive behind those first dates.

But soon it became more. Bob wasn't a Christian, but he was nice. He was exciting, too. Somehow more alive, more real, than the kids at church. He didn't swear or anything like that. And even that occasional smoke and his having beers now and then with the guys when she wasn't around didn't seem so important.

Of course, there was less time for church. Then the kids started pressuring her, telling her she shouldn't date Bob. When her folks found out, her dad really hit the roof. It wasn't fair, jumping on Bob like that, she said, when they didn't even know him.

Then it got worse at home. At school, Bob was the only one to turn to. But now—and this was more than anyone had expected—just a week ago they had gone away and been secretly married. Even now no one knew about it.

The next day, with that sinking feeling that grew and grew, it was clear to her that it was wrong—all wrong. But whom could she tell? Not her folks. They would never understand. Or the kids. There was no one, no one except maybe Mr. Jack at church.

But would he understand? Maybe he would condemn her too. She have to be careful. See what he thinks about—about kids like Bob. Maybe he would think it was all right to see unsaved fellows and witness to them. Maybe he would understand how a girl could get pushed by family and friends into even marrying an unsaved fellow. Maybe he wouldn't. Maybe she just won't commit herself. Just feel him out. She's just got to tell someone. Someone's got to help.

And there are others: kids like Mark, bound by his perfectionism; kids like Sherrill, disturbed by conflicts at home, uncertain how to respond; kids who are facing life, eager to live it meaningfully and well but somehow uncertain, sensing their inadequacies and looking for ways to live responsibly.

Sometimes the problems are really big ones, like Jan's. Sometimes they seem smaller. But in each case the central need is not for release of emotions or for an explanation of present bondage in terms of the past or a dispassionate presentation of facts. *In each case the central need is for decision, for a response that is adequate and will be freeing*—if not freeing from the situation, at least freeing for the personality.

The Bible tells us this kind of freedom is found in obedience, not the sullen obedience of one forced against his will, but the joyful obedience of the believer who trusts God and trusts Scripture's revelation of what is right and best. Obedience is what Jesus speaks of when He says, "If you are faithful to what I have said, you are truly my disciples. And you will know the truth and the truth will set you free" (John 8:31–32).

Counseling situations, then, are those in which young person and adult wrestle together to find freedom through obedience to God. *Counseling focuses on the choice to obey.*

This clarification helps us see more clearly what must be accomplished in a counseling situation. For one thing, the problem at the root of the counselee's present inadequacy must be identified. There also has to come an understanding of God's revelation concerning the situation—a grasp of reality as revealed in Scripture, reality on which to base the obedient response. And finally there must be motivation to act.

Most secular counseling approaches are inadequate for the accomplishment of these three necessary tasks. We must seek an understanding of how to "counsel," not in counseling theory, but in the scripturally revealed dynamics of Christian leadership.

APPROACHES TO COUNSELING

There are various approaches to counseling that attempt to deal with (or have ignored) the three tasks that I have suggested must be accomplished. I am aware that any attempt to simplify and sketch must lead to unfair distortion. Yet it seems necessary to highlight certain suppositions and patterns in various approaches as background for the counseling approach I will suggest. So, with apologies to proponents of other views for the unfairness that simplification must involve, I would like to compare and evaluate three distinctive approaches.

Directive counseling — The pattern of directive counseling is quite clear and simple. Although the process that a skillful directive counselor may use will be far more subtle, the philosophy underlying the approach is something like this. The counselee comes with a problem, which he reveals to the counselor. The counselor provides the answer. The counselee is expected to go out and act on it.

Diagramed, with the counselor's part boxed, directive counseling looks something like this:

There are several drawbacks to the directive approach. Given even that the counselor is a wise man and knows the right answer, an externally imposed solution, like advice, is unlikely to be followed. I mentioned earlier that an intellectual-spiritual ministry is unlikely to move people. Simply telling another person what is best for him usually is inadequate to motivate action.

But now, how about our supposition that the counselor is a wise man? Can even the wisest of men play God to others? Most counseling situations do not face us with a clear-cut moral issue, where the biblical imperative "Stop!" applies. In most situations the individual needs the personal guidance of the Holy Spirit in showing him just how to apply relevant biblical principles. A directive approach, in which the counselor tells the counselee what to do, puts the counselor in the position of playing God—often with tragic results. For as human beings we cannot know just in what way, how, and when God wants another to act.

But even if the counselor were correct in his solution and his instructions, would he help the counselee grow as an independent, responsible person? His counseling is far more likely to lead the other to depend on *him* rather than on God! Even the best directive counseling tends to establish a dependency relationship between counselee and counselor—a relationship that does not foster growth toward maturity.

Although it is relatively easy to introduce biblical content and the biblical perspective in the directive situation, doing it effectively, to motivate acceptance and response, is very difficult.

Nondirective counseling — The pattern of nondirective counseling is significantly different. In nondirective counseling the counselor does not provide an answer: instead, he views his role as listening and reflecting feelings, so helping the counselee understand his own problems. With the issues clarified, the counselee is expected to come to his own solution, based on his own personality, perceptions, and values.

Diagrammed, with the counselor's role again boxed, nondirective counseling looks something like this:

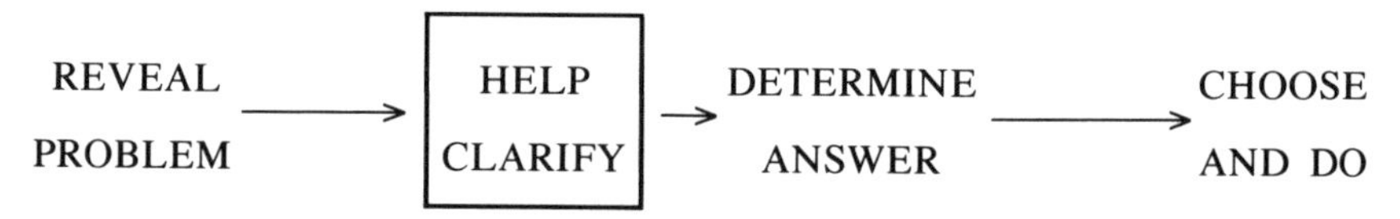

While nondirective counseling avoids the "playing God" aspect of directive counseling, it has other problems. One of these is the difficulty of introducing new information and insights. The nondirective counselor essentially stands *outside* of the counselee. He is concerned, but distant. His job is to feed back to the counselee his own feelings and perceptions about the problem until the counselee is able to come to his own solution, based on his own values and ideas about life. In nondirective counseling the counselor does not intrude his own values or solutions.

This is an extremely difficult position for the committed Christian to take. Believing firmly that Christ provides the answer for each human need, convinced that the biblical revelation must be understood if we are to have an adequate guide to knowing God's will or understanding life, the Christian *has* to introduce distinctive biblical values and perceptions in counseling.

While many of the techniques of nondirective counseling are valuable and used by counselors of every school, the underlying concept, that one must stand outside and, out of respect for the integrity of the counselee as an individual, not share himself or his values, must be rejected.

It is important to notice the relational aspects of both directive and nondirective counseling. *In each the counselor stands apart.* In neither does he seek to establish a relationship, described in the last chapter, that marks the context for ministry. In neither is he a *"person with."*

Identification counseling — A third approach, which I have called identification counseling, is represented in the ministry of Swiss psychiatrist Paul Tournier. Rather than standing outside, to reflect or direct, Tournier seeks to share himself with the counselee as the counselee shares, and, when each senses his identification with the other, he, the counselor, seeks to to share solutions he has experienced in Christ.

This last approach harmonizes with what we have been saying in the last two chapters, for it permits the counselor to serve as a model who is trusted because of his humanity. I believe this is also what the apostle Paul speaks of to the Corinthians, when he talks of God as the "source of all mercy and comfort." He goes on to say that God

> gives us comfort in our trials so that we in turn may be able to give the same sort of strong sympathy to others in theirs. Indeed, experience shows that the more we share Christ's suffering, the more we are able to give of his encouragement. This means that if we experience trouble we can pass on to you comfort and spiritual help; for if we ourselves have been comforted we know how to encourage you to endure patiently the same sort of troubles that we have ourselves endured (2 Cor. 1:3–8).

The common experience of trouble provides the basis from which we can speak meaningfully to the troubles of others and share what has comforted and encouraged us.

If we were to diagram identification counseling as we have the other two types of counseling approach, it would look something like this (with the counselor's actions again indicated in boxes):

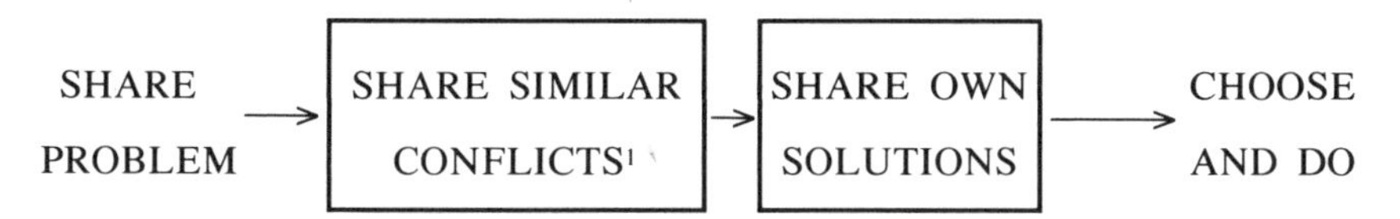

This process has been diagramed in greater detail by Bill Gothard, whose analysis is presented in figure 5 and explained in this chapter.

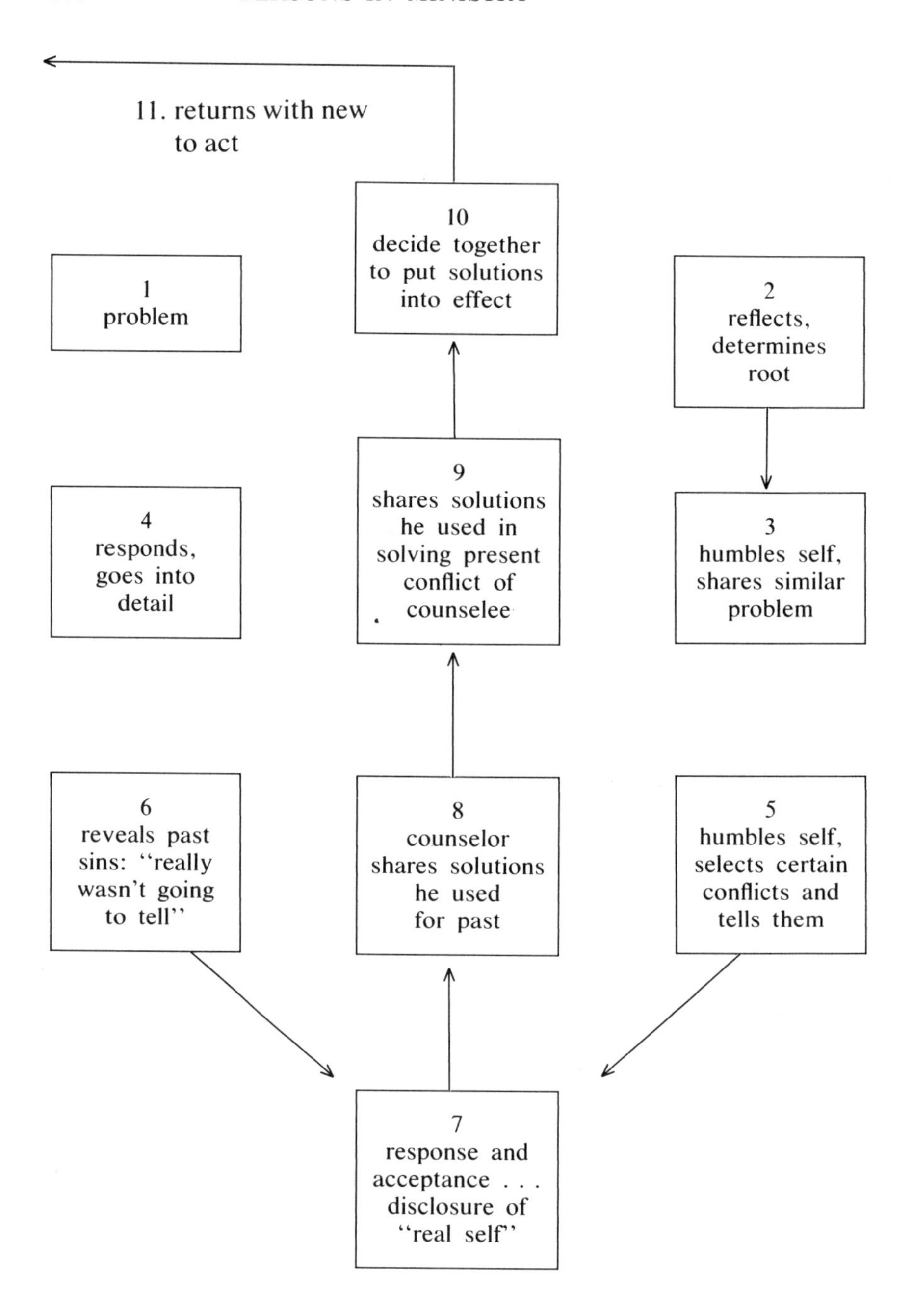

Figure 5
The Process of Identification Counseling

Steps

1–2. Most counseling processes seem to start here, with the counselor using nondirective technique to encourage the counselee to express the problem. The chart shows the purpose of this process in identification counseling to determine the "root"—that area common to human experience from which the problem arises.

3. Contrary to other counseling approaches, this approach accepts self-revelation and the premise that the counselor must become a *person with* the counselee. After locating the problem area, the counselor shares a similar problem, seeking common ground with the counselee.

4–7. These steps show the process of mutual self-revelation that gradually leads to mutual trust and acceptance. More than one conversation may be represented here, though if the counselor has established in his ministry with the young people the relational context described in chapter 8, the whole process may take place in a single meeting, including resolution of the problem.

8. With counselor and counselee in a mutually accepting open relationship, the counselor is able to introduce the solutions he has found to the conflicts they have had in common. In biblical terms, the counselor has revealed the trouble he has experienced; now he is able to share the comfort and keys to endurance God provided for him. *The biblical perspective, then, is shared not in an intellectual-spiritual setting, but in a deeply personal, emotionally real, whole-person setting: "This is what* I *have experienced."* With rapport established, the content shared is acceptable to the counselee and wins the hearing it might not have had if presented in another setting.

9–10. The biblical perspective and experience of the counselor are then used by both to reevaluate the counselee's situation and needs, leading to a decision as to how the counselee will respond. The impact of shared decision is not to reduce responsibility but to support the counselee's determination to act. The counselee returns to the life-situation and acts on the new insights gained and decisions made.

HOW IDENTIFICATION COUNSELING WORKS

I noted earlier in the chapter that there are three tasks that must be accomplished if counseling is to have its desired impact: (1) The counseling relationship must free the counselee to reveal and explore his problem, (2) it must permit the effective introduction of God's perspective on the problem, and (3) it must facilitate decision to act. In other words, the counselor must help his counselee express the problem, must introduce biblical content, and must motivate an obedient response to God.

The goal of counseling is important to keep clearly in mind. Counseling is not concerned so much with words as with life—with behavior. The New Testament speaks without apology of behavior. "No more evil temper or furious rage," Paul warned the Colossians. "No more evil thoughts or words about others, no more evil thoughts or words about God, and no more filthy conversation. Don't tell one another lies any more, for you have finished with the old man and all he did and have begun life as the new man, who is out to learn what he ought to be, according to the plan of God" (Col. 3:8–10). The Christian is called to go on in life *as a new person:* to find in Christ the power to break the chains that bind him. *Counseling in Christian ministry is not to help a person understand himself, but to become himself.* And the Christian becomes himself by making the right choice of obedience; will he obey the demanding insistency of the sin and inadequacy that bind him, or God, who calls him to transformation through obedience? The goal of counseling is to help a person respond to God, to find freedom in the words and power of Jesus Christ.

How does identification counseling work toward this goal and seek to accomplish each task that lies on the pathway?

Discovering the problem — Most persons who seek help are hesitant about revealing their problems. They are deeply concerned about how the others will respond and whether the counselor will still accept them and like them. When the counselor makes himself vulnerable by sharing his own conflicts, he demonstrates acceptance and trust. He shows that he views himself as on the same level as the counselee and takes his stand with him or her, not as his judge, but as *simul justus et peccator.*

Sensitive self-revelation[1] normally encourages additional revelations by the counselee. I have noted that even when I fail

[1] I recommend the reading of my book *How I Can Fit In* (Grand Rapids: Zondervan, 1979) for important background on this process. Self-revelation is a mutual process, which can proceed only as fast as each person is ready for it. *How I Can Fit In* goes into greater detail as to the background and nature of building relationships through self-revelation.

to grasp the root problem, self-revelation encourages further explanation. "No," I have been told, "it's not like that. It's like this. . . ." Self-revelation lets the other know that we are meeting *person-to-person,* that there is no "relating down."

Introducing content — The difficulty in introducing the biblical perspective so vital to Christian solutions to life problems is not in making the perspective clear but in creating a willingness to hear. I noted earlier that ministry is not so much intellectual-spiritual as emotional-spiritual. We need help to grasp on a basic, common-sense level what God's way of life means—not merely help to crystallize concepts and doctrines. To some extent, any presentation of biblical truth that is divorced from experience comes across as intellectualized, idealized. But when God's truth is seen incarnated and realized in the personal experience of others whom we see as being like us, it has the ability to grip and to compel.

Identification counseling seeks to build a personal relationship on that real-life, common-ground level. In the initial process of mutual self-revelation, each person has come to know and appreciate the other and to trust him as one who understands—as someone who is real. *When rapport has been gained, experience of the reality of God's Word can be shared as well as one's essential vulnerability to life.* In the rapport relationship, the biblical perspective comes across as more than theory, more than doctrine, more than "faith." It comes across as reality.

This may be one reason for Paul's great "if." "If we ourselves have been comforted we know how to encourage you" (2 Cor. 1:6). Only someone who has himself experienced the reality of God's comfort and guidance when in trouble is qualified to counsel. For counseling, like leadership itself, is the sharing of oneself so that in the servant-leader's example others also might find inspiration and trust to respond to God, in full obedience.

Motivating response — Although each person must be treated as a responsible individual, it is important to remember that responsibility is *not* independence. The most responsible of us need others to support and encourage us. The identification process first links counselor and counselee together through mutual self-revelation, until rapport and trust are established. Then the counselor is free to share the divine perspective, revealing how the biblical truth has infused and transformed his experience and provides a basis for solution of his conflicts. So the biblical perspective has been explored by both as a basis for solving the counselee's problem, too. Ideally, the counselee has made a tentative decision to act on God's truth, to seek release and freedom through obedience.

At this point, where both directive and nondirective counselors leave those who come to them, the identification counselor continues in relationship. He prays for and with the counselee; he shows that he continues to care; he encourages. He helps the counselee realize that he is not alone. God is with him, and in the person of the Christian friend God demonstrates His continuing love.

PROBE

case histories
discussion questions
thought-provokers
resources

1. Many who work with youth suggest that rather than waiting for teens with problems to come to them, leaders need to set up preventive personal conferences. Bill Gothard suggests several objectives for such a session. The following material has been adapted from his "Basic Youth Conflicts" lecture series.

   a. show personal love and concern
   b. build genuine interest in his life and future
   c. put him at ease about sharing personal problems
   d. discuss where he is in spiritual growth
   e. stimulate faith by setting reachable spiritual goals
   f. establish a bond of prayer

   One of my friends suggests a different format for the initial personal conference. The conference is preceded by asking the teens in the group to write on a card three areas in which they would like to change. These then become the general topic for conversation in the first counseling interview.

   I may note here that, although I have used the terms "counselor" and "counselee" throughout this chapter, I really do not like them. They seem to me to imply a superior-subordinate relationship that is so deadly to ministry. My own commitment is very much to the identification process, so much so that when young people or others come to talk with me, I tell them I am not a counselor or someone with answers. But I am more than willing to share—person to person. And very often in the process, God shows His grace in meeting needs. I much prefer to think of such situations as simply times to share and to seek God's guidance together.

2. You may be interested in some modern theories of counseling that parallel quite closely what I have said in these chapters. Interestingly, some of these theories also spring from a theological base. Here are summaries of two, presented by Alexander Bassin in *Marital Counseling*.[2]

BASIC CONCEPTS OF INTEGRITY THERAPY

Any wrongdoing, past or present, that someone decides to keep secret causes that individual to become walled-off from others in various ways. The person feels anxious, ill-at-ease, uncertain, depressed, uncomfortable, on guard all the time to keep from being exposed as a type of person he or she is but doesn't want to be—dreading what others would think if they knew the facts. Integrity therapy insists, however, that what the person must do is work up enough courage to admit past mistakes frankly to others. Frequently, others will then accept the individual more completely than he or she ever thought possible, and that will make the individual begin to feel better, too. The more one actually begins to practice honesty with others, the easier life will become, and the symptoms will slip away. There may also be some surprise to notice that others become more open to the individual; they also have been holding secrets of their own that they would like to get off their chests and thus feel better, too. One person dropping a curtain of secrecy encourages another to do likewise.

Listen, say the integrity therapists, to that "still, small voice" within us, because what it "tells" us will help keep us psychologically satisfied. Unfortunately, this "voice" can be throttled to such an extent that it grows all but silent. Then we have no internal gyroscope to guide us, and we are in trouble. All sorts of symptoms emerge with the message: "Get back on the integrity track!"

Integrity therapy emphasizes the need for self-revelation, confession significant to others. It also insists that confession must be followed by restitution and good works. Mowrer has explored the history of primitive Christianity and notes how frequently public confession was a required ritual of group living; and he believes the original vitality of early Christianity may well be related to this procedure, which insures honesty and integrity in interpersonal relationships. He notes how frequently the most effective of the self-help groups—Alcoholics Anonymous, Gamblers Anonymous, and others—succeed where more conven-

[2]Alexander Bassin, "Integrity Therapy in Marriage Counseling," in Hirsch Silverman, *Marital Counseling* (Springfield, Ill.: Charles C. Thomas, 1967).

tional approaches fail dismally in rescuing a victim from a life of shame and despair.[3]

REALITY THERAPY

Reality therapy, the main component of which is emphasis on *responsibility,* is the brainchild of Dr. William Glasser, an extraordinarily warm, friendly, unassuming young psychiatrist.

The therapist within the framework of reality therapy must be a highly responsible person—tough, involved, sensitive, and human. He must be willing to fulfill his own needs and to discuss some of his own struggles so that the person he is trying to help can see that acting responsibly is possible, even though difficult. The therapist is neither aloof, superior, nor sacrosanct, nor would he ever imply that what he does or what he stands for or what he values are unimportant. He must have the strength and courage to become involved, to have 11s values tested by the client, and to withstand intense criticism by the very person he may be trying to help. He must submit to have every fault and defect of his picked apart by the other. He must be willing to admit that, like the client, he is far from perfect but is a person who can act responsibly even if it takes effort.

THE TECHNIQUE OF REALITY THERAPY

In various addresses, Dr. Glasser has explained the methodology of his treatment procedure. He warns, however, that, in contrast to conventional psychiatry (the theory of which is difficult to explain but the practice easy), reality therapy has a simple theoretical base that can be explained in fifteen minutes but a treatment procedure that is extremely difficult to follow.

1. *Become involved.* The first and most difficult phase of reality therapy is the gaining of the *involvement* that the client so desperately needs but which he has been unsuccessful in attaining or maintaining up to the time he presents himself for treatment. Unless the requisite involvement develops between the responsible therapist and the irresponsible client, there can be no therapy, Glasser asserts. The guiding principles are directed toward achieving the proper involvement: a completely honest, human relationship in which the client, for perhaps the first time in his life, realizes that someone cares enough for him, not only to accept him, but also to do so with the purpose of helping him to fulfill his needs in the real world.

---

[3] Mowrer, 105.

How does a therapist become involved with a patient so that the patient can begin to fill his needs? Glasser asks. The therapist has a difficult task, for he must quickly build a firm emotional relationship with the patient who has failed to establish such relationships in the past. He is aided by recognizing that a patient is desperate for involvement and is suffering because he is not able to fulfill his needs. The patient is looking for a person with whom he can become emotionally involved, someone he can care about and who cares about him, someone who can convince the patient that he will stay with him until he can better fulfill his needs.

Unless the client is convinced that the therapist genuinely cares about him, there can be no prospect for change. Glasser extends this thesis to all areas of human interaction, whether it be in marriage, school, or work.

2. *Reveal yourself.* Glasser differs from Mowrer in terms of emphasis of confession as an essential ingredient for therapy, but he does insist that involvement cannot be obtained if the therapist maintains the aloof "stone face," the impersonal posture that is taught in conventional psychotherapy. On the contrary, the therapist must be prepared to *reveal himself* as a person, with a family, with a car, with his own ups and downs.

3. *Be subjective and personal.* Glasser feels that orthodox psychiatry, in its insistence on being objective and impersonal, is laboring under an almost impossible handicap. People simply do not change in that kind of interpersonal situation. Furthermore, not only should the therapist be subjective and highly personal, he or she must demonstrate this attitude by constantly speaking of himself, using first-person pronouns. For example, in working with a student who is not handing in his term papers, the reality therapist does not say, "The school administration expects you to do your homework," but "I would like you to work."

4. *Emphasize behavior, not feeling.* In conventional psychiatry, which is very much concerned with providing a forum for the expression of feelings, Glasser notes, no one ever explains what the therapist is supposed to do with these feelings once they have been expressed. Glasser, on the contrary, suggests that the person speak about concrete behavior and deeds rather than philosophy and rumination. He holds that feelings are beyond our control; behavior is not. We can't tell ourselves to start feeling happy, for example, but we can tell ourselves to *do something*. Best of all, if we can do something responsible rather than something irresponsible, our behavior may help us feel better. The reality therapist does not mind discussing this and other concepts of his craft with the client, rather than acting as

though he were in possession of some great esoteric final truth that is beyond the comprehension of mere laymen.

5. *Force a value judgment!* The most important single component of reality therapy as a method, next to obtaining involvement, is to so direct the conversation that the client makes a value judgment about his behavior. For example, to use a situation mentioned by Glasser, if a kid punches a teacher in the nose, we ask him, "Now, did that behavior do you any good?" If the student responds that it did, there is very little you can do about it except drop the matter for discussion at a later date. But, Glasser insists, in ninety-nine out of one hundred cases, the boy will think for a moment and then respond, "Naw, I guess it didn't. Just made a big hassle and now I'm in more hot water than ever." The client must be pressed, again and again, to evaluate the responsibility of his behavior. Is it helping him meet his needs? Is it interfering with other people's meeting their needs? Is it doing him or others any good? These are the inquiries the reality therapist throws at the client after a firm involvement has been achieved.

Having looked over these five points, how would you say each approach is similar to what I have been saying in this chapter? How does each differ?

3. I suggested several situations in this chapter that might be characterized as counseling situations. To get the feel of the concepts I have sketched, look back over these situations and think about how you might approach each person from the stance of different counseling theories.

   For example, let's think about Jan (p. 139). Her youth leader, Mr. Jack, had been aware that something was wrong. Let's suppose that, as Jan is approaching his office, he is thinking about how to handle the situation.

   Jan has been so sharp. But these last few months she sure has lost interest. She was cheerful—so open, too. Now she backs off from the others. She sure doesn't seem to respond to spiritual things, either. Maybe she's even close sometimes to becoming rebellious.

   The whole pattern seemed to fall into place a few weeks earlier. Then Mr. Jack heard that Jan had been dating an unsaved fellow—in addition to taking a beating from the church gang and heavy opposition from her parents.

   Looks like I'm finally going to have a chance to help. Glad she asked for that private talk. Could be she's under real conviction. Let's see, what are some good Scripture verses to use with her? . . .

   In this sketch, Mr. Jack sounds as if he will be a directive counselor, planning to tell Jan what to do about what he believes to be her problem.

Write out a dialogue that represents what you think each will say and do if he does take a directive approach.

Now, looking over the identification approach again, do another dialogue. What will each say and do if he takes the identification approach?

If you wish, do the same with other situations described in the chapter until you begin to "feel" the difference and the interpersonal implications. For even greater value, role-play these situations with a friend, taking turns alternating as counselor/counselee and attempting to get the feel of each approach.

Part Three

PROCESSES OF MINISTRY

YOUTH IN SCRIPTURE
YOUTH IN BODY RELATIONSHIP
YOUTH IN LIFE

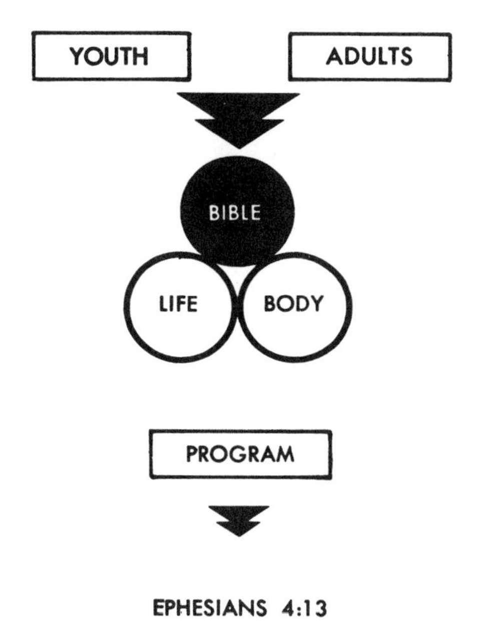

YOUTH IN SCRIPTURE

CHAPTERS

10. CONFRONTING REALITY

11. INVOLVED, TOGETHER

10

CONFRONTING REALITY

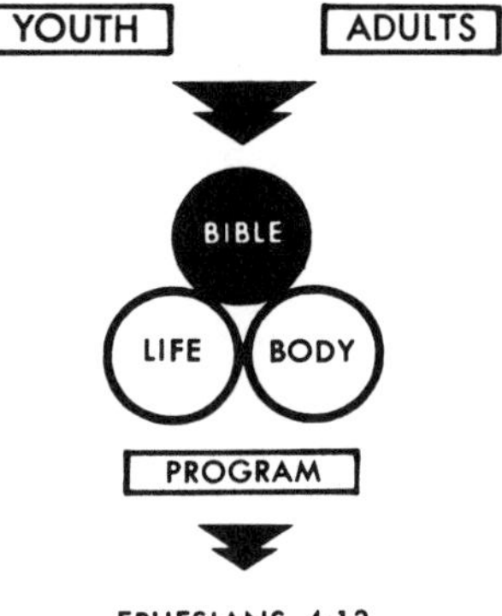

Charles Gragg, in evaluating the training given young people for careers in business management, has commented on the idea underlying most such training. The present approach, he says, which rests on the idea of giving carefully selected young persons information and general principles that others have acquired in years of business experience in order to give them a head start, "rests on a decidedly questionable assumption: namely, the assumption that it is possible by the simple process of telling to pass on knowledge in useful form. This is the great delusion of the ages. If the learning process is to be effective, something dynamic must take place in the learner."[1] The passing on of information—no matter how important that information may be—should never be mistaken for that dynamic something happening within.

The assumption that "telling" passes on knowledge in useful form is a delusion that has long plagued Evangelicals. Convinced that Scripture is God's Word containing information that we need and that has a vital meaning for us, we have been quick to emphasize communication of biblical content. But we have not been as quick to check and see if we communicate it in useful form—if our reading and teaching of the Bible has had God's intended impact on lives.

Probably nowhere in youth ministry has our intellectual-spiritual orientation been more in evidence than in our interaction with Scripture. And probably nowhere in youth ministry do we more need to involve youth as whole persons with the biblical Word, which speaks out decisively about their whole lives.

Somehow we need to bring young people into that kind of contact with God's Word that carries them beyond understanding it to the place where the divine perspective permeates personality, reshapes values, and is expressed in decision.

[1]Charles I. Gragg, "Because Wisdom Can't Be Told" (address as head of the Harvard Business School).

The following statement by Kaltsounis highlights what a secular educator sees as essential to an educational approach that focuses on decision-making—essentials distinctly parallel to approaches Christians need to take in communicating God's Word.

> *It should be made clear that decision-making does not minimize the value of concepts, generalizations, inquiry, social sciencing, and the like. It simply shifts their position from ends to means.*
>
> Decision-making involves three basic elements: knowledge, values, action.
>
> Values, which include the feelings, dispositions, attitudes and beliefs of the decision maker, are just as important as knowledge in making decisions. *At times, value factors can be more important than knowledge.* For example, a person may inquire into the unfair treatment of the minority groups. He may conclude and declare that discriminating is evil. Yet, when it actually comes down to supporting an open-housing policy for his neighborhood, he finds all kinds of excuses to oppose it. He might say, for instance, that he does not object to having a minority person move into his neighborhood, but he is concerned about what this might do to property values.
>
> During the past, the school has done a great deal to increase children's knowledge. The more recent emphasis on concepts and generalizations has strengthened this function even more, but little has been done in the area of values. There is a need for the school to expand its role and devote more time to designing ways that will stimulate children to discover their inner world of values, to analyze them, and to modify or perhaps reorganize them.
>
> Finally, decision-making requires action. It is this step that has the potential of making social studies exciting and useful to the individual as well as to society. It is in action that the child will see the relevancy of what he knows and is learning.
>
> Taking action gives the child an opportunity and the stimulation to bring out his inner feelings and values. He can test their vitality in the light of related information and the feeling and values of his classmates, and other persons closely associated with him.

> *Decision-making, then, takes the social sciences beyond simple intellectualization concerning the society and into the realm of positive social action.*[2]

Each point made by Kaltsounis is directly relevant to our ministry with youth. Scripture has not been inspired by God for "simple intellectualization." Rather, God's Word bursts upon us with the demand that we submit ourselves to it, permitting God to reshape our personalities through His revelation. And the test of our commitment, as well as the process through which growth in Christ takes place, is decision. Decision takes the Bible and our faith beyond the realm of "belief about" and into the realm of positive, obedient response—into the realm of action.

It is important to view Scripture in a reality framework rather than simply in a truth framework. By this I especially mean to insist that the Bible's teachings are not merely to be believed (a response that is appropriate to an objective but impersonal truth) but also are to be acted on (a response that is appropriate. to a confrontation with reality). There is an immense difference between these two teaching goals—and the way they can be reached.

In school I have learned many things that I accept today as true—but that make absolutely no demand on me for response. In high school I learned (and passed tests to prove that I had learned) how many representatives and senators there were from our state, what the powers of the Supreme Court were, etc. In college I was forced to take botany and zoology, and in the process I learned the parts of a flower, the make-up of cells, and even the body parts of some huge South American frogs that I had cut up with distaste. I accepted as true what I was taught, and in some cases I even discovered in the laboratory by personal investigation that certain statements were true. *But the truths I learned and accepted had no impact on my life.* They called for no particular response and demanded no change in my values or my actions.

This kind of learning requires only a simple "acceptance of x as true" and normally has little impact on life—even when potentially it has implications for life. Thomas Cook's study of

---

[2]Theodore Kaltsounis, "Swing Toward Decision-Making," *Instructor* 25 (April 1971): 35–56.

the effects of confronting a belief with its implied response in action is quite revealing here.[3] Cook and others communicated to a group of college students a message that had potential life implications. Cook showed the students that an untrained person has the ability to help mentally retarded children in institutions. Student groups were given this message, alternately with and without the information that they had easily available an *opportunity* to help in a local institution. With the added information, the message not only had potential action implications but also confronted the students with the necessity of making a decision.

What were the results? Students who were not confronted with a perceived-action consequence—and therefore with the necessity of making a decision—accepted the information as true: they believed an untrained person could be of help. Students who were confronted with the action consequences—and who were thus forced to make a decision—rejected the information, refusing to believe an untrained person could be of help, and "the costly action was totally resisted."

Somehow a "truth" that implied something for the improvement of others' lives but did not demand a decision to act represented no threat, and so could be believed without cost!

It is important to understand that our present educational system is designed for the communication of cheap truth. It focuses on the transmission of information that can be accepted (believed) without any necessary change in behavior, without personal decision. In fact, the whole approach to teaching and learning that characterizes our schools is suited to just this kind of teaching.

Kaltsounis's article and many like it forcefully point out that when an attempt is made to communicate costly truth—truth that demands decision—*an entirely different educational approach is required!*

Turning to Christian education, we note that our teaching and learning approaches are in fact largely patterned after, and in many ways are like, the secular—suitable only to the communication of cheap truth. But the Bible communicates a costly truth—the kind of truth that not only has potential implications for life, but also in fact demands decision. Thus, the Scripture says, "Don't, I beg you, only hear the message,

---

[3]Thomas D. Cook, John R. Burd, and Terence L. Talbert, "Temporal Effects of Confronting Belief With Its Action Consequences," a report financed by a grant from the Council for Research at Northwestern University, Evanston, Ill..

but put it into practice; otherwise you are merely deluding yourselves'' (James 1:22).

God's truth *can* be heard as a message that requires only assent, involving no costly decision to respond. *But it must not be. For Scripture is by nature a revelation of reality, and each human being must come to terms with reality.*

REALITY REVEALED

G. A. Kelly makes a point restated by many in many different contexts: our universe is open to interpretation, and our interpretation is important. In fact, decisions and choices in life are ultimately based on our perception (conceptual and affectual) of the world. He declares:

> The universe is real; it is happening all the time; it is integral; and it is open to piecemeal interpretation. Different men construe it in different ways. Since it owns no prior allegiance to any one man's construction system, it is always open to reconstruction. Some of the alternative ways of construing it are better adapted to man's purposes than are others. Thus, man comes to understand his world through an infinite series of successive approximations. Since man is always faced with constructive alternatives, which he may explore if he wishes, he need not continue indefinitely to be the absolute victim either of his past history or of his present circumstances.[4]

Looking at the world from different viewpoints, then, opens up new options to action, options that free us from various dead ends. For instance, the mechanistic physics of the nineteenth century set a pattern of determination that spilled over into the social as well as physical sciences. Dr. Werner Heisenberg's work on atomic physics, leading to the replacement of deterministic concepts by those of randomness and probability opened up exciting new avenues of research in the physical sciences and led to drastic revisions of thinking in the social sciences as well. This new ''construction system,'' or way of understanding the world, changed not only our generation's way of thinking about the world, but also our way of interacting with it.

[4]G. A. Kelly, *The Psychology of Personal Constructs* (New York: Norton, 1955), 39.

When an issue involves a reconstruction of our understanding of reality, our way of living must always change.

Illustrations from the physical world will perhaps help us to see how a perception of reality affects behavior. When we want to enter buildings, we—because of our reality orientation—look for doors rather than try to walk through walls. Similarly, because of our reality orientation, we hesitate to cross the street in the face of onrushing traffic. Our perception of reality tells us that we cannot walk into walls without hurting ourselves and that a mistake in gauging the speed and nearness of an oncoming automobile can prove to be our last mistake. *When we are fully convinced that something is rooted in reality, we modify our behavior to harmonize with it.*[5]

This principle operates in the social and moral world as well as in the physical. If we lie, ultimately it is because we see reality as something we can manipulate by falsehood, rather than understanding life as truly under the control of a God who is sovereign, and who is involved in our lives. A biblical reality orientation frees us to be finished with lying and to speak the truth with our neighbor (Eph. 4:25). Again, if we adopt the playboy philosophy of sex, it is because ultimately we accept the animalness of human beings and are willing to treat other persons as *things to use* for our pleasure. Our response to people, to situations, to all of life, is based ultimately on our whole-person (conceptual and affectual) orientation to reality.

What is involved in a reality orientation, then, begins to come clear.

First, there is the universe itself: the physical and social and spiritual world we live in. Secular thought sees the universe as "open to interpretation" and reconstruction. For to the non-Christian the universe is essentially impersonal, without meaning or purpose or goal. And so man can make of life what he will and choose his own values on the basis of what seems to work best for him. But the Christian has a different view of the creation. He understands the universe as essentially *personal,* created and sustained and guided by a God who involves Himself with us human beings to infuse His own loving purposes and give life ultimate meaning. We joyfully proclaim

[5]Let me stress again that "fully convinced" is not merely a statement about intellection. I present no such argument as Plato, that the person who knows the good will always choose it. Rather, "conviction" here refers to a person's whole perception of a situation: his understanding and emotional commitment. In familiar terms, I am talking about one's believing in something "with all his heart."

that "reality" is *not* something for man to construct for himself. Reality is the physical and social and spiritual world as God has made it and knows it to be.

The secularist has only human experience to guide him in his attempts to approximate reality and come to grips with life. But the Christian has an entirely different source for his understanding of reality—God's revelation. God's own understanding of the meaning and purpose of life and the principles on which we are to operate is made available to us in His Word. Only God truly understands what people fumble with in their mean attempts to find meaning. "Who could really understand a man's inmost thoughts except the spirit of the man himself?" the Bible asks. "How much less could anyone understand the thoughts of God except the very Spirit of God? And the marvelous thing is this, that we now receive not the spirit of the world but the Spirit of God himself, so that we can actually understand something of God's generosity toward us" (1 Cor. 2:11–12). And the Scriptures go on to point out that God's Spirit has acted to impart God's grasp of reality to us "in words not taught by human wisdom but taught by the Spirit" (1 Cor. 2:13 RSV). The conviction that we have revealed in God's Word an accurate and trustworthy portrait of reality underlies our attitude to such biblical exhortations as this: "Live for the rest of the time in the flesh no longer by human passions but by the will of God" (1 Peter 4:2 RSV). Because the Gospel message is anchored in reality Paul says, "Whatever happens, make sure that your everyday life is worthy of the gospel of Christ" (Phil. 1:27). The Gospel, as well as the entire Word, reveals reality, not irrelevant truth, and so demands that we live in harmony with it.

The conviction that Scripture is God's revelation of reality is central to our understanding of the role the Bible must take in Christian education of youth, and it is determinative for our understanding of *how* to communicate it.

A second thing to note about a reality orientation is that it involves a personal commitment that is reflected in behavior. Reality always demands a response and is hard on those who make a mistaken response. Every winter there are snowmobile drivers who dash at full speed out onto a frozen lake or river and plunge to their deaths through the ice. They think the ice is safe, but in reality, it is not thick enough to support them.

We can play with ideas, but we can't play with reality. We live in harmony with it or suffer the consequences.

Thus, we need to communicate reality, not only so that people come to understand it intellectually, but also so that they subjectively accept and act in harmony with it. To attempt to communicate Scripture in the way we communicate true but irrelevant information (for acceptance, without requiring decision and response) is to violate the essential nature of Scripture itself. God's Word must always be communicated so as to demand and invite decision to act.

Cook's experiment (pp. 155–56) gives us insight into what happens when we attempt to communicate reality in ways suitable only to the communication of true but irrelevant information. Remember that Cook succeeded in conveying information about the ability of the untrained person to help retarded children so as to gain acceptance of it as a belief—when that communication was framed as an undemanding truth. But when the same message was communicated in the same way with its reality orientation made plain ("if you believe this, go to an institution and volunteer to help"), then the information was rejected.

Something more than true information is required in order to produce decision.

Communicating a reality orientation is in fact distinctly different from simply communicating true information. It has different goals and requires a distinctive approach. We should be very clear on this: the communication pattern appropriate to one is not appropriate to the other! Something very different is demanded of the learner who is coming to grips with reality from that which is demanded of the learner who merely masters and accepts information that has no reality orientation for him.

INFORMATION INADEQUATE

Earlier we saw that to Kaltsounis subjective factors in teaching for decision making are values. Values, he says, "include the feelings, attitudes and beliefs of the decision-maker."[6] Scripture presented in a reality orientation brings a confrontation with values. "What we regard as important" may very well not be what God says is important. Man's essentially

[6] Kaltsounis, "Swing," 35–36.

self-centered view of life is in direct conflict with the biblical teaching that in reality the route to fulfillment is self-denial. Human wisdom finds it difficult to accept the fact that the leader must learn to function as a servant. Yet when we are confronted by God's view of reality, we are forced to choose: to decide to reject the biblical statements, to relegate what the Bible says to the realm of true but unimportant information, or to explore and restructure our own values and ways of life according to God's values. If we take this last course, we involve ourselves in a painful reordering of our feelings, dispositions, attitudes, and beliefs—a reordering of our inner person to bring our values into harmony with the objective revelation of reality God has shared with us in Scripture.

"Teaching the Bible" or "getting people to study the Bible," then, demands that we pay attention not only to accurate transmission of biblical information and concepts, but also to what must happen within learners when they confront a reality that demands response and change. And this we must never forget. The Bible, understood as God's revelation of reality, contains costly, not cheap, truth. As such a revelation, God's Word must be taught for decision, not for "acceptance."

We need, then, to reject educational approaches that are designed only to gain acceptance of truth (as illustrated in the secular "classroom" to teaching and learning) and develop distinctive educational ministries that will free learners to explore and change their values.

If we continue to teach the Bible in old ways, youth may well accept its teachings as true but file that truth away as irrelevant to life.

If we use old structures in teaching the Bible as a reality structure that demands decision and action, young people may well reject its viewpoint as being in conflict with their own unexamined but dearly held values.

If we teach the Bible in contexts where youth are confronted with God's revelation of reality (and thus are faced with the necessity of decision and action) *and* where they are free to explore, express, and change their values, then and only then can we expect transformed lives.

What context frees persons to change and develop new values? I pointed out in an early chapter that values are formed in and through interpersonal relationships—with parents, peers, and other significant persons. In chapter 9 I stressed the importance of the leader's developing a *"person with"* relationship with youth. If the leader is to have an impact, he needs to be in a relationship with youth in which life-to-life communication can take place—a relationship in which the objective reality revealed in the Word can be seen incarnated; where God's truth can be perceived in the experiences, feelings, emotions, and behavior of a Christian example as well as in his beliefs and ideas. To deal with what Kaltsounis calls values we need to have honest sharing of affective as well as cognitive data. (I am using "affective" here as Parry does when he describes affective data as "all messages meant to convey the quality of moods, preferences, values, emotions, hedonic tones, strivings, pleasant and unpleasant conditions, physical or mental, volitions and attitudes."[7] Only when there is an open and loving *relationship* between adults and youth in the teaching/learning situation, with freedom to share feelings as well as to discuss concepts in the study of God's Word, is there likely to be that kind of study that leads to decision and the personal discovery that God's Word actually *is* truth.

GUIDELINES

To this point, then, I have argued that our attempts to involve young people in Bible study must rest on certain understandings and presuppositions. These are, to summarize:

1. God's Word must always be understood as a revelation of reality.

2. As such, it must always be taught for decision, to produce action that is in harmony with the reality it reveals.

3. Secular education is designed to communicate information as "truth to be believed," usually not as a reality demanding decision.

4. When action implications are specified in an "information" teaching-and-learning setting, the information itself is more likely to be rejected than is merely the specified action.

[7] John Parry, *Psychology of Human Communications* (New York: American Elsevier, 1968), 65.

5. The problem with the information process is that it does not deal with values, the "what's important to me" that is the basis on which most of us accept or reject various points of view.

6. Only an approach to teaching and learning that seeks to deal with learners' values in a context of open, honest, and loving personal relationships is likely to bring learners to accept and live by a particular view of reality.

Understanding Scripture as God's revelation of reality—a revelation that demands decision and commitment—has many practical implications for youth ministry. We want to lead youth into God's Word. But we want to do it in such a way that they respond with a decision to live by it.

This understanding of Scripture provides criteria by which we can evaluate some of our present approaches for involving youth in Bible study. Are our classes and meetings information-centered? Is there a free expression by youth and adults of feelings and attitudes and beliefs in the study situation? Is there exploration together of the life response that is demanded by taking this particular portion of God's Word seriously? Is there a shared expression of commitment? Is there actual life change (observed and reported) taking place on the basis of a biblical understanding of life and an adoption of biblical values?

Although the answers to these questions may often be discouraging, the same questions give us guidelines for developing contexts in which meaningful study of God's Word with youth can take place. For God's Word does portray a reality that each of us is invited to experience in Christ. And the Holy Spirit, working in our lives through his Word and through one another, is uniquely able to set young believers on the pathway to maturity and vital relationship with Jesus Christ.

PROBE

case histories
discussion questions
thought-provokers
resources

1. One of my friends described the Sunday school class of a seminarian. Look over his description below and see how successful you think he is in communicating God's truth in its reality setting. Can you see strengths and weaknesses in his approach? How would you teach differently? What would you do in the same way that he does?

Earlier this fall I talked with one of the grad fellows who is a Sunday school teacher; in the course of the conversation he shared some of his views about teaching. By the way, he is not a Christian-education major and has never had a C. E. course! At any rate, I wanted to talk to him some more but I didn't want to make it an interview in any way. Well, today we had lunch together—and the topic came up so naturally that I didn't even have to initiate it.

Rusty feels:

Content is very important. Bible knowledge is a must. Methods can never outweigh Bible knowledge.

We need to experience biblical principles rather than just read about them. We need to see what the Bible says and then put it into practice in daily life.

Curriculums that have students merely fill in blanks are not good, not teaching the student anything.

How he structures the Sunday school hour is important. The president of the class welcomes visitors, makes announcements, leads in prayer, and then calls on Rusty. Rusty begins with a "gossip time"; everyone has to share something. Then they have Bible study. They're in Romans now. They're in small groups with a group leader. Rusty gives them assignments, so they have specific questions to answer. He supplies Bible dictionaries, atlases, concordances. Findings are written out; each student keeps his own notebook. Each student writes how the passage applies to his life. Groups come together to share at the end. He also has something special: an album, an article, or something they discuss—some current issue.

He gives homework assignments, expects students to prepare at home. He feels it's wrong not to demand work. He keeps them busy all hour, tries to vary his "something special" every Sunday. He feels this is important. I asked if there would be any trouble getting a substitute teacher now when he's gone for vacation. Oh, no, he said, they don't need a sub. They have their assignment and know what they're supposed to do; they'll get along just fine without a teacher.

Rusty feels it's terrible that our people know so little about the Bible. He thinks this may be because teachers have taught out of commentaries and quarterlies rather than getting right into the Bible. That's why he's so strong on Bible knowledge. Then he said that we need to train teachers to communicate Bible knowledge effectively. And with that lunch was over.

2. Like Rusty, I have some pretty strong ideas on how Bible content needs to be communicated. The concept of Scripture as a reality that demands response has definite implications for structuring the teaching-and-learning situation, whether for the traditional Sunday school hour or for a small-group meeting.

   In this book I will not attempt to go into structuring the teaching-and-learning situation for the Sunday school because I have written an entire book, *Creative Bible Teaching* (Moody Press), that works this out in detail. For those whose ministry involves Sunday school teaching, I suggest you consider reading that book carefully.

3. In this chapter I suggested that we need to develop a Bible-study setting in which youth feel free to explore, express, and change their values and attitudes as they study Scripture.

   To a great extent this kind of freedom depends on the interpersonal context. Only when we feel the love and acceptance and concern of others do we feel free to share honestly. When we are dealing with values, we are exploring the very roots of our personalities, exposing thoughts and feelings and experiences that are often emotionally charged. The same context of mutual self-revelation that frees persons in the counselor/counselee setting is necessary in group Bible study.

   The following example of a Bible study that seeks to encourage facilitating relationships as well as an exploration of the content of Scripture is drawn from *Fruit of the Spirit*,[8] one of a series of Discipling Resource Bible study guides that I developed with Norm Wakefield. The goal of these studies is to help students explore the realities of Scripture and their own lives in the context of open, accepting relationships.

---

[8]Lawrence O. Richards and Norm Wakefield, *Fruit of the Spirit* (Grand Rapids: Zondervan, 1981), 37–45.

SHALOM 4

"My peace I give. . . ."
What an
important promise
for us,
living as we do
in a tangled world.
Opening our lives
to welcome
His gift of peace
is part of the joy of discipleship.

THE SEARCH

I looked for peace outside my house but all I found were strikes and recession and Russian troops in Cuba and Cuban troops in Africa and nuclear-plant accidents and the dollar losing value and crime and pornography and drugs in grade schools. I decided to stay inside.

I looked for peace inside my house but all I heard was TV and my kids whining and my wife yelling at me to go out and work and the phone ringing and bills and one bathroom for five people. So I decided to go to the basement.

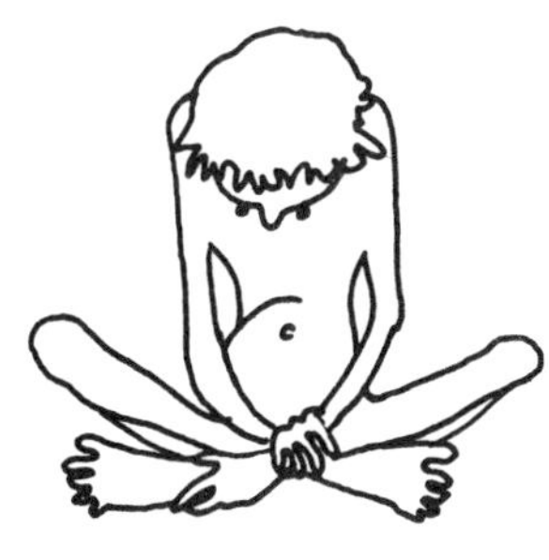

I sat in the basement and looked for peace by contemplating my navel. But all I could think about was why my parents didn't love me, and my ulcers and how I failed on my last job and how I wanted to be a writer but got married and how I'm getting old. So I stayed in the basement.

Where else is there to look?

READ

this psalm.

The Lord is my shepherd, I shall lack nothing.
He makes me lie down in green pastures,
He leads me beside quiet waters,
He restores my soul.
He guides me in paths of righteousness
for his name's sake.
Even though I walk
through the valley of the shadow of death,
I will fear no evil,
for you are with me;
your rod and your staff,
they comfort me.

You prepare a table before me
in the presence of my enemies.
You anoint my head with oil;
my cup overflows.
Surely goodness and love will follow me
all the days of my life,
and I will dwell in the house of the LORD
forever.

Psalm 23

RESPOND

to the cartoon
and psalm.

What is the
critical difference
between
the views expressed
by the cartoon
character
and the psalmist?

IDENTIFY

a tense situation
in your own life now.
Describe here
some characteristics
of the situation.

SHARE

with three
other persons.

A WORD FROM LARRY

The word "peace" occurs often in the New Testament. It's found in every book except 1 John. But roots of the biblical concept of "peace" are Old Testament.

There we are introduced to *shalom,* a term that speaks of "wholeness, completeness." In Joshua the word describes an *uncut* stone (Josh. 8:31); in the little Book of Ruth it describes *full* wages (Ruth 2:12 KJV). In Hebrew thought, *shalom* affirms well-being, in the widest sense of that word.

Typically the world views "peace" as the absence of war or tension. Men search for peace by changing the circumstances of their lives. But Jesus, who promises His followers peace, has a different concept.

"Peace I leave with you," Jesus promised. "My peace I give you. I do not give to you as the world gives. Do not let your hearts be troubled and do not be afraid" (John 14:27).

Jesus, who knew rejection, was possessed by peace. Jesus, who knew opposition, remained whole in spite of pressures. Jesus, who knew deep weariness, remained unshattered. Even the active hatred of men for which he came to earth to give His life did not shake His composure or His confidence.

In the same context as that in which He promised peace Jesus prophesied a difficult life for His disciples. "If the world hates you," Jesus taught, "keep in mind that it hated me first. If you belonged to the world, it would love you as its own. As it is, you do not belong to the world, but I have chosen you out of the world. That is why the world hates you. Remember the words I spoke to you: 'no servant is greater than his master.' If they persecuted me, they will persecute you also. If they obeyed my teaching, they will obey yours also. They will treat you this way because of my name, for they do not know the One who sent me" (John 15:18–21).

Notice that Jesus expects his followers to know external kinds of tension. Antagonism, even persecutions, are not to be unexpected. And like other men, we live as members of a twisted society, subject to inflation and crime and all the ills that mar our culture.

What then is the secret of the peace that Jesus promised us? What is the secret of what Jesus called "my" peace, in contrast with the kind of peace provided by the world?

We see the answer in His prophetic warning. Peace—a wholeness, a completeness, a true inner well-being—is found in our personal relationship with God, a relationship defined in Jesus' warning in John 15.

We do not belong to the world, but we belong to God. Because the whole life of the unbeliever is oriented to his experience in the material universe, circumstances can shatter his sense of security. Our life is oriented to God. No circumstances can shake Him or change Him, or threaten the certainty that "I am His, and He is mine. Forever."

We have been chosen by Jesus. Our relationship to God is no accident. His own active seeking of us is at the root of our relationship. It is because we know we are loved; we know with certainty that God is for us, that the foundation of our peace remains secure.

We share Jesus' experiences in the world. Some promote the notion that God does (or should) protect His children against all disappointments and strains. But Jesus came to be God's servant and to pay the price to communicate the love and sufficiency of God. We are now servants, too. And we are not to expect any life different from that of our Master. Because we share in His struggles, we must find a source of peace that gives His peace. A peace that is found in wholeness—not in escape from the tensions of life in the world.

Thus, the word *shalom* has deep meaning and a precious promise for us. Shalom is a peace that exists in spite of circumstances. Shalom is a peace that exists because we find our wholeness, and our security, in our relationship with God.

The psalmist found peace even walking "in the valley of the shadow of death." We can find our peace, in our extremities, just where he found it.

"I will fear no evil, for you are with me."

MEDITATE

Read through this exploration of "peace" again thoughtfully. As you reread, circle the *three* thoughts or phrases that are most meaningful to you in view of the personal "pressure" situation you wrote down a few minutes ago.

WRITE OUT

your own psalm,
telling God of your
confidence in Him
in the situation
you described
earlier.

SHARE

Then with the
whole group together,
share your psalm
one person at
a time . . . and tell what
it expresses of your situation.

And pray.

THIS WEEK

Meditate on this week's Scripture passage and what it suggests about peace. How would it help in the tense situation you are presently facing? What action(s) do you need to take according to the verses? Jot down your thoughts in your journal.

11

INVOLVED, TOGETHER

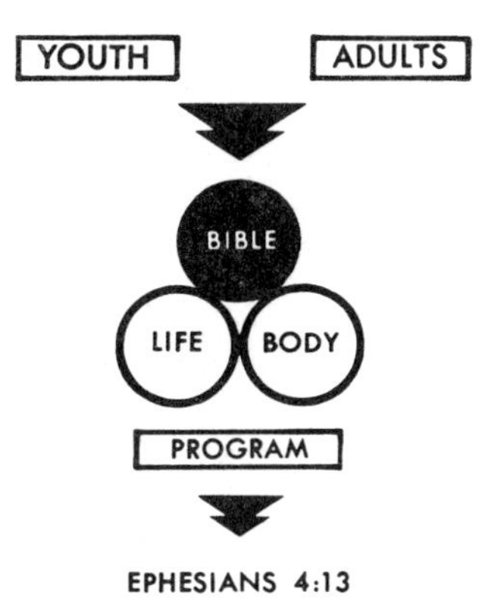

The Bible plays a central and utterly vital role in Christian ministry with youth. God's Word provides our only trustworthy guide to reality, for it is God's revelation in words of His own accurate knowledge of the meaning and purpose of our lives and how we can live them "in Christ." For anyone to live and mature as a Christian, he simply must learn to see life from God's viewpoint and respond to everything in life on that basis. In terms of what I suggested in the preceding chapter, youth must come to grips with God's Word as His revelation of reality and learn to act on it.

In the preceding chapter I suggested that a decision to act involves more than possession of accurate information. It involves opening up our personalities and our values to change. I also suggested something that will be developed in the next section of this book: the need for a distinctive context of interpersonal relationships to free us and motivate change.

Youth ministry, then, must confront young people with God's Word as a reality demanding their decision and must permit them to explore this reality in open, supportive relationships with others.

How can we bring about such a confrontation in the local church and create the necessary relational context? Clearly this approach to Bible study demands very different skills, knowledge, motivation, and acceptance of responsibilities from those of the traditional approach, which requires little of youth except that they come to "class" and listen to an adult "teach." While more detailed guidelines to both Sunday school and small-group Bible study remain the province of the two books noted in chapter 10 (*Creative Bible Study* and *Creative Bible Teaching*), we can perhaps sketch here the characteristics of study situations with which youth ministry must be particularly concerned.

Perhaps the most helpful approach to thinking about involving youth with God's Word is first to ask ourselves, What, specifically, do we want to accomplish? What are our goals in involving youth in Scripture?

There are a number of ways to state goals, but probably it is best to translate them from general statements to specific, observable behaviors. That is, to state what a person who has attained a certain goal will *do* that gives evidence of attainment. Simply making generalizations ("We want kids to trust the Bible") is not very helpful. We cannot tell from such a statement what "trust the Bible" means. Many people "trust the Bible" in an abstract, impersonal way. Others "trust the Bible" in a deeply personal and committed way and demonstrate their trust by acting in accord with God's Word even when alternative ways of response to a situation may seem easier or "safer" or more charming. What we must do, then, is state goals in general terms but go on to specify clearly just what behaviors we can accept as evidence that the youth are being reached.

There are several sources of evidence that we might want to consider. Probably the simplest is the kind represented in passing a paper-and-pencil test. This source of evidence is most appropriate for measuring achievement of knowledge goals. Does a teen know the books of the New Testament? Give him a paper and pencil and let him write them down. Does a teen know what it means to become a Christian? Sit down with him and ask him to explain the gospel.

It should be clear that while this kind of test gives evidence of knowledge, it may indicate nothing about personal response. A young person may be able to explain clearly how to become a Christian without having a personal, saving relationship with Jesus Christ. Knowing about the Bible is *never* to be equated with response to God. Certainly such knowledge is basic. But as we saw in the preceding chapter we need to be concerned with more than knowledge. We care about *knowledge* and *values* and *decision*. Bible knowledge is a means to an end in youth ministry, but never the end in itself. The end is a decision: action.

How can we measure decision? How can we tell if our young people have gone beyond acceptance of the Bible as information to respond to God's revelation of reality? Two sources of evidence seem open to us. The first is the young people's report of their own experiences. Do they tell of finding guidance or strength through Scripture? Do they report on looking into the Word of God for comfort or understanding? Normally, what happens inside people or how they act when we

YOUTH/SCRIPTURE GOALS

	Goals stated in general terms	Behavioral statements	R	O	T
			sources of evidence of achievement*		
KNOWLEDGE	I. Have overview of the content of Scripture.	I. List with 80% accuracy the 14 periods of Bible history including (a) approximate times, (b) books of Bible written then, (c) major persons, and (d) major events.			x
		Match with 60 of the 66 biblical books a statement of the distinctive message or thrust.			x
		List for 20 of 25 basic Christian doctrines at least two passages of Scripture which express or define them.			x
		Etc.			
	II. Be able to approach the Bible as a reality revelation.	II. Given a list of 5 common youth problems, develop answers to four and express them in essays appealing to reality as revealed in Scripture.			x
		Take a passage of Scripture and show its relationship to his own life today, including its guidance for response to his own life-situations.		x	x
		Etc.			
SKILLS	III. Actually seek solution to personal problems and questions by searching the Scriptures.	III. When faced with uncertainty concerning a value-based choice, seek out guidelines for his decision in Scripture.	x	x	
		When feeling discouraged or unhappy, read Scripture for comfort and/or understanding.	x	x	
		Keep notes of at least four weekly time in Bible study that revea probing for life-application.	x	x	
		Etc.			
ACTION	IV. Share responsibly in Bible study with others.	IV. Meet weekly with other Christians for prayer and Bible study.	x	x	
		Speak honestly and self-revealingly in the weekly meeting with other Christians.	x	x	
		Prepare, as required by the group, for sharing by personal independent study of Scripture during the week.	x	x	
		Etc.			
	V. Live in accord with the reality revealed in Scripture.		x	x	

Sample goals for youth's involvement with Scripture stated in general and behavioral terms

*R: self report of experience
O: observation of behavior
T: test

are not with them is something we can discover only as they reveal themselves to us.

There is also a second test of decision: our observation of behavior. How does he or she respond in a Bible study group? What attitudes does the young person reveal? How do the young people behave in various situations? What values are expressed in choices we see them make? Is their life and character in harmony with the Word? Or, in Paul's terms, are their everyday lives worthy of the gospel of Christ? When the report that young people give of their experience and our observation of their behavior harmonize, we have evidence that they have gone beyond Bible knowledge—that they are using their knowledge to make decisions and to form a basis for action.

Let's go back, then, to the question of what goals we want to set for youth ministry. What involvement with God's Word can we expect of youth, what does this involvement mean in behavioral terms, and how will we know if youth are growing in the ways we have said are important? On page 185 is a simple chart specifying sample goals and behaviors, as well as the most likely sources of evidence that goals are being reached. This is not an exhaustive set of goals nor a complete specification of behaviors that might serve as indicators of achievement. But they do demonstrate (1) several basic goals that we must be concerned with in youth ministry and (2) how to move from general statements of goals to specify the behaviors they imply. Thus, the chart shows a helpful way for a youth leader to approach goal setting in this important area of ministry.

SETTINGS FOR INVOLVEMENT

The chart on the preceding page indicates that we need Youth/Scripture goals in several areas—*knowledge goals, skill goals,* and *action goals*. The first two of these are actually means to reaching the third. Yet in practice the first two are normally products of the third! Only as young people become convinced of the meaning of God's Word for their life and begin to discover reality by living in obedience to Christ are they motivated to learn more about the Word. And skill in Bible study develops through just that kind of practical, relevant searching of Scripture that reaching action goals implies.

Thus, *involving youth in the kind of study of the Bible that leads to and demands response is our first concern in youth ministry.*

Where there is not decision-focused, decision-motivated Bible study involvement, there will be little growth in either knowledge or skills. Our priority, then, must be to develop a setting for reality-based, value-shifting study. Until this is successfully accomplished, little can be done to reach *any* of our Youth/Scripture goals.

So let's evaluate the potentials of various settings readily available to us in youth ministry for interaction with Scripture.

The "class" setting — Most local churches consider the Sunday school the "Bible-teaching arm of the church" and see the ministry of the Word centered there. When we evaluate the class setting objectively, we can see that it has both advantages and drawbacks as a teaching and learning situation.

The drawbacks are those shared with other formal teaching and learning settings. And the Sunday school has much in common with the secular educational approach. Each operates within strict time boundaries ("We have forty-five minutes for class today, so let's get on with it"); each tends to cast an adult in the role of teacher (giving him primary responsibility for preparation and presentation); each operates with a curriculum that specifies what will be studied that day or week.

The time boundary is one of the most serious drawbacks, for it tends to limit expression in class to the concept level. Put bluntly, it is very difficult to have free expression of feelings and honest exploration of values when time is so strictly limited. Meaningful expression of personal concerns and self-revelation takes longer than expression of thoughts and ideas. But this is vital for the teaching and learning that leads to decision. Normally when there is freedom of expression in the class, there is little time for facing action implications of Scripture and coming to decisions. *At some point in the teaching/learning process the lack of time will unfortunately keep teens from interacting at necessary depth.*

This drawback can be overcome to some extent by changing the traditional "teacher" role. As I noted above, the formal learning situation casts the adult in the role of teacher and makes him or her primarily responsible for lesson preparation. Teens come to class unprepared and unready to participate. However, when teens have been involved as responsible participants and have prepared through personal Bible study for class, the Sunday school hour can become a most meaningful time.

In *Creative Bible Teaching* I have suggested that four processes are required for meaningful interaction with Scripture in the class setting. These processes, successively, lead learners to do the following:

1. Locate and define an area of life in which they sense needs and become sensitive to ways in which the Bible portion to be studied is important to them.
2. Study the selected Scripture passage, discovering the reality it reveals, so coming to understand God's point of view on the original issue.
3. Continue to examine the life issue they originally explored in studying the Bible, seeking to understand how the biblical revelation sheds light on their lives. How do the present values and behavior of each person match up with the Word? If a person takes the Word seriously, how might his or her life and values be changed?
4. Decide, on the basis of this last exploration, to act on the Word—and return to daily life to do so.

When students come into a classroom unprepared, each of the above four processes must either take place or be initiated in the class hour. So the class time may be diagramed as follows:

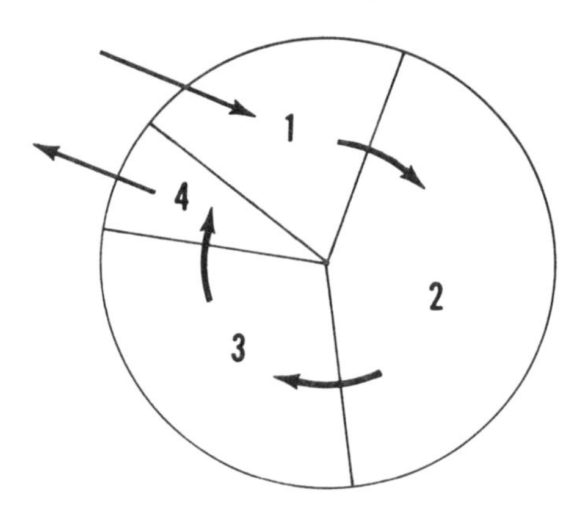

Figure 6
The Teaching/Learning Process
Limited to the Sunday School Class Hour

On the other hand, when young people take responsibility for study outside of class, the Sunday school hour can be used in a distinctively different way! Rather than attempt to squeeze all four processes into this limited time, the first and second processes and part of the third can be accomplished through individual preparatory study. Then when the teens come together, they can focus on the third process—the very process of exploring values and present experience in the light of Scripture that is not only essential for decision, but also requires the relational context that group study can provide.

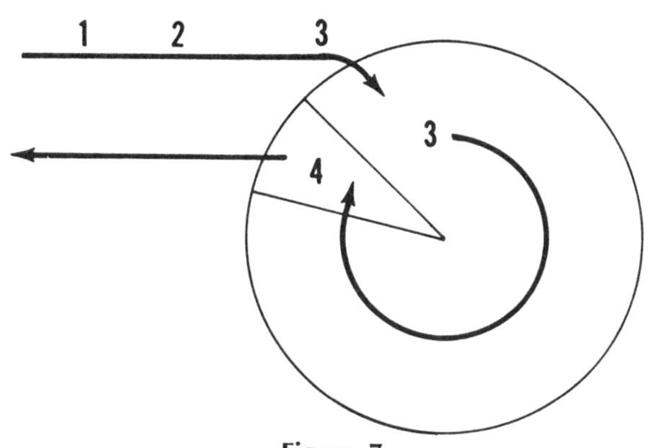

Figure 7
The Teaching/Learning Process
Not Limited to the Sunday School Class Hour

The Sunday school, then, *need not* be a formal learning situation just because it happens to meet at 9:30 on Sunday morning. But if it is to function as something other than a formal situation, it is preferable that close personal relationships between class members be developed before teenagers meet together as a class. (A fall retreat might be used to help members of new classes come to know each other as persons and become free to share honestly with each other in the learning setting.) Meaningful exploration of life and values requires a level of trust not created by mere acquaintance.

Curriculums, though often thought of as drawbacks, are not necessarily so. Today very excellent curriculums, designed to involve youth in just the processes I have noted, are available. It is true that, as some object, curriculums do not encourage opening up the class to discussion of immediate and felt needs. We can't simply sit down and say, "Well, what's bugging you today?" But we need to remember that Scripture is the essential guide for our lives; it is inspired by God and is profitable. We all need to expand our vision beyond those things our problems make us sensitive to.

It certainly is true that in our ministry with youth we must be sensitive to their life situations and their concerns, and we must be ready to work with them to help each discover God's guidance in Scripture. But we need to do more: *we need to start from God's viewpoint* and expand our awareness of the meaning of our lives. Today's youth curriculums often feature studies that are carefully chosen for their importance to youth and their relevance to adolescent concerns.

The Sunday-school hour, then, while it has drawbacks that may hinder involvement of teens in reality-oriented Bible study, is nevertheless a potential center for such study.

There is another possible use for the Sunday school that many are exploring today. That is to recognize the formal characteristics of the hour, and take advantage of the strength of the formal situation as an opportunity for the communication of information.

As I noted in the goals specified earlier, it *is* important for the Christian to have a working knowledge of the Word. Yet few in our churches have a firm grasp of Bible content. Knowing what the Bible talks about, its main themes and doctrines, the historical setting of the books and the distinctive message of each is tremendously helpful for reality-oriented Bible study. A good knowledge of the content of Scripture will help us to know in what passages we can best seek God's personal guidance and keeps us from misinterpreting verses and paragraphs by tearing them from their contexts.

Thus, many today try to make Sunday school a "school of the Bible," offering electives and knowledge-oriented courses, issuing notebooks and giving examinations, even providing certificates for those who enroll in a course and successfully complete it. This approach certainly has merit, *provided that somewhere else youth are being involved with God's Word as a decision-demanding reality*. Ultimately the Word of God must be approached as reality revelation, and to such a revelation only obedient response is appropriate. Studying the Bible for knowledge is valid as an aid to true Bible study; it can never be a replacement for it.

Small groups — The small-group setting merits much attention. As used today, the phrase "small groups" refers to more than size. Groups do usually include only a few members (five to twelve is most common), but the picture the phrase conveys is primarily one of close, intimate personal relationships. Size, in fact, is determined by this function: we can get to know well only a few others at a time.

These small groups are usually formed because Christians sense a need to get to know one another as persons, to move beyond the superficiality that marks so much of our contact with others, and to find friends who will love and care about them.

Sometimes small groups fail to move beyond deepening relationships and for this reason have been criticized for "encouraging exclusiveness." But in this chapter we want to see the small group (that coming together of persons who are learning to know and accept and care about one another) as a setting for Bible study. When such groups are involved in meaningful Bible study together, sharing a commitment to the Word as authoritative for their lives, the potential dangers of the small group can be avoided and the group setting can become a dynamic power for personal spiritual growth and effective witness.

Small-group Bible study can perhaps be most clearly seen in contrast to the traditional Sunday-school approach. In small group studies the time is usually open: there is room for sharing and mutual self-revelation, the development of those close interpersonal relationships that are so vital for changing values and making decisions.

Thus, the format of the small-group meeting differs significantly from that of the Sunday school. While there is no standard procedure, the following illustrates a common pattern:

1. "Temperature check"—members sharing their feelings, experiences of the past week, and any problems and concerns they may have.

2. Bible study—reading, discussing, and exploring Scripture, the passage chosen either by predetermined plan ("We'll study Acts 3 next week") or on the basis of group members' concerns ("Carol, you've been bothered by that, too? Let's look and see if we can find some help in Scripture.")

   The Bible study itself may take place before the meeting as an individual responsibility, during the class meeting individually, or as a group experience, by simply reading and talking over a passage.

3. The Bible passage that has been studied is explored for its impact on members' lives. At this point what has been shared at the beginning often seems to be excitingly illumined by the Word and often definite guidance is discovered.

4. A time of prayer for each member—asking God to help the members act on their responses as they show and express mutual concern and commitment to live the Word.

The duration of these meetings, as I mentioned, is best left open. But it is not unusual for them to take three hours or more, with up to an hour given to each of steps 1, 2, and 3–4.

Not all youth in our churches are ready for this kind of in-depth involvement. But it is important to provide such opportunities for those who *are* ready and to encourage those who become involved to constantly demonstrate their love and concern for others who are not yet involved with them.

Personal Bible study — Many reports of teenage devotional habits bear out what we know intuitively. Few young people have regular interaction with God's Word. Those who do not regularly study the Word of God give various reasons for their failure to do so, typical reasons being difficulty in concentration, interruptions, inability to stay awake, lack of interest, no place to be alone, lack of regularity, and inability to get up early enough. Yet all these simply reflect a more basic failure. The root problem may well be that few young people today find the Bible interesting or meaningful.

The solution is not to resort to exhortations to "have a daily quiet time," but to provide in our youth ministry both motivation for study and an opportunity to learn how to study. The solution is to make youth's involvement in Scripture meaningful and exciting.

Such motivation and meaning are best discovered through study with others. Linking what teens study privately to what they share when they meet with others (whether in Sunday school, a small group, or person-to-person with the youth leader) provides an impetus to study. Sharing perceptions with others and learning to see fresh meaning in the Word do much to foster awareness of the value of personal Bible study.

MOTIVATING BIBLE STUDY

There are several sources of motivation for involvement in God's Word. These, in order of priority of introduction in a local youth ministry, are:

Responsibility to others — In the next section we will explore in some detail what are called in this book "body ministries." Underlying the concept, however, is awareness that God has joined us with others because we need them and must develop commitment to them. Mutual self-revelation, a coming to know others as persons, has often been alluded to in this book. It is the way we come to know others in the body and sense our unity with them. When we have come to trust and accept one another in Christ, this relationship itself is highly motivating. A sense of responsibility, then, to those to whom we become committed, is a primary and initial motivation for personal Bible study. When studying God's Word is no longer viewed as the role of a "teacher," but when each person involved accepts his responsibility to share with and minister to others, individuals can be expected to study and prepare for group meetings.

Where no group yet exists, the leader himself can tie into this motivation by developing close personal relationships with individuals and meeting with them privately for prayer and Bible study.

Probably seeking to help youth become involved in this way with others, so they accept responsibility for personal study, is *the* crucial starting place in motivating teens in any youth ministry.

Awareness of relevancy — When young people discover how excitingly the Bible speaks to their individual situations, another important motive for study is created.

Such an awareness can be developed in either of the group settings discussed in this chapter. But we need to remember that one's underlying attitude toward Scripture is critical. The way an individual perceives the tone of Scripture is unquestionably going to affect his responsiveness to a Word he learns is relevant to his life. Thus, a nagging mother may be heard by a teen to say something relevant—but a nagging mother is hardly welcomed or responded to! In leading youth to see the Word as relevant, we *must* make sure that they view God's involvement in their lives in a positive way.

Experience of reality — The ultimate motivation for continued involvement in God's Word is a person's own experience of reality. Christ said to a disciple who questioned how He would make Himself real to believers after His death and resurrection: "If a man loves me, he will keep my word, and my Father will love him, and we will come to him and make our home with him" (John 14:23 RSV). Living by the words of God sets us free (John 8:31–32); love-motivated response to God makes Christ real.

Just as our love for persons grows as we come to know them better, so our love for God grows as we come to know Him better. And the one pathway God has provided for us to know Him as a Person is through responsive obedience to what He says to us in His Word.

Our goal, then, in seeking to tap other motivations for Bible study is to lead youth into a vital relationship with Jesus Christ—a relationship that submerges other motives in an overriding desire "to know Him."

PROBE

case histories
thought questions
discussion questions
resources

1. Put yourself in the place of a person called to minister with youth at Typical Local Church. The teens there are not particularly enthusiastic about church. Half of those associated with the church come to Sunday school, fewer to Sunday evening "Youth Group." More of them attend the frequent socials the church sponsors. After a few weeks you discover two or three young people who seem to be honestly concerned about their relationship with God. Most of the others have at best a superficial interest.

   In this setting, (1) develop a set of goals concerning the teens' involvement in the Word—goals for the first six months, for the first year, for five years. Then (2) plan a strategy of approach you would take to reach the goals. What study settings would you use? What motivations would you try to establish? How would you do this?

2. I mentioned that good curriculums are available for the ministry with teens. Evaluate several in terms of the processes discussed on pages 188–90. Include also in your evaluation the small-group approach reported on pages 131–33. Watch particularly for their attitude to Scripture as a reality that demands response.

   Materials are helpful not only for classes, but also for personal devotional aids. A survey of two hundred young people taken by some of my students shows that those who use printed helps are significantly more involved in personal devotions than others.

   Printed helps, however, may either aid or hinder young people in interacting with the Word as a reality revelation. Devotional "thoughts" often totally neglect the need for personal response.

TEENS WHO USE PRINTED HELPS		TEENS WHO DO NOT USE PRINTED HELPS
39%	Have daily devotions	19%
52%	2 or 3 times weekly	25%
9%	sometimes	49%
—	never	7%

The Ignatian Method for Experiencing Jesus as Friend

3. Shelton describes a meditation/devotional method of interaction with Scripture that has a long tradition in Catholicism. It is a method developed and explored in the writings of St. Ignatius, linking prayer and Bible study. What is your evaluation of the usefulness of the historic approach in your own devotional life and in the life of teens? Here is Shelton's description:

Let us now come back to the point made earlier in our discussion: It is solitude that allows the adolescent to experience Jesus as friend. Thus, we need to discover what method allows this friendship with Jesus to be experienced.

St. Ignatius's method of prayer may prove useful. The ancient monastic tradition spoke of prayer in several stages: *lectio* (reading the mystery of scripture), *meditatio* (applying this reading to oneself), *oratio* (petitioning, asking God for help and enlightenment), and *contemplation* (contemplation, the unique personal experience of God in prayer). St. Ignatius was influenced by this tradition, and it is revealed in his own spiritual writings. For St. Ignatius, contemplation is an "organic" experience that involves the total self-thoughts, memory, feelings, imagination, and will. We experience the self with God through the mystery of Scripture. We can propose that the adolescent try to encounter God in this way. It is this friendship model, one that is crucial for adolescent development, that provides the opportunity for the adolescent to experience Jesus in this most intimate way.

Scripture and the friendship model — One way to adapt the Ignatian method to the adolescent's life is to work with scripture and the friendship model. By encountering Jesus in scripture, the young person experiences a deepening knowledge of Jesus as a friend. By contemplating the actual words of Jesus (and incorporating the perspective of a "low Christology"), the adolescent can become better acquainted with Jesus as friend. The adolescent can then share Jesus' own feelings, thoughts, and experiences. In other words, Jesus becomes a real friend with whom the young person can share his or her own life.

Just as the adolescent allows the Lord into his or her life, so too does Jesus (as a real friend would) invite the adolescent to share His life with Him. This, of course, does not mean that every event in the gospel is a literal, historical, occurrence in Jesus' life. Our knowledge of scripture tells us that the Gospel writers wrote to understand more deeply the message of salvation that Jesus had proclaimed. At the same time, though, we can view the scriptural words and accounts of Jesus as not only relating much of what the real Jesus was actually experiencing, but also giving us glimpses into who this man Jesus was. We invite the adolescent to penetrate scripture with his or her imagination so that he or she can experience more deeply the personal call and actual life of Jesus in friendship.

In attempting to capture the experience of Jesus as friend, we can turn to the Gospels and view passages that reveal to us who Jesus is. The following list suggests some passages that might help us to capture the humanity of Jesus:

Prayer—Mk 1:35 (withdrawing to prayer); Mk 6:9–15 (the Our Father); Lk 5:16 (Jesus retiring to pray); Lk 9:29 (prayer before the Transfiguration).

Being tempted—Lk 4:1–13 (Jesus enduring temptation).

Compassion—Mt 15:32–38 (Jesus feeds the hungry); Lk 7:11–17 (Jesus has compassion for the widow).

Hunger—Mk 11:12 (leaving Bethany); Mt 4:2 (fasting in the desert).

Anxiety—Mt 26:36–46 (agony in the garden).

Surprise—Mt 15:21–28 (encounter with the Canaanite woman).

Friendship—Jn 11:1–44.

Tears—Lk 19:41 (viewing Jerusalem).

Frustration—Lk 22:38 (response to the disciples).

Forgiveness—Lk 23:34 (on the Cross).

Relaxation—Lk 10:38 (visiting Mary and Martha); Lk 11:37 (dining with Pharisees); Jn 2:1–11 (wedding feast at Cana).

Discipleship—Lk 9:23–27; Mt 10:16–27; Lk 9:57–62; Mt 16:24–28; Mk 10:17–22.

Anger—Mt 21:18–19 (the fig tree); Mt 23:25–26 (warning to the Pharisees); Jn 2:13–16 (driving money changers from the temple).

Love—Mk 12:28–34 (the great commandment); Lk 10:25–37 (the Good Samaritan); Mk 10:43–44 (serving others); Jn 15:9–17 (the commands to love).

Openness to others—Mk 3:31–35.

Borrowing from the Ignatian method, an adaptation of the format for adolescents might include the following forms of prayer:

Preparation—Suggest that the adolescent imagine the importance of friendship: What does a friend really mean to the young person? How important are friends to him or her? Spend a few moments on this.

Grace—Have the adolescent ask Jesus to share His life with him. The adolescent can ask Jesus some questions about Himself, His life, His experiences.

Setting—Read about a scripture passage, such as John 11:3–6, for example, which describes the friendship of Jesus, Martha, Mary, and Lazarus. Then, ask the adolescent some questions dealing with the theme of the passage. In this instance, the young person could imagine himself or herself with Jesus when He learns of the death of Lazarus. Or the adolescent could go with Jesus as He talks with Martha and Mary, or accompany Jesus to the tomb.

Colloquy—Reflect with the adolescent (or have the adolescent reflect alone) on what his or her reactions are. Ask the following questions: What are you feeling? What are your reactions to Jesus now? What kind of friend do you find yourself being to Jesus?

Many other scripture passages can be included and this format can easily fit into a classroom setting, a weekend retreat, or an individual spiritual counseling session. In addition, the use of scripture and the friendship model offers several advantages for the adolescent. First, these exercises allow the adolescent to be aware of his or her affective life and to incorporate this aspect of the personality in his or her relationship with Jesus. Other benefits are also derived from this approach; for example, insights about how the adolescent relates to others can often emerge. Second, the adolescent experiences Jesus in a relationship that is both personal and special. Third, this model takes into account the current developmental level of the adolescent and provides support for it.[1]

---

[1]Charles M. Shelton, *Adolescent Spirituality: Pastoral Ministry for High School and College Youth* (Chicago: Loyola University Press, 1983), 130–32.

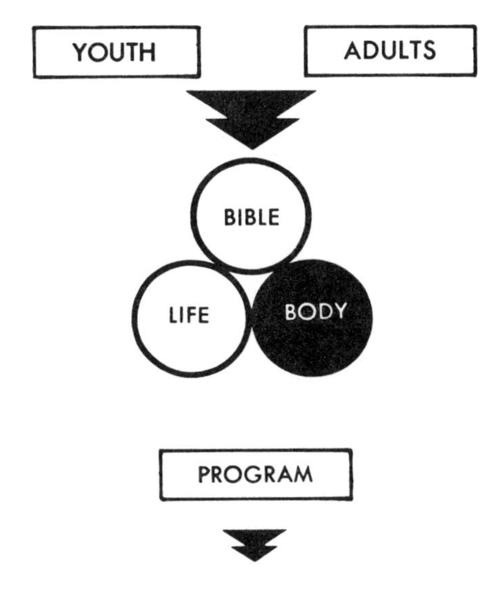

YOUTH IN BODY RELATIONSHIP

CHAPTERS

12. THE NEW COMMUNITY

13. COMMUNITY, NOW

12

THE NEW COMMUNITY

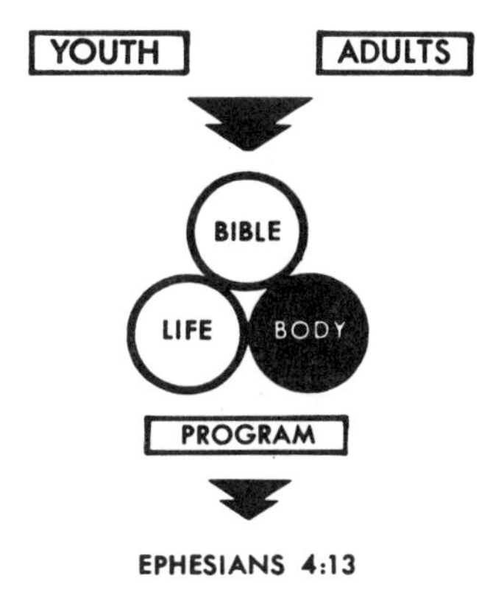

As I noted in earlier chapters, values are communicated and personally formed in the context of interpersonal relationships. But not all kinds of interpersonal relationships are helpful or effective conductors of values. The social sciences recognize several possible products of group influence, including compliance, identification, and internalization. Only the last of these, internalization, implies the character transformation for which God has called believers together "in church."

The local church as an association of persons does not automatically or necessarily function as a transforming community. As in many types of associations, the influence of the church group on the believer may in fact produce only conformity—a situation in which the lowest level of acceptance of biblical values may produce a high degree of conformity in public statement.[1] Simply having a group we call our "church youth group" or "youth fellowship" is no guarantee that the purposes God has in mind for the church will be fulfilled. For a group of Christian young people to function as Christ's church is intended to function, it must develop the kind of interpersonal relationships that are to characterize His body.

And at this point we can depart from all reliance on the social sciences for direction of the life of the body. For God's Word gives clear and distinctive directions for our life together—directions we must take seriously in youth ministry if we are to tap the dynamic power of the Holy Spirit released when God's people come together as the body of Christ—the new and transforming community.[2]

---

[1] See Allen's discussion of Kelman's theoretical formulation in "Situational Factors in Conformity," in Leonard Berkowitz, ed., *Advances in Experimental Social Psychology* (New York: Academic Press, 1965).

[2] The implications of this truth for the local church as a whole are discussed in my book *A New Face for the Church* (Grand Rapids: Zondervan, 1970).

At several points in this book I have emphasized relationships: in chapter 4 it was to note the impact of others on an individual's emerging self-concept; in the section on leadership the dynamic of Christian leadership was an example provided in a mutually self-revealing, open and honest relationship; and in chapter 11 this same kind of relationship in a group is viewed as providing the most meaningful context for Bible study. Now, at last, it is necessary to go into some detail about Scripture's revelation of the quality and function of relationships that are to exist between believers in Christ's church and, as part of that church, in youth ministry.

LOVE, THE FIRST PREREQUISITE

Jesus' words to His disciples pick up a theme that is reflected often throughout the New Testament. "I am giving you a new command–love one another. Just as I have loved you, you must love one another. This is how all men will know that you are my disciples, because you have such love for one another" (John 13:34–35). It is tremendously impressive to page through the Scriptures and see the emphasis given to love in Christ's church. At the risk of losing your attention (I find that my own tendency when I come to a string of quotes is to skip them!), I would like to reproduce just a few of the many references to love. As you look them over, note the significance each passage invests in love.

"Now that you have," says Peter, "by obeying the truth, made your souls clean enough for genuine love for your fellows, see that you do love one another, fervently and from the heart" (1 Peter 1:22). Fervent and genuine love is a major theme of both Pauline and Johannine Scriptures. Paul writes:

> Keep out of debt altogether, except that perpetual debt of love we owe one another. The man who loves his neighbor has obeyed the whole Law in regard to his neighbor. For the commandments, "Thou shalt not commit adultery," "Thou shalt not kill," "Thou shalt not steal," "Thou shalt not covet," and all other commandments are summed up in this one saying: "Thou shalt love thy neighbor as thyself." Love hurts nobody: therefore love is the answer to the Law's commands (Rom. 13:8–10).

> Above everything else, be truly loving for love is the golden chain of all virtues. Let the peace of Christ rule in

> your hearts, remembering that as members of the one body you are called to live in harmony, and never forget to be thankful for what God has done for you (Col. 3:14–15).
>
> You should be free to serve one another in love. For after all, the whole Law toward others is summed up by this one command, "Thou shalt love thy neighbor as thyself" (Gal. 5:13–14).

John, particularly in his first letter, discusses in depth the love relationship that is to exist between Christians.

> We know that we have crossed the frontier from death to life because we do love our brothers. The man without love for his brother is living in death already. . . . We know and to some extent realize the love of God for us because Christ expressed it in laying down his life for us. We must in turn express our love by laying down our lives for those who are our brothers. But as for the well-to-do man who sees his brother in want but shuts his eyes—and his heart—how could anyone believe that the love of God lives in him? My children, let us love not merely in theory or in words—let us love in sincerity and in practice (3:14–18).
>
> The test of the genuineness of our love for God's family lies in this question—do we love God himself and do we obey his commands? For loving God means obeying his commands, and these commands are not burdensome, for God's "heredity" within us will always conquer the world outside us (5:2–4).
>
> To you whom I love I say, let us go on loving one another, for love comes from God. Every man who truly loves is God's son, and has some knowledge of him. But the man who does not love cannot know him at all, for God is love.
>
> To us, the greatest demonstration of God's love for us has been his sending his only Son into the world to give us life through him. We see real love, not in the fact that we loved God, but that he loved us and sent his Son to make personal atonement for our sins. If God loved us as much as that, surely we, in our turn, should love one another! (4:7–11).

There is something both vastly moving and extremely practical about the love God's Word describes as the essential mark of Christian community. This love is not cast in Scripture as an impractical or abstract ideal. It is a motivating drive that finds constant and daily expression in interpersonal relationships. "Love one another fervently." "Serve one another in love." "Express love. . . ." "Love in sincerity and practice."

The same Scriptures that exhort love also leave us multiple examples of love in action. Some of the clearest examples of how love is expressed are found in context with a simple phrase: "one another." Here the command to "love one another" is illuminated as various dimensions of the reciprocal relationship are etched in the most graphic terms. While a full-fledged study of every occurrence of "one another" in the New Testament is well worth our time, only a sampling can be given here of the many portraits of love in action.

"Welcome one another . . . as Christ has welcomed you" (Rom. 15:7 RSV). This instruction to the church in Rome, which Paul addresses as Christ's body, highlights love as welcoming or "receiving" other believers into fellowship. The Greek word here is *προσλαμβανω*, which means "receive or accept into one's society, into one's home or circle of acquaintances."[3] This same word is used in Romans 14:1: "Welcome the man whose faith is weak—but not with the idea of arguing over his scruples." The Bible portrays everyone who knows Christ as Savior as "accepted in the beloved." In Jesus Christ every Christian has been welcomed by God into the community of the saints; every Christian has become a member of Christ's body. Love recognizes this shared relationship to Jesus Christ and eagerly welcomes other believers into the inner circle of friends who love and care for one another as members of a close-knit family.

Note that this welcome is not conditional. It is not dependent on a person's acceptance of our particular point of view, or of our scruples concerning doubtful practices (see Romans 14). Welcome is not, as a pastor friend of mine once stated, dependent on his subscribing to exactly the same doctrinal statement we subscribe to. If a person knows Christ, he *is* a member of God's family, our brother or our sister, and love demands that we welcome him and love him wholeheartedly.

"In honour of preferring one another" is the way the King James translates Romans 12:10. Phillips says it this way: "Let's

---

[3]The source for the definitions of Greek terms in this chapter is William F. Arndt and F. Wilbur Gingrich *A Greek-English Lexicon of the New Testament and Other Early Christian Literature* (Chicago: University of Chicago Press, 1957).

have no imitation Christian love. . . . Let's have real warm affection for one another as between brothers, and a willingness to let the other man have the credit." The root idea of the word rendered "preferring," *προηγεομαι*, seems best taken as "try to outdo [one another]." In this and other meanings, love is seen as creating a relationship that is marked by the opposite of competitiveness. This is a portrait of Christians coming together eager to listen to, and to respect, the views of others as important. There is no attempt here to force others to one's own point of view. There is no "politicking" behind the scenes. Love finds expression in Christ's church in the realization that each person is important—that each has a place, for God speaks through each. And so love seeks to help each find God's place for him, not through competition, but by encouraging everyone to contribute, and by hearing contributions with respect.

Christians are able to "*admonish one another*." This statement of Paul in Romans 15:14 points up a fascinating dimension of the love relationship that is to exist in the church and mark our fellowship. The word "admonish" is the Greek word *νουθετεω*, which means to warn, admonish, and instruct, with the general connotation of "helping through warning and rebuke." It is particularly striking that in a fellowship of persons who welcome and show respect for one another love is also expressed by rebuking. Here echoes of Paul's command to "speak the truth in love" are heard; family love often demands rebuke of a son or brother. So, too, in the church of Christ love may demand warning and admonishing a fellow Christian. And even from this negative expression of concern love is not to draw back.

In our culture we hesitate to rebuke even those we are closest to. "If you can't say something nice about someone, don't say anything," is a proverb that is not normally applied to saying something *about*—but certainly is applied to saying something *to*. Confrontation is avoided—as the mouthwash ads that feature arguments over "who will tell the boss about his bad breath?" seem to count important. But real love is impelled to speak out even in rebuke when it is necessary for a brother's good. And it is this kind of risk-taking love that the Christian community is to know.

"*Provoking one another*" is an archaic phrase we find in Hebrews 10:24, which in the original means "to consider, to notice [in a spiritual sense], to fix the eyes on." The thought here is that the Christian community should draw attention to and concentrate on that which needs to be done.

In the context of "one-anothering" we might better translate "provoking" as "stimulating" or "encouraging." The meaning is quite clear. Christianity is an action religion. We are called to live our faith, not simply to "believe" it. And so when Christians come together as the church, one of the ways they minister is by encouraging one another to active faith. Love is expressed by stimulating other believers to step out and live the life of Jesus.

"*Bear one another's burdens* and so fulfill the law of Christ" (Gal. 6:4 RSV) is the last description of love we will take time to note. This one is particularly important, for it is directly connected with the command to love (love is the "law of Christ" referred to in the text). And because bearing one another's burdens implies at least two corollaries: first, that we care deeply about the troubles and needs of other believers and seek to shoulder them in prayer, in encouragement, in expressed concern; and second, that the burdens of believers are shared with others. The only way I can know of the needs of another person is if he tells them to me. If he shares. So this "one another" phrase tells us much about love in action. Trusting love honestly and openly expresses its needs and weaknesses and burdens to others: responsive love rejects criticalness and condemnation to express concern and care. Love takes the neighbor's burden as its own.

Now, whatever can be said about the love that the Bible speaks of as central to life together in the church of Christ, we must say this:

> This love is marked by in-depth involvement of believers in the lives of one another.
>
> This love is marked by an active sharing of one another's life and experiences.

Love in the Body encourages, bears burdens, welcomes, admonishes, and performs a host of other simple ministries that cannot possibly exist without a deep knowing of others as individuals.

A "JUST AS" LOVE

So far in this chapter I have tried to sketch (all too briefly) something of what Scripture has in mind when it speaks of love, and how Christ's command to love calls us to involvement and deep personal relationship with other Christians. We need to note two other aspects of the biblical love, aspects that seem to stand in such contrast to each other that they appear almost to exist as a paradox. These aspects are rooted in Jesus' expression of the new commandment. There He gives us definite instructions as to the way in which we are to love each other: "even as I have loved you."

The standard of love among Christians is God's love for us. And so in the New Testament we often find directions like "Be as ready to forgive others as God for Christ's sake has forgiven you" (Eph. 4:32). God's love is the pattern on which love in the body must be modeled.

Here we must remember, as I discussed on pages 73–74, that God's relationship with us is linked to acceptance and rooted in forgiveness. God "knows our frame." He operates under no illusions when He invites us into relationship with Him through Jesus Christ. Before our salvation, the Bible honestly portrays us as "spiritually dead" (Eph. 2:1; Col. 2:13—"dead in our sins," KJV, NEB). We all "drifted along on the stream of the world's ideas of living, and obeyed its unseen ruler (who is still operating in those who do not respond to the truth of God). . . . We all lived like that in the past, and followed the impulses and imaginations of our evil nature, being in fact under the wrath of God by nature, like everyone else" (Eph. 2:2–3).

There was and could be no basis in ourselves on which God might say, "I accept you." No sincerity, no efforts of our own, no suffering or fleshly dedication could give God grounds for saying, "You're trying—so I'll accept you for that." The Bible is utterly clear that Jesus died to provide the ground of our forgiveness and that God is One who "justifies *the sinful*" (Rom. 4:5). God's love goes out to us *as we are,* and in His offer of forgiveness for Christ's sake He accepts us freely and fully for love's sake.

Most of our human relationships have had a performance-linked basis. An employee is valued because of the work he does. A husband or wife is appreciated when he or she meets the other's expectations—and may be rejected for failures. Young people are welcomed when their hair and clothing suit our idea of what is respectable, or when they seem to accept adult wisdom without question. Performance-linked acceptance says, "I value you for what you do. And when you displease me, I reserve the right to reject you."

This conditional attitude toward others is one that Jesus Christ decisively rejected in His life and in His death. His love went out to sinner as well as to disciple, and only those who refused Him, as did the Pharisees, found themselves cut off—not by His choice but by their own. Christ expressed the principle of unconditional love in His Sermon on the Mount in these words: "You have heard that it used to be said, *'Thou shalt love thy neighbor and hate thine enemy,'* but I tell you, Love your enemies, and pray for those who persecute you, so that you may be sons of your Heavenly Father. For he makes his sun rise upon evil men as well as good, and he sends his rain upon honest and dishonest men alike" (Matt. 5:43–45).

No, an entirely different basis for relationship is seen in Christ's love: He accepts others *as they are*—and loves them anyway.

This is particularly important in Christ's church. We believers are still human beings, still sinners, still flawed by the selfish drives and desires that bring us into conflict with God, with ourselves, and with others. Our flaws do bring us into conflict with other believers. (Otherwise the Word's many reminders to "forgive one another" would have no meaning. Only where there is injury and sin is there a need for forgiveness.) Our flaws—the sin that threatens to trip us up—often succeed and cause us to fail our God and one another. It is particularly because we are sinners who are at the same time saints that we need assurance that other Christians love us *just as* Christ loves us—that other Christians accept us and welcome us and value us *as we are*.

Certainty that we are loved as we are frees us from the need to pretend with one another and lets us share our burdens and our inadequacies. "Perfect love casts out fear" (1 John 4:18). When we are loved, we can open ourselves up to one another and cast off all hypocrisy.

Yet many claim to see a danger in this kind of acceptance-linked love. They fear (and not without reason) that a love that asserts, "I love you *as you are*," gives license for all sorts of sin and looseness in living. But here the Bible speaks in an exactly opposite vein. The Bible presents a love that accepts persons as they are, yet insists on a disciplined, discipled life. In fact, the Bible suggests that a Godlike love that meets and accepts people where they are actually energizes an amazing transformation. Accepting and loving people as they are implies no abandonment of them to present bondage. Instead, it is the first step toward their becoming.

So Paul exhorts believers to put their old life behind them. "No more evil temper or furious rage: no more evil thoughts or words about others, no more evil thoughts or words about God, and no more filthy conversation. Don't tell one another lies any more, for you have finished with the old man and all that he did and have begun life as the new man, who is out to learn what he ought to be, according to the plan of God." For the new person, "Christ is all that matters, for Christ lives in . . . all [believers]" (Col. 3:8–11). The same thought is repeated over and over in the Word. "Finish, then, with lying, and tell your neighbor the truth. For we are not separate units but intimately related to one another in Christ" (Eph. 4:26). "Live together in harmony, live together in love, as though you had only one mind and one spirit between you. Never act from motives of rivalry or personal vanity, but in humility think more of one another than you do of yourselves. None of you should think only of his own affairs, but each should learn to see things from other people's point of view" (Phil. 2:2–4).

No, the experience of an acceptance-linked love—a love that accepts us, knowing full well all that we are—is no invitation to continue in sin. Instead, it is God's open door to transformation—to actually become in daily life what we are potentially in Him. Thus, Scripture reminds us, "Consider the incredible love that the Father has shown us in allowing us to be called 'children of God'—and that is not just what we are called, but what *we are*. Our heredity on the Godward side is no mere figure of speech!" (1 John 3:1–2). So Scripture also urges us, knowing the completeness of God's love for us: "With eyes wide open to the mercies of God . . . as an act of intelligent worship, give him your bodies, as a living sacrifice, consecrated to him and acceptable by him. Don't let the world around you squeeze you into its own mold, but let God remold your minds from within, so that you may prove in practice that the plan of God for you is good, meets all his demands and moves toward the goal of true maturity" (Rom. 12:1–2).

REMOLDING LIVES

We can perhaps now see more of the concepts that underlie the titles of this section and this chapter. In youth ministry, we must see our young people in body relationships, experiencing together the new community.

The Bible speaks much of the body of Christ, focusing our understanding of the local church as well as the universal church through this figure. If we take the body concept seriously, we are driven to the awareness that Christians who come together in churches are to form no mere association of individuals who band together for a common goal or a common set of purposes. Instead, God binds Christians together in a supernatural unity; individually we are members of Christ, together we are His body (1 Cor. 12:27). The unity that exists because of our common share in Christ does not need to be created, but it does need to be "maintained in the bonds of love." *We need to experience the reality of a relationship that God's Word affirms does exist.*

The Bible is utterly clear on the cement that binds the Christian community together as a body. That cement is love. Hence the constant emphasis in the New Testament on love among believers. Only when we love one another, become involved in one another's lives, care for one another, bear one another's burdens, and live openly and forgivingly, do we experience the meaning of the body.

Christ's "just as" helps us see the nature of the love we can have for each other, and the purpose of the body. By nature Christ's love is forgiving love, accepting love—love that recognizes failures but joyfully asserts the worth and value of the individual. Jesus' love is a giving, self-emptying love. Jesus' love was expressed in His commitment to live, and even to die, for others. And it is just this kind of love—*love that commits us to live and even die for the benefit of our brothers*—that is to exist and be expressed in Christ's church.

But even more, Christ's love reflects the purpose of the body. The love of God is a freeing, transforming thing. Along with forgiveness God gives each believer a new heredity, a capacity to become a new person. And so all of a person's life opens outward to newness once he or she comes to know Christ.

Life in Christ's church has exactly this same impact. Through the body of believers unified in love and commitment to one another, God opens and remolds our personalities. He transforms us into the image of His Son.

This must, in fact, be central in our understanding of the church, His body. The body exists, and we are called together in unity, to be changed persons through ministries the Holy

Spirit performs for each of us through the others. So the Bible says, "Serve one another with the particular gifts God has given each of you, as faithful dispensers of the magnificently varied grace of God" (1 Peter 4:10). *Every passage in the New Testament that speaks of the body speaks of the spiritual gifts.*[5] And—the New Testament is clear about this—*each* believer has one of these spiritual gifts, a capacity to be used in ministry to others and to be a means God uses to remold personalities. Spiritual growth individually and corporately depends on the active involvement in mutual ministry of each believer, for Scripture says that "the whole body, as a harmonious structure knit together by the joints with which it is provided, grows by the proper functioning of individual parts to its full maturity in love" (Eph. 4:16).

Strikingly, the Scripture's teaching concerning spiritual gifts leads to the conclusion that they are not exercised so much through organizational roles as in the context of interpersonal relationships. All the ministries mentioned earlier as practical expressions of active love—welcoming, preferring, exhorting, provoking, bearing one another's burdens—are occasions (in individual or group situations) when gift-ministry takes place. So, as the Scripture says, "let us think of one another and how we can encourage one another to love and do good deeds. And let us not hold aloof from our church meetings, as some do. Let us do all we can to help another's faith, and this the more earnestly as we see the final day drawing ever nearer" (Heb. 10:24–25).

Love, then, not only unites the body through commitment of Christians to one another; love expressed (in welcoming, rebuking, encouraging, etc.) is the medium in which spiritual gifts operate. When Christians are involved in one another's lives in loving ways, God's creative and transforming power is unleashed for transformation. "God works through different men in different ways, but it is the same God who achieves his purposes through them all. Each man is given his gift by the Spirit that he may use it for the common good" (1 Cor. 12:6–7). *The supportive, loving concern of Christians gathered in body relationship is, together with the Word of God, the primary means God uses to remold us from within—a dynamic, divine power that growth in Christ demands we experience in life*

[5]Spiritual gifts are best understood as particular ways the Holy Spirit works through believers to strengthen, motivate, and transform other Christians toward maturity and Christlikeness.

together as a new community; a community created and marked by love.

MORE THAN A PEER GROUP

In an earlier chapter we saw something of the influence of the peer group on youth in our culture. Reasoning from what is known through observation and the social sciences, many who are engaged in youth ministry have written compellingly of the power of the peer group and have suggested approaches for developing a strong peer group in the church. Usually one rationale for social and recreational activities in the church is drawn from the premise that doing things together socially is one way to build a peer group.

I hope it is clear that what I am arguing for in this chapter goes far beyond the "peer group" concept—and speaks of a far deeper relationship than can be established by "doing things together in a social situation." At best, in the local churches attempts to develop peer groups bring teens together in loose *association*. But what we must do in youth ministry is bring Christian teens together *as Christ's body*. And for this, the normal activities on which we have tended to rely are tragically inadequate. The community of love to which we are called in Christ goes far beyond what most of us have dreamed of experiencing.

In summary, the community we need to build in youth ministry among Christian teens, the community that permits the experience of Christ's body, is characterized by:

1. deep involvement in one another's lives, sharing of concerns, caring, supporting, and encouraging;

2. each person's seeking to minister to and help others in every way he can;

3. honesty and self-revelation in all ministry situations, made possible by the conviction that each loves and is loved by the others;

4. commitment of each Christian young person to the others in the group, to consider their needs before his own.

These qualities are indeed necessary, for they constitute together the practical expression of Christ's love: the love that Christ commended to His disciples as a "new commandment

. . . that you love one another; even as I have loved you, that you also love one another" (John 13:34 RSV).

When this love fills and infuses our youth, and they begin to live with each other in love, Christ's body becomes an experienced reality to them, and one of God's necessary conditions for maximum spiritual growth is met.[6]

PROBE

case histories
discussion questions
thought-provokers
resources

1. In the next chapter we will explore ways of building the new community of love in youth ministry. But before we do, we need to get a better feel for the body concept introduced in this chapter. To put the concept in biblical perspective, look over the following three Bible passages that deal with Christ's church as His body.

   You will want to examine each passage for several salient features:

   a. What is the nature of the body revealed here?

   b. What are the functions of individuals as body members? What is the result if they do function in ministry? What is the result if they do not function?

   c. What does each passage indicate about the relationship context in which gift ministries operate? Why is there so much stress here on interpersonal relationships?

   It is well worth taking time to explore these passages now, and to think seriously about the specified areas of examination.

   1 Corinthians 12 and 13

   As the human body, which has many parts, is a unity, and those parts, despite their multiplicity, constitute one single body, so it is with Christ. For we were all baptized by the Spirit into one body, whether we were Jews, Greeks, slaves or free men, and we have all had experience of the same Spirit.

   Now the body is not one member but many. If the foot should say, "Because I am not a hand I don't belong to the body," does that alter the fact that the foot *is* a part of the body? Or if the ear should say, "Because I am not an eye I don't belong to the body," does that mean that the ear really is not part of the body?

[6]In the long run, we need to build this same kind of community across the generations, to mark the life of the whole church. In such a church, many distinctions between youth and adult will be (and in several churches with which I am acquainted, *have been*) reduced, and youth and adult accept one another as valuable members of the body, who need and love each other.

After all, if the body were all one eye, for example, where would be the sense of hearing? Or if it were all one ear, where would be the sense of smell? But God has arranged all the parts in one body, according to his design. For if everything were concentrated in one part, how could there be a body at all? The fact is there are many parts, but only one body. So that the eye cannot say to the hand, "I don't need you!" nor, again, can the head say to the feet, "I don't need you!" On the contrary, those parts of the body which have no obvious function are the more essential to health; and to those parts of the body which seem to us to be less deserving of notice we have to allow the highest honor of function. The parts which do not look beautiful have a deeper beauty in the work they do, while the parts which look beautiful may not be at all essential to life! But God has harmonized the whole body by giving importance of function to the parts which lack apparent importance, that the body should work together as a whole with all the members in sympathetic relationship with one another. So it happens that if one member suffers all the other members suffer with it, and if one member is honored all the members share a common joy.

Now you are together the body of Christ, and individually you are members of him. . . .

As we look at the body of Christ do we find all are his messengers, all are preachers, or all teachers? Do we find all wielders of spiritual power, all able to heal, all able to speak with tongues, or all able to interpret the tongues? No, we find God's distribution of gifts is on the same principles of harmony that he has shown in the human body.

You should set your hearts on the best spiritual gifts, but I shall show you a way which surpasses them all.

If I speak with the eloquence of men and of angels, but have no love, I become no more than blaring brass or crashing cymbals. If I have the gift of foretelling the future and hold in my mind not only all human knowledge but the very secrets of God, and if I also have that absolute faith which can move mountains, but have no love, I amount to nothing at all. If I dispose of all that I possess, yes, even if I give my own body to be burned, but have no love, I achieve precisely nothing.

This love of which I speak is slow to lose patience—it looks for a way of being constructive. It is not possessive: it is neither anxious to impress nor does it cherish inflated ideas of its own importance.

Love has good manners and does not pursue selfish advantage. It is not touchy. It does not keep account of evil or gloat over the wickedness of other people. On the contrary, it is glad with all good men when truth prevails.

Love knows no limit to its endurance, no end to its trust, no fading of its hope; it can outlast anything. It is, in fact, the one thing that still stands when all else has fallen.

Ephesians 4:1–24

As God's prisoner, then, I beg you to live lives worthy of your high calling. Accept life with humility and patience, making allowances for one another because you love one another. Make it your aim to be at one in the Spirit, and you will inevitably be at peace with one another. You all belong to one body, of which there is one Spirit, just as you all experienced one calling to one hope. There is one Lord, one faith, one baptism, one God, one Father of us all, who is the one over all, the one working through all and the one living in all.

Naturally there are different gifts and functions; individually grace is given to us in different ways out of the rich diversity of Christ's giving. . . .

His "gifts unto men" were varied. Some he made his messengers, some prophets, some preachers of the gospel; to some he gave the power to guide and teach his people. His gifts were made that Christians might be properly equipped for their service, that the whole body might be built up until the time comes when, in the unity of common faith and common knowledge of the Son of God, we arrive at real maturity—that measure of development which is meant by "the fullness of Christ."

We are not meant to remain as children at the mercy of every chance wind of teaching and the jockeying of men who are expert in the crafty presentation of lies. But we are meant to hold firmly to the truth in love, and to grow up in every way into Christ, the head. For it is from the head that the whole body, as a harmonious structure knit together by joints with which it is provided, grows by the proper functioning of individual parts to its full maturity in love.

This is my instruction, then, which I gave you from the Lord. Do not live any longer as the gentiles live. For they live blindfold in a world of illusion, and are cut off from the life of God through ignorance and insensitiveness. They have stifled their consciences and then surrendered themselves to sensuality, practicing any form of impurity which lust can suggest. But you have learned nothing like that from Christ, if you have really heard his voice and understood the truth that Jesus has taught you. No, what you learned was to fling off the dirty clothes of the old way of living, which were rotted through and through with lust's illusions, and, with yourselves mentally and spiritually remade, to put on the clean fresh clothes of the new life which was made by God's design for righteousness and the holiness which is no illusion.

Romans 12:3–18; 14:5–15:7

As your spiritual teacher I give this piece of advice to each one of you. Don't cherish exaggerated ideas of yourself or your importance, but try to have a sane estimate of your capabilities by the light of the faith that God has given to you all. For just as you have many members in one physical body and those members differ in their functions, so we, though many in number, compose one body in Christ and are all members of one another. Through the grace of God we have different gifts. If our gift is preaching, let us preach to the limit of our vision. If it is serving others let us concentrate on our service; if it is teaching let us give all we have to our teaching; and if our gift be the stimulating of faith of others let us set ourselves to it. Let the man who is called to give, give freely; let the man who wields authority think of his responsibility; and let the man who feels sympathy for his fellows act cheerfully.

Let us have no imitation Christian love. Let us have a genuine break with evil and a real devotion to good. Let us have real warm affection for one another as between brothers, and a willingness to let the other man have the credit. Let us not allow slackness to spoil our work and let us keep the fires of the spirit burning, as we do our work for the Lord. Base your happiness on your hope in Christ. When trials come endure them patiently; steadfastly maintain the habit of prayer. Give freely to fellow Christians in want, never grudging a meal or a bed to those who need them. And as for those who try to make your life a misery, bless them. Don't curse, bless. Share the happiness of those who are happy, and the sorrow of those who are sad. Live in harmony with one another. Don't become snobbish but take a real interest in ordinary people. Don't become set in your own opinions. Don't pay back a bad turn by a bad turn, to *anyone*. See that your public behavior is above criticism. As far as your responsibility goes, live at peace with everyone. . . .

Again, one man thinks some days of more importance than others. Another man considers them all alike. Let every one be definite in his own convictions. If a man specially observes one particular day, he does so "to the Lord." The man who eats, eats "to the Lord," for he thanks God for the food. The man who fasts also does it "to the Lord," for he thanks God for the benefits of fasting. The truth is that we neither live nor die as self-contained units. At every turn life links us to the Lord, and when we die we come face to face with him. In life or death we are in the hands of the Lord. Christ lived and died that he might be the Lord in both life and death.

Why, then, criticize your brother's actions, why try to make him look small? We shall all be judged one day, not by one another's standards or even our own, but by the judgment of God. It is written:

As I live, saith the Lord, to me every knee shall bow,
And every tongue shall confess to God.

It is to God alone that we have to answer for our actions.

Let us therefore stop turning critical eyes on one another. If we must be critical, let us be critical of our own conduct and see that we do nothing to make a brother stumble or fall.

I am convinced, and I say this as in the presence of the Lord Christ, that nothing is intrinsically unholy. But none the less it is unholy to the man who thinks it is. If your habit of unrestricted diet seriously upsets your brother, you are no longer living in love toward him. And surely you wouldn't let food mean ruin to a man for whom Christ died. You mustn't let something that is all right for you look like an evil practice to somebody else. After all, the kingdom of Heaven is not a matter of whether you get what you like to eat and drink, but of righteousness and peace and joy in the Holy Spirit. If you put these things first in serving Christ you will please God and are not likely to offend men. So let us concentrate on the things which make for harmony, and on the growth of one another's character. Surely we shouldn't wish to undo God's work for the sake of a plate of meat!

I freely admit that all food is, in itself, harmless, but it can be harmful to the man who eats it with a guilty conscience. We should be willing to be both vegetarians and teetotalers if by doing otherwise we should impede a brother's progress in the faith. Your personal convictions are a matter of faith between yourself and God, and you are happy if you have no qualms about what you allow yourself to eat. Yet if a man eats meat with an uneasy conscience about it, you must be sure he is wrong to do so. For his action does not spring from his faith, and when we act apart from our faith we sin.

We who have strong faith ought to shoulder the burden of the doubts and qualms of others and not just to go our own sweet way. Our actions should mean the good of others—should help them to build up their characters. For even Christ did not choose his own pleasure, but as it is written:

The reproaches of them that reproached thee fell upon me.

For all those words which were written long ago are meant to teach us today; that when we read in the scriptures of the endurance of men and of all the help that God gave them in those days, we may be encouraged to go on hoping in our own time. May the God who inspires men to endure, and give them a Father's care, give you a mind united toward one another because of your common loyalty to Jesus Christ. And then, as one man, you will sing from the heart the praises of God the Father of our Lord Jesus Christ. So open your hearts to one another as Christ has opened his heart to you, and God will be glorified.

2. Take a moment to compare what I have suggested in this chapter and what you have seen in the biblical passages above with your own experience in the church, or with the pattern of relationships that now exist among the youth with whom you minister.

   Describe briefly the relationship patterns you observed the last five times you saw or brought your teens together for any purpose. (This may include a Sunday school class, a "youth group" meeting, an officer's meeting, a social occasion, or just a chat with several young people, etc.)

   Now, compare what you have just described with the kind of relationships the chapter and the Scriptures speak of. How does what is actually happening in your group compare? How is it like, and in what ways is it unlike, what I've described?

   What conclusions do you draw from your evaluation and comparison?

3. I know that it is hard to visualize body relationship—especially when so few have experienced it. The following is a report written by two girls about their relationship as roommates for a quarter. Both were in my class in Youth Ministry at Wheaton College and ran into some of the ideas I have been discussing in the chapter. I think you will find their perceptions and their experience together helpful in communicating the emotional tone of what I have been trying to say. What they began to experience as their relationship grew is very much like the body relationship that has been the main burden of this chapter.

ANALYZING A ROOMMATE SITUATION: PERSONAL RELATIONSHIPS

In this project, we—Karol and Jan—analyze a rooming situation. We tried to determine what kinds of things were really important to us in our relationship. We both sat down and wrote our reactions to each other from the first time we met to the last night of our being together as roommates. And then after reading each others' reactions we sat down at the typewriter and reacted together to what we had written. Even in writing about each other we expressed our feelings in relation to how the other person had affected us. It was not only a great learning experience, it was also a tremendous sharing experience and a wonderful way to end our quarter of rooming together.

KAROL

January

The first time I met Jan was in March of last year. I had just had my hair cut, and I guess that it was a release for my emotions, because I was crying. The girl in the room across from me had hurt her foot, so the two of us were standing out in the hall, crying, and neither of us could stop. This was when Jan tromped up. She was tall and seemed like the motherly type. Automatically she became sympathetic. I just had the impression of a very kind girl, very free with love and expression of it.

Our first real meeting was on the steps of Evans Hall. I was going out with a guy she knew and was concerned about spiritually. That whole evening (it was quite long) was very Christ-centered and started off a friendship very deeply.

We were deep, but never close friends. Due to circumstances that developed in December, we were both in need of roommates. I thought it would be really fun to room with her, but I was afraid of pushing myself on her, because she was so kind that she would never refuse, and I didn't want her to have to feel pressured. One day I came to her room and presented the idea. She immediately squealed and jumped up to give me a big huge hug, and I just knew that she meant it.

I went into the situation without reserve. My opinion of her at the beginning of the quarter was extremely high. She was close to Christ, outgoing, very pretty (I didn't think that she was very smart), but she was completely accepted. I felt that she had absolutely no interest in guys, and she seemed like such a strong girl that I figured she would never be able to be married happily, in a submissive sense. And she was superspiritual.

I pretty much felt that there were things that she was above. Not snobbishly, but just not even concerned about such trivia that I (inwardly) was really interested in.

She was consistent with herself, and acted pretty much the same with everyone she was with. She was very motherly, and when we were together she was always very sure to see that I was included in everything. This was really good, because I was so used to being the big advisor and mother. It felt good to have somebody looking out for me.

So began the first week of Winter Quarter.

February

At the end of the first week I began dating a guy Jan knew pretty well, and this brought us closer. From my way of thinking, we were beginning to develop a normal girl-girl relationship. We began to share concerns (small, picky things) I had never thought of expressing before, and this added bonds to a growing friendship.

Our big breakthrough in our own lives and in our relationship (based on humanness) came on the 8th or 9th of February. Within two days we were both torn down from pedestals, and one night we just began to really open up our lives to each other. We had both given the impression of being extremely mature, "spiritual," goody-goody, "hard to get"; and to those who just saw us and didn't know us at all, we could both be mistaken for loose girls.

For the first time in my life, I opened up parts of my life that were just icky, and she understood. One of us would say something and the other one would understand and be able to relate a very similar instance. We had come up different paths and hit the same fork.

Together, we came to face the blackness in our lives, and it helped so much to have each other at a time like this.

I began to see Jan as an equal—equal, not somebody who was "superspiritual." I had often been a counselor and sometimes when I would start to share something with someone, would get a response something like this: "You think you've got problems, you should hear about what happened to me!" And I loved that, but once in a while I just wanted to feel a hand that was just a little stronger and firmer than my own when it was faltering.

Jan was so much like me. We were up until 4:30, and we were both constantly sharing, because it was all the same. There was finally somebody who was standing very near me, and we were both pushing the other just a little. We were able to tell each other things we had never told anyone before, and it helped us both to break down false images.

We've both grown up as "Miss Perfections." And that night we had to finally admit that we both had flaws. Jan and I both had guy problems—the problem of having guys flip, without our having any feelings. This had put both of us on the defensive, and we were beginning to harden toward the male sex.

I had always seen a beautiful, patient, near-perfection (just what I rebelled against) person in her, and to know that she felt some of the same defenses that I did, helped me to feel much closer to her again. Jan is so giving and loving but, just like me, she can put up fronts of snootiness and cutting with guys who can be pains. Our being together has helped us to be able to see so much more of ourselves, and to talk about it, and admit it.

Our defenses came from weakness, not from strength, and our putting up barriers meant just so many more to tear down. Super-strong Karol and Jan had holes in their armor—and we could finally see them.

Jan and I have not prayed together very often, but our lives together revolve around Christ. That is one very beautiful thing that I really treasure.

Faith is in Christ and Christ's love. I get so tired of philosophical arguments and intellectual discussions. Just to be able to experience Christ's love with a person and share it is one of the most beautiful gifts. Christ has given her more love and concern than just about anyone else I've ever met—and I've seen it constantly. All I can do is praise Him.

March

Tonight was our last night together, and I miss her. She has changed, in my mind, from a "spiritual Sally," who was just too involved with Christ to become upset, to a very real, beautiful human being. I used to think that she had just gobs of compassion, but no empathy, and I've been allowed to see the empathy so much and so beautifully.

We've also become close as human beings, and girls. She really gives me encouragement and love—she's always so willing and ready. Most evenings we would have at least a few minutes of sharing and going through our days—just like girls.

We have to separate next quarter, but even in that I can see God's planning. We were put together for one quarter in order to learn from each other and to support each other in some hard times. These hard times are very uncommon for both of us, and God provided us for each other.

Now He has taught us, and we have to learn to apply it. Maybe we can stand that better if we're apart from each other.

We've developed a friendship, and a deep-rooted love has grown. She's even more than I ever imagined her to be, because she has weak spots and she's shared them with me.

I had a higher opinion of her than just about any other girl on this campus, and through the last quarter, seeing the shakiness and humanness in her, my original opinion has been solidified.

JAN

My first recollection of Karol was at a dorm meeting early in January when she was part of a skit that was advertising the coming dorm banquet. We were both members of the freshman class here at Wheaton, but we had never met, even though we were in the same dorm. Perhaps it was because she lived up on the fourth floor and I was on the first floor. She played a really corny part in the skit and I remember asking the person next to me just who that girl was. I felt that she had to have a lot of nerve to get up in front of the whole assembled dorm with that stupid costume and makeup and do those silly things. I remember thinking that I had never noticed her before and to be quite honest, after that skit I wasn't any too anxious to make her acquaintance. I suppose that was really having a closed mind and attitude, but it never once occurred to me that night that we would ever meet, much less become close friends and eventually good roommates.

My first actual encounter with Karol occurred up on her floor later on during that year in March. I had come up to the floor to visit her roommate whom I had met and gotten to know quite well at band camp before the freshman year had started. When I got up on the fourth floor, a girl with short, brown, curly hair was sitting in the middle of the hall, crying her eyes out. I immediately thought that something terrible had happened and I asked my friend what was wrong with the girl. She quickly told me that the person was Karol, who happened to be her roommate and had just had her hair cut. She told me not to worry because Karol had informed everyone on the floor beforehand that she was going to cry as soon as she realized that her long, dark hair had been cut. I remember saying a few words to Karol but nothing really significant remains in my mind from that encounter.

Our first *real* encounter as two individuals occurred within the dorm again around the middle of May, right before the baseball banquet. I had found out *who* Karol was going to the banquet with, and one night when I asked her about how she was feeling about the dating situation. That conversation turned out to be a real sharing time, and we discovered that we both had *real relationships* with our Savior and Friend, Jesus Christ, and could turn to Him in times of frustration and worry. We prayed together and after that meeting I really felt that I had met a true "sister" in Christ. Even then I could sense that we had a lot in common as far as attitudes, spiritual insights, etc., were concerned.

When Karol presented me with her problem of not having a roommate, I didn't at first think of the possibility of her moving in with me. I considered the problem to be a "dorm thing," and since I lived within another dorm, I felt like a friend listening to a situation with no real answer or comments to give. I think I *did* offer her a place in my dorm, but the actual possibility of that coming about didn't really hit me. For one thing, I never really considered that Karol would want to move out of the dorm with all her friends living there and also it just seemed like a remote possibility in many ways. But I was overjoyed the night that she came over and told me that the arrangements had all been made with Mrs. Hackman and that she'd be living with me second quarter and "did I mind?" Of course not! I was truly happy. Especially after having lost my other roommate, I was lonely and was eager to have someone live with me. So it was settled before Christmas that she would move in with me after winter break, until spring when we believed Eunice, my other roommate, would be coming back.

When Karol first moved in with me in January, it was all new and fresh. We weren't really close friends, but I knew that we were a lot alike basically. She was funny but could be serious, and I enjoyed it, for I was a lot like her. Of course, there had to be some adjusting, but I feel that this was mainly due to our lack of knowledge about each other. I don't feel that either of us *really tried* to fake each other out concerning our own personalities, but we just needed time to get to know and understand each other.

I suppose the point at which the "getting to know each other" period finally culminated into a deep, full understanding and friendship was during the first week in February. One night we just talked until four in the morning and let it all out. We seemed to discover so many things that were alike in our basic personality make-ups. Our spiritual ideas seemed to match as only God could match them and our lists of personal hangups, priorities, ideals, problems, etc., were almost awesome in their similarities. At times one of us would say exactly what the other person had been thinking or feeling. I felt completely on a level plane with Karol that night, with no personal barriers placed before me, so I could really see "Karol" and I think she really saw "Jan."

And it's been basically like that since then. This winter quarter has been fantastic in so many ways. I personally have learned quite a bit. God has shown me so many things about myself and my relationship with those around me. Karol and I, I feel, can *and do* talk about almost anything, especially our own personal problems, which are usually the hardest points in our characters to reveal. I've grown to love Karol more and more every day, and Christ is teaching me to love even more through her. My attitude toward her most definitely has changed, for I didn't really know her before. And even during the first weeks in January, I didn't know her. I think that although we didn't try to fake each other out, certain aspects of her personality were revealed a little later than others. I must say that I was relieved in one sense. When friends would find out that I was to have Karol as my roommate, they would often say something like, "Oh, she's so funny—you'll have a riot!" until I was almost afraid that I was going to have a comedienne on my hands. But as it turned out Karol's brand of humor is basically the same as mine—Praise the Lord! For I truly think that He gave me a prize. We *both* grew. And I think we both grew out of being on top of our lofty spiritual-social pedestals into a realization of what it's really all about and where it *really* is. It, of course, meaning life, and life is only evident or possible through God—and *that's* where it really is. Karol and I, I think, finally not only knew this, but really knocked away some of that strangling pride. Praise the Lord!

BOTH OF US

Well, we've just read each other's critiques and it blows our minds. What one of us meant to say and didn't, the other did. And we really think that both of us meant to say the same thing. As we were reading them, we both squealed or made some other kind of unusual noise. At the same points in our papers we would squeal. One thing that has really hit us both is that this roommate situation has not only shown us that we are two very similar people but that we've both grown together in the same direction and the same ways. And all the growth has been through Christ.

We both had rather narrow conceptions of each other, and these conceptions broadened slowly during the first four weeks of our stay together, and all of a sudden one night our misconceptions didn't seem to matter anymore, because we were seeing the real people and not the outer shells. It seems to us that both of our real personality hangups had grown from a good amount of spiritual pride, especially in the area of dating in which we thought that we were such "superstrong women" who were always looking down at these "poor weaklings" of men we were always tromping into the ground as they flipped over us. We thought we were living it up. Well, right now we're living it up in just writing down the thoughts that came into our conversations.

In reality these "poor guys" were the strong ones. They were putting themselves on the line for us, which really took a whole lot of strength, courage, and honesty. If in the course of our lives we had ever fallen over any guy, we couldn't even admit it to ourselves, never mind anyone else and especially the guy! We were too afraid of someone doing to us what we were becoming known for. Do you want to know what we were? We were "strong, secure, dominant, idealistic, and proud-of-it women with the most humble and modest attitudes." We didn't even *realize* that we were beautiful, kind, considerate, sought-after, admired, and least of all we didn't realize that we were up on pedestals. We kept wondering where those pedestal-cleaning bills were coming from!

One of our greatest defenses were our mouths. Sarcasm came quite easily whenever we felt we were in danger. This is something that wouldn't have hit us quite as hard if we hadn't roomed together last quarter. Tonight is our last night together as roommates and the full impact of what God has really shown and taught us together this quarter is really hitting us. We have tried too hard to be "like" Christ; and that is just plain stupid. There is no way that we can ever be "like" Christ, for He, and He alone, is perfect. All we can do is look at Him. In Matthew 6 it says, "The lamp of the body is the eyes; if therefore your eye is clear, your whole body will be full of light." Only Christ has light that can penetrate into that inner realm of darkness. And only in this way can we really be living for Him. Trying to be like Christ puts too much emphasis on ourselves and on our own efforts, but looking at Him, His glory is so overpowering that we can't even see ourselves.

Within a two-day span two pedestals were knocked down. In the same hands that handed us hurt, we were handed balm. We had grown up being little Miss Perfectionists. We had heard so much of this that we were beginning to rely on our strength, rather than just following at Jesus' feet. He didn't push us down; He gently and lovingly took His hand and laid on just enough pressure to help us down on our knees.

It's been a rather hard quarter because God has given us a speed course in human relations. But our identical end reactions have given us reason to praise Him. We both grew so much, and it was only through His goodness, His guidance, His grace, His loving care, and His perfect love. And it was only when we took our eyes off ourselves (where *all* problems have their beginning) and looked to Him, that He was able to teach us. Praise the Lord!

13

COMMUNITY, NOW

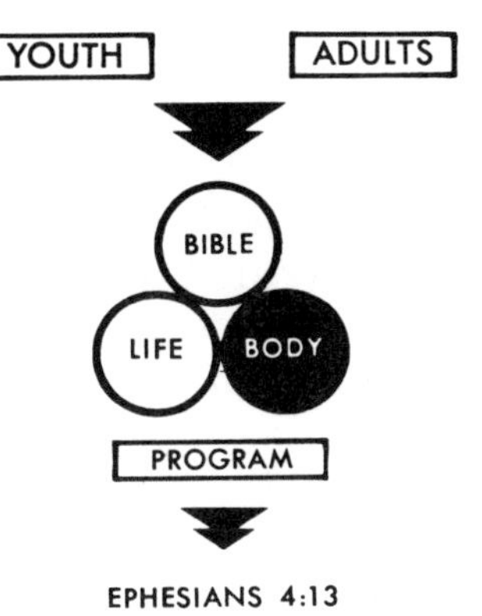

Jan and Karol (PROBE, pp. 218–24) broke through the barriers of superficiality that exist between persons and came to know the "real" Jan and Karol underneath. In the context of honesty and self-revelation that marked their sharing, weaknesses were exposed, as well as strengths. But even the "icky" was accepted: they discovered that they loved each other *as they were.*

The involvement in each other's lives that they began to experience did more than bring them closer as persons. Both girls talked about "growth." Both discovered truths about themselves that they had been blind to, ways that sin had been warping their personalities and their relationships with others. Pedestals were knocked down, the girls related. And rejecting the discovered reliance on their own strength, they turned to "following at Jesus' feet." So God used each to minister to the other and so, in their words, helped them back down to their knees.

This is how Christ's body is supposed to function—accepting and loving other believers as they are, opening up our lives to one another, discovering needs in each life and finding encouragement for change—with all of it gently turning our eyes back to Jesus, to follow Him. This is life together in and as Christ's body.

How do we develop this kind of love among believers? Even if we could put the youth of our churches into roommate situations, like that of Jan and Karol, a body relationship wouldn't necessarily develop. How, then, do we move toward developing Christian community? How do we build and maintain the unity of the Spirit in the bonds of love?

There's probably no more significant or challenging aspect of youth ministry than working toward body relationships. Significant, because mutual ministry "in body" is essential to the life together of Christians. Challenging, because in most situations development of body life may be slow.

The slowness stems from several sources. Many teens will not be far enough along in their own development to fit comfortably into mutually self-revealing relationships. Although there are churches where unusual closeness has grown among junior high youth (ages twelve to fourteen), research shows that distinctly different friendship patterns exist in young, middle, and older adolescence. In early adolescence, friendships seem to focus on activities rather than on personal interaction. A friend is someone you do things with, but typically friendships display little depth of feeling. In middle adolescence young people feel a great need for security. The highest values in friendships are loyalty and trustworthiness. Girls particularly show great insecurity in friendships and a fear of rejection at around fifteen years of age. One or two close friends become more important for stability and acceptance in a larger group. "Best friends" are valued in middle adolescence for intimacy, loyalty, and giving help.

The tremendous importance of friendships in middle adolescence and the stress associated with friendship relationships make a body-building ministry particularly appropriate and necessary during these years.

What is the essential of a body-building ministry? Just what we looked at in the preceding chapter: *love*—a love that involves itself in the lives of others in mutual self-giving and self-revelation, love that commits itself to loyal caring for others, love that seeks only the good of others.

MEANS GOD USES

There are two primary contexts in which we can work toward development of body relationships. The first context is individual, and the means God uses is the person and example of adults or other teens. The second context is the small group.

The leader's example As we have seen in earlier chapters, Christian leaders always lead by example. *There is no other way to guide people into growth.*

I know that some of my writings on the church have been criticized by those who feel I have left no place for the pastor and other church leaders in my approach to renewal. I am concerned about this reaction, because it is clear from Scripture that leadership *is* vital to the health and growth of the church—including every local church. What I have suggested, however, is not leaderless churches, but *churches in which leadership functions in the biblical way. The church must have leaders, but it must have leaders who lead by example.*

Example leadership is not demonstrated primarily in the sermon from the pulpit or in the chairing of committee meetings. Example leadership isn't demonstrated primarily in the planning of programs and the making of plans and preparations. *Example leadership is demonstrated and exercised by personal involvement with people in ministry*—by talking with and listening and sharing, by teaching another person how to love by loving and how to reveal himself by revealing yourself. Example leadership is an informal, interpersonal involvement with the *persons* to whom we minister.

In youth ministry, the first prerequisite for building the body is that the adult sponsor or leader comes to know and love individual teens. There will, of course, be times when he speaks to the group and makes plans and preparations. But nothing must be allowed higher priority than teaching kids to love by coming to know and love them. *Anyone who works with youth and is not building this kind of relationship with individuals and small groups will never succeed in developing the body relationship.*

The small group — We can know on the intimate level implied in this and the preceding chapter only a certain number of persons. As time goes by, we find it easier to move quickly into body relationship with other believers and to function as a body in larger, congregation-sized meetings. But there are compelling reasons for bringing Christians together to share with one another in small groups. I have expressed some of these in an earlier book.

> To learn to trust and to become trustworthy—to learn to love, and become loving—we must become deeply involved in the lives of others to whom we commit ourselves in Christ. To develop this kind of relationship we need to share ourselves with others, and they need to share themselves with us. All of this demands time. More than this, it requires a face-to-face relationship—a relationship we can have with only a few others at one time. And, thus, a church is forced to move to a small group structure.
>
> "Small," then, suggests a size which permits and encourages face-to-face relationship. It is not so large that any will be cut off from deeply and personally sharing himself with others, and in turn receiving from them. How large is this? Some research in group dynamics suggests

> that five may be the optimum number! But often groups of eight or twelve are suggested for church fellowship groups, and this range seems to have advantages.[1]

Often small natural groupings already exist among teens, and on these we can build toward the body. For instance, in many churches today youth attend more than one high school. The youth from each high school form a natural group, and we can work toward development of a supportive body relationship among them as a base for witness in that school.

In most school systems a distinction is made between teens by grade level, with the tenth graders and the twelfth, for instance, carefully distinguished. Where such distinctions are also made within the church (as is normal in larger churches), groups can be established by age and grade level, thus corresponding roughly with Sunday school classes as well.

Although small groups will grow naturally as body life develops, and can be used creatively to foster body life, the example of the servant leader is still central and essential. I believe it is a mistake to attempt to develop body life in youth ministry wholly through the operation of small groups. The first foundation and the continuing impetus to formation of the new community are and must be the adult involvement with individuals in the group, teaching them how to love by first loving them.

Figure 8 illustrates a development pattern for body life in a youth ministry, showing the central role of adult example, with *subsequent* development of small groups and change in the character of larger group meetings.

(1) The leader seeks out those who are committed to Christ and by example teaches them how to love and be committed to each other.

(2) These in turn reach out to other teens, forming small and natural groupings of youth who begin to experience body life together.

(3) As more and more of the youth group become involved and experience one another's love, more and more freedom exists when the whole group is gathered for worship or study.

---

[1]Lawrence O. Richards, *A New Face for the Church* (Grand Rapids: Zondervan, 1970), 153.

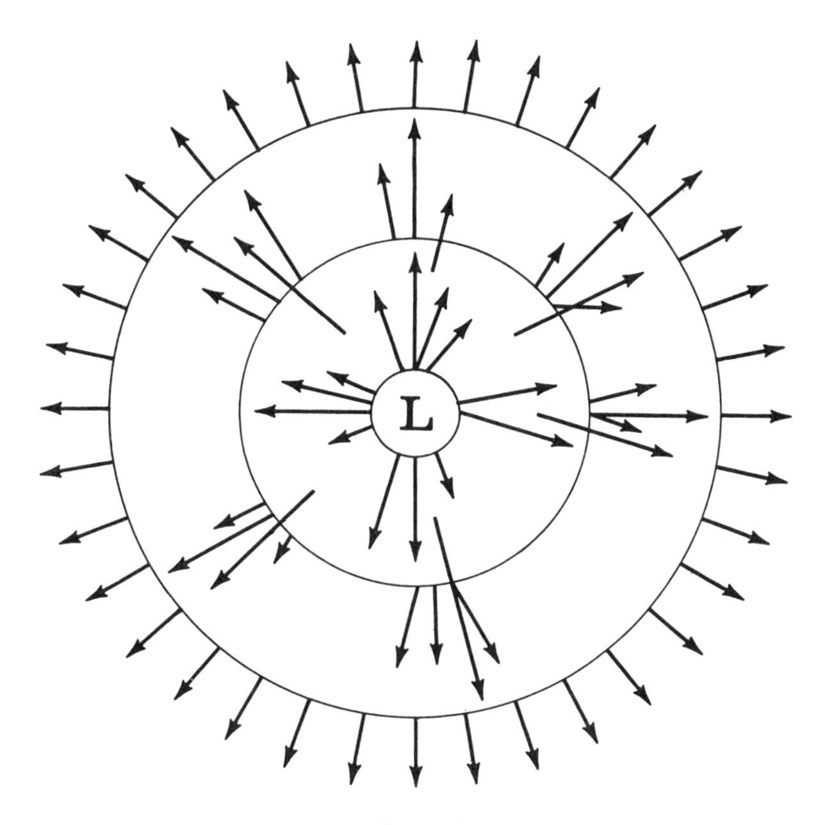

Figure 8
The Process of Development of Body Life
(begins in the center and moves outward)

PROBE

case histories
thought questions
discussion starters
resources

1. The viewpoint expressed in this chapter is in fact a very simple one. The key to building the body relationship in youth ministry is the person of the leader. Still, the practical implications are very hard to grasp, for few of us have ourselves been so led! To make the process as clear as possible, I am including here the responses of a man in youth ministry whom I have asked, "How did you go about building a body relationship in your ministry with youth?" Here, in a well-articulated statement, is his reply:

TALKING ABOUT "BODY RELATIONSHIPS" IN THE BODY OF CHRIST

J. Bristol

First let me share what is really behind our youth ministry, and actually this is a principle that's not simply behind the youth ministry, but behind all phases of our ministry in our church. I think that we take as our goal (we as pastors on the staff are very much agreed) the proclamation of Christ, as Paul says in Colossians 1:28, 29: "Him we proclaim, exhorting every man [or admonishing every man] and teaching every man in all wisdom that we may present every man mature in Christ." This is the focal point—the underlying verse, the underlying purpose, the underlying concept that guides all we do. That's rock bottom, right there.

Now, we seek to carry this out by means of certain principles laid down in the Scripture. First of all, I think we could build a model from the bottom up. We have principles; we operate on what we discuss to be spiritual principles concerning how to go about the work of the church, the work being admonishing and teaching in order to present people mature in Christ. And this we carry out through the scriptural principle of equipping the saints for ministry. In Ephesians, Paul writes that the Lord has given certain people to the church—prophets, apostles, pastors and teachers—for equipping the saints *for* the work of ministry *for* the building up of the body of Christ. We who are pastors see ourselves essentially as coaches in this.

We start off with principles and then we have above that the promise that the Lord makes again in Ephesians, that the body will function smoothly—each joint, each ligament becoming stronger so that the body may grow qualitatively and quantitatively. This is the promise He's made, that when we follow these principles, our body will grow. And from this springs our program. So, we always put principles first, then the promise that comes to us, and then the program will always come from the principles. We think programs vary from church to church as God leads people differently in different situations. But we feel the principles do not vary.

With this goal in mind, let me speak with regard to what we're doing in the junior high youth program at this point. We have on Sunday morning approximately 200 to 250 junior high school kids in our Sunday school department, and each class has two teachers. We have a co-teacher arrangement. I'm always for this, because I like to see the kids exposed to Jesus Christ through two different personalities. What Sunday morning gives us is what we would term a "pool of kids"—a large number of kids. Some of these kids are Christians; some *have* to come because their parents make them; some are inquiring kids, wondering about Christianity; and some of them simply aren't Christians at all. I'm sometimes puzzled why some of them come, but at any rate, we have a large pool of, say 200 kids. From that pool we draw anywhere from 30 to 75 kids on Wednesday evening, when from 5 o'clock to 6 we have what we call our time of "Bible Rap and Body-Life Sharing." This is a time when some of the more serious-minded kids come out. We don't offer any gimmicks; we simply say, "We're going to study the Scriptures; this time is for those of you who are serious in your relationship to Christ, and who want to spend time studying the Scriptures, talking about different problems that you have on your mind, different questions that you come up against at school, or just in your own thinking. Come on out."

Now this meeting that we hold from 5 to 6 on Wednesday has two emphases or thrusts to it. First of all, we have a time of praise. That's not exactly a thrust, but we have a time of singing, with guitars and ukuleles; we sing some of the more contemporary songs. Then we have a time of scriptural input. We always go through the Scriptures. The kids sit there with their Bibles. We've been working our way through *James* recently. But as we go through the Scriptures, we seek not only to learn what they have to say to us about Jesus and about our commitment to Him, about where we stand in relation to Him and to our brothers and sisters and those outside of Christ. We're also seeking to teach the kids to learn to feed themselves from the Scriptures. This is one key thrust of what we're trying to do—to get them to learn to feed themselves, so that they don't become dependent on a pastor, a youth worker, or a Sunday school teacher, but that with just the Bible they can put spiritual food into their souls. This is one of our thrusts, then: a study of the Scriptures.

After that, we have a time of body-life sharing. This is a free time when we begin by asking, "What has the Lord been doing in your life?" and, "If there's something we can pray about, can we have some prayer requests"; and "We don't want to pray for Aunt Suzie down in Tampa who sprained her ankle; we want to pray about *you,* where you're hurting. How can we, as brothers and sisters in Christ, bear your burden?" A scriptural mandate for this is Jesus' words in John: "By this shall all men know that you are my disciples, that you have love one for another." And then also Paul, in Galatians 6:2, said, "Bear one another's burdens and so fulfill the law of Christ"—which is the law of love. But we can't bear each other's burdens unless we are acquainted with each other's burdens. So this is the time when we share both our burdens and our joys. So we throw it open, and it takes time for real honesty to develop. And I wouldn't say we've by any means arrived; we have a long way to go, but there are flashes, and I think honesty is contagious, and burdens are shared and hearts are opened up.

We pray for unsaved parents and about the problems in their homes. Some kids have confessed that their moms and dads are fighting, and we need prayer for the healing of that relationship. Others have fallen out with their friends and they feel that this has been a blow to their witness—and they want to be effective witnesses for Christ, so will we pray for reconciliation between them and their friends? One boy was flunking English, and his dad's an English teacher—would we pray for him? Another girl wanted us to pray that she'd be able to control her tongue, because she's had a lot of problems with it. After we get a number of these requests, I write them briefly on the board and say, "Well, now, who'll pray for Meg here, or who'll pray for Ken, or who'll pray for Joe? If some request is particularly pressing or needful, several of us will pray for it. And the kids will raise their hands, and say, "I'll pray for him"; "I'll pray for her," and then we go to prayer.

We also encourage spontaneous prayer as the Lord leads. We simply take this time together to pray. It's really good; it's really rich to have these kids hear people in their own peer group praying for them, and bringing their petitions before the Lord. And of course the kids then really learn how to pray in a group. We also have sentence prayers sometimes—for different people or different outreaches of our church—different concerns. And this is our time of sharing. Now I've found that in the group, when these needs come up, afterwards kids will just put their arms around other kids (even in junior high) and say, "Boy, we're going to be praying for you this week, brother." And it's beautiful to see. Sometimes it even breaks me up. I think there was one time last year that was really something. There were about seventy-five kids there, and we had a season of prayer that lasted for forty-five minutes. A lot of it was spontaneous and beautiful and real. One kid would confess something and another one would pray for the person who had just confessed a fault—a prayer of encouragement, which showed acceptance and love and concern for this person. It was really beautiful. So this is why we call it "Body Life"—the body is alive to bearing each other's burdens. Now we don't only bear burdens; we praise the Lord for answers to prayer when a person becomes a Christian! I'm sure at least half a dozen of the kids will praise God for this. We just praise the Lord together and really make that Christian feel welcome, and accepted and loved. It's really great.

After this time from 5 to 6, we usually just go en masse to McDonald's and load up on hamburgers and fries. Then we come back and play all kinds of games for about an hour and a half in the gym. And the kids let off steam in this way.

So here's the picture. We have this big "pool" that comes on Sunday morning—a couple hundred kids, then about fifty or sixty on Wednesdays, and then from this Wednesday group, I reach in again and I have a smaller group. This one is only of boys that I'm working with, and these are more intimate disciples.

2. I commented in this chapter that working through small groups is not sufficient, in itself, to build a body relationship or to establish mutual ministries. Still, it is helpful to the development of the body to plan retreats, Bible studies, etc., around small groups, and to use this form to support and stimulate the development of the body.

   The following retreat program[2] is an example of the kind of thing that may be done to draw teens closer together as persons and help them come to know each other in deeper ways. A retreat like this can well be used over Christmas or Easter holidays with natural groupings that have already developed (using Sunday school classes or other previously established associations as the basis for group assignment), or it may be used at the beginning of a school year to introduce to one another persons who will be together in some such natural association.

RETREAT OUTLINE 3

"UNIFY YOUR GROUP"

By Virgil Nelson

A retreat designed for simple and effective group building

Any time is a great time to give special focus to helping your group members get to know each other as persons and to develop a common sense of purpose and commitment to God, each other and the goals of the group for the year.

In retreat planning, some basic decisions need to be made in light of the "givens" in your group at the moment, and your goals for your group and the weekend.

THE PLACE

You may have a regular place you go for retreats and all you need to do is check schedules and make reservations. Or, someone in the group may have a home that could accommodate the group. You may have a friend in

[2]This retreat plan is taken from *The Group Retreat Book* (Loveland, Colo.: Group Books, 1983). Used by permission.

a distant church and your group could arrange to stay in that church building for its retreat. Or you may have state or county parks that would be ideal. Make your choice, and make your reservations.

STRUCTURE

If a primary goal is helping your group members know and love each other, consider determining room assignments before the retreat so that persons who do not know one another well will be together.

If you choose to structure group contact tightly in other parts of the program, then you may want to give participants free choice regarding rooming arrangements and let natural friendships be honored. For example, if people are together in small groups during group sessions, and are assigned to work together in food preparation, then somewhere in the weekend they need to have a "no pressure" choice.

Theme scripture: Colossians 3:12–17

IN TRAVEL

The process of travel can be a conscious part of building and developing friendships and group process. Try this game entitled "Chicken Roulette."

Step #1

Each car is given a number. Slips of paper with that number are put into a hat. If you plan five passengers in car #1, then put five #1 slips of paper in the hat. Each participant draws a number which assigns him/her to a car.

Step #2

Once in the assigned car, each person writes his/her name on a piece of paper, which again goes into a hat. The hat goes around and each person draws a name.

Step #3

One at a time, each person reveals the name drawn. The people in the car then try to guess the answers to the following questions about the person whose name was drawn. Each passenger gets one guess for each question. Go one question at a time. After hearing all guesses, the named person can give the real answer. If there is further discussion/sharing, let it continue.

Questions

1. Guess how this person likes his/her chicken prepared (barbecued, crispy, old-fashioned, boiled, broiled, etc.).
2. Guess birthdate.
3. Guess favorite TV program.
4. Guess color of eyes (without looking).
5. Guess favorite hobby.

POSSIBLE SCHEDULE

FRIDAY EVENING

3:30 p.m.	Register at the church; final payments; cabin room assignments here or later at the camp
4:30 p.m.	Departure for the retreat (actual time depends on the driving distance to the center)
6 p.m.	Dinner on the road: individual cars on their own, or agree on a specific location and all meet there
8 p.m.	Arrival at center: unload and move in
9 p.m.	Opening session: "God's Chosen People: Who's Here?"
10:30 p.m.	Free time: snacks, games
Midnight	In the sack; lights out (This and other ground rules need to be agreed upon in advance of the weekend. Rules depend on the age/maturity of the group, rules of camp, program goals, morning schedule, etc.).

SATURDAY

7 a.m.	Up and at 'em
7:30 a.m.	Personal devotions
8 a.m.	Breakfast
9:30-11:30 a.m.	Morning session (with break): "God's People: Clothed With Compassion"
Noon	Lunch
Afternoon	Free time, with some structured optional choices: group games (see references); tournaments; swimming; outings, etc.
5:30 p.m.	Dinner
7-9 p.m.	Evening session: "God's People: Macramed (or Woven Together) in His Love," including film "The Nail"
9:30 p.m.	Free time

SUNDAY

9:30 a.m.-Noon	Morning sessions including break and worship: "God's People: Thankforgivefulness"
12:30	Lunch and evaluation: most/least valuable activity for our group in its spiritual development; changes I would suggest; other comments

WEDNESDAY

Leaders' meeting to look over evaluations and reflect upon the strengths and weaknesses of the weekend.

Step #4

The second and fourth persons whose names are drawn get to answer the "Chicken Roulette question of the day." Each person guesses a question that #2 or #4 might be "chicken" to ask. Persons #2 and #4 are free to acknowledge if each question is truly one they'd be afraid to ask or not. If not, they may respond with another question that they really would be afraid to ask someone. If a genuine question is asked, you shouldn't feel any compulsion to answer it. Move on; it can come up again later as appropriate.

If the trip is over two hours, plan to change cars in the middle, using the same process twice.

FRIDAY EVENING SESSION (1½ hours)

1. Group singing (10–15 minutes).
2. Put all the participants' names into a hat. Each person draws a name, and becomes a "secret friend" to that individual during the retreat, without the other person guessing that he/she is in fact a "secret friend." During the worship service on Sunday there will be an opportunity for revelation of who the secret friends have been during the weekend.
3. Find your identity. Number the group by counting around to end up with groups of eight persons. Each number is assigned a song tune to hum in order to find the other seven persons in the group. This should be done with eyes closed, on your knees, on the floor. (Possible songs: "Old MacDonald," "Clementine," "Home on the Range," etc.) When all the group is found, stand and sing the song out loud at the top of your voice. (10 minutes) Stay in this group.
4. Names Are No Game. Ask the groups to subdivide into groups of two persons. Share around the following questions:
   a. How do you feel about your name? Anything unusual about it? How did you get it?
   b. If you could change it, would you? To what? (5–7 minutes)
5. Names—What's the Fame? Have the groups of eight reassemble.
   a. Share briefly about the person you met and his/her name. (5–7 minutes)
   b. Individually share with the entire group. If you could be famous for something, go down in the Guinness Book of Records, be written up in the annals of history, end up in future editions of the Bible, what would you like it to be for? Allow two minutes of reflection before starting. Begin with the person whose eyes are bluest. (15 minutes)
6. Mini-presentation (5–7 minutes) on the theme passage. Or, simply read the passage aloud to the entire group from two different translations without comment.
7. Prayer by leader for the total group, or within small groups using sentence prayers.
8. Announcements and overview-reminder of ground rules/assumptions for the weekend. Tell people to remember which persons are in their group.

SATURDAY MORNING SESSION (2 hours)

1. Group singing (10–15 minutes).

2. Form same groups as Friday evening. Read aloud to the entire group the theme scripture Colossians 3:12–17.

3. Reflection sheet on key theme words. Print 8 ½ x 11 sheet with the following words listed down the left side (distribute over entire length of page):
COMPASSION/KINDNESS, HUMILITY, GENTLENESS, PATIENCE, FORGIVENESS, LOVE, and THANKSGIVING.
Vertically divide the page into three columns with the following headings at the top, from left to right:
WHEN I HAVE EXPERIENCED THIS, WHEN I GAVE THIS, A TIME WHEN I NEEDED THIS.
   a. Have each person reflect and make notes in silence. (5 minutes)
   b. Divide into pairs and share feelings and responses. (7–10 minutes)

4. Bible study based on Colossians 3:12–17. (30–45 minutes) Print Bible study instruction sheet as follows (or read instructions to the group):
   a. Reread the scripture to your group of eight. Focus on what the Holy Spirit is saying to you about the meaning of the passage in your life. Reflect on the meaning of this passage in the life of your group. Share. (10 minutes)
   b. Then create a way to share or demonstrate the meaning of the passage using the vehicles/tools suggested below. Groups must pick different categories until they are all taken and then there can be repeats. Creations will be shared during the Sunday morning session with the entire group.

Pick one word from the list of theme words in the passage listed above and:

a) **Letter writing:** Pretend you are Paul writing a letter to your group on the meaning of this word and this passage in the life of your group. Now read this letter as though it were the year 2180. You may want to write individual letters and then compile a "group letter."

b) **Poetry:** Pick one word and use the French poetry form "cinquain" (sin-kane) to express the meaning of this passage. It is difficult for more than two people to work on one verse, so work as individuals and in pairs so your group can create several.

CINQUAIN FORM

			________	title (one word)
		________	________	describe title (2 words)
	________	________	________	feeling (3 words)
________	________	________	________	action (4 words)
			________	one word summary

Members of the group may want to use other poetry forms also.

c) **Crafts:** Using the craft materials available, make something that symbolizes, represents or demonstrates the truths of the scriptural theme passage. (Have available an assortment of colored paper, string, glue, wire, rubber bands, paper clips, straws, crayons, Play-Doh, sticks, toothpicks and the like.)

d) **Slides and/or music:** Select slides (bring a bunch from family trips, etc.) to express the meaning of this passage. Or select one song from a record and pick slides to go with it. Or you may choose your own music and sing it live along with the slides.

e) **Song creation:** Use the tune of a popular song or TV ad and create new words to express the meaning of this scripture in your life as an individual or as a group. (Several may want to work with one tune, others with another. Or you may want to work in pairs writing different verses for the same tune.)

f) **Commercials:** Think up ad lines from radio, TV or magazines. Take the line and convert it to convey meanings around the theme and the truths of this scripture.

g) **Soap opera:** Create a skit, pantomime or role play that illustrates or demonstrates the meaning of the passage in a real-life situation.

5. Closing prayer by leader with the total group, or within small groups (sentence prayers).
6. Announcements; include a request for crazy skits for tonight, talent to sing, dance, etc., as a part of the evening session.

SATURDAY EVENING SESSION (2 hours)

1. Game: Divide group in half, on either side of an imaginary line, or use a line of chairs or a rope. Play balloon volleyball or Nerf volleyball, using two balloons or Nerfs at once. Play to 7 points.
2. Singing as a group.
3. Fun 'n dumb skits, plus musical and other talent. You'll need one coordinator and an emcee for this event. Watch your time limit.
4. One or two songs as transition to the film.
5. Show film "The Nail." (20 minutes) In pairs (does not have to be someone from your base group of eight) share:
   - feelings about the film
   - if you were a person in the film, which person would you most likely be?
   - what does this film tell you about being God's people bound together in love?
6. Prayer and close.
7. Announcements, reminders, etc.

SUNDAY MORNING SESSION (2½ hours)

At breakfast announce that each person is to bring something to the morning session from outside the building—for example, an object from the world of nature.

1. Group singing.
2. Small groups of eight meet to review or prepare their creations from the Saturday morning session. (15–20 minutes)

3. Come back together in groups of eight all in the same room. In pairs share the object you brought and how this object reminds you of God. Then share how this object reminds you of your group as it has been in the past.

Then, share one final question: "How does this object reflect how I want our youth group to be in the future?" (20 minutes)

4. Self-rating scale: On a scale of 1–10 rate yourself in the following:

I feel loved:	I am patient:	I am loving toward:	I am thankful for:	I express my thanks to:
___ self	___ with self	___ self	___ self	___ self
___ by parents	___ with parents	___ parents	___ parents	___ parents
___ by peers	___ with peers	___ peers	___ peers	___ peers
___ by God	___ with God	___ God	___ God	___ God

Share responses to these with one other person in your group of eight. (10 minutes)

5. Each group shares its creation from the Saturday morning session. Affirm each in a way appropriate—applause, etc. (15–45 minutes)

6. Each group by itself should discuss who in their school, community, and church needs to have human love (and God's love) given to them? Make a list of specific groups and even individuals. What are we going to do about it? List possible actions. (10–20 minutes)

7. Revealing of secret friends—go to your secret friend and share with that person.

8. Close in song and prayer.

9. Provide evaluation forms at lunch.

RESOURCES

1. Games: **The Best of Try This One; More . . . Try This One;** and **Try This One . . . Too,** Schultz, Group Books, P.O. Box 481, Loveland, CO 80531.

2. Songbooks: **Songs,** Songs and Creations, Box 559, San Anselmo, CA 94960.

3. Film: "The Nail," available from American Baptist Films, Valley Forge, PA 19481.

4. In this chapter I have suggested that the most crucial role of the person ministering with youth is that of *example*. And this requires personal involvement with kids—loving them, and teaching them to love each other.

   If you are presently ministering with youth, it might be helpful to do an analysis of your contacts with your teens. The chart on page 240 will help you analyze the pattern of your ministry in terms of the kind of contacts, the roles, the purposes, and interrelationships it supports.

   If you agree with the priorities in youth ministry that I have suggested in this book, you will perhaps be interested on completion of the chart to ask, What are my priorities? What do my activities indicate my priorities are? Do any changes in my approach to ministry and investment of my time seem to be needed?

INTERPERSONAL CONTACT EVALUATION CHART

Occasions when I am with the youth (in class, committee mtgs, socials, counseling, etc., *in order of* amount of time spent.	1. Decribe briefly what happens in the contact situation. State, specificlly, the *goal* of the contact (study, decide plans, etc.)	2. What is my role in this contact situation? Am I teacher, leader, coach, motivator, "person with," or what?	3. To what extent do I get to know the teens as *persons* in this contact?	4. To what extent do they come to know me as a person—in self-revealing depth?

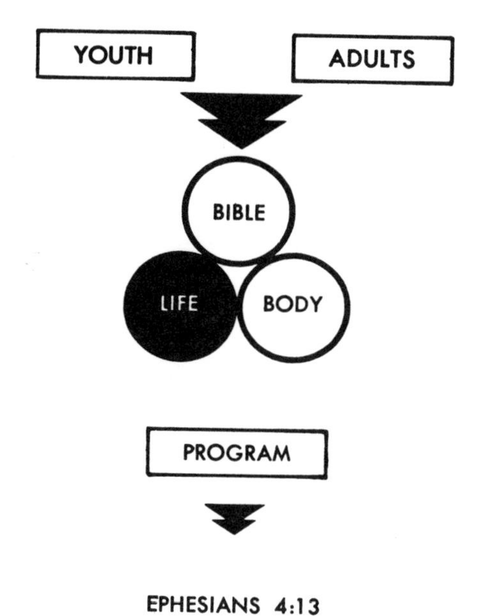

YOUTH IN LIFE

CHAPTERS

YOUTH ADULTS

BIBLE

LIFE BODY

PROGRAM

EPHESIANS 4:13

14

THE SHARING LIFE

From the earliest days of the church, believers in Christ "went throughout the country, preaching the good news of the message" of the gospel (Acts 8:4). And each new company of believers established by the early apostles became "a sort of sounding board from which the Word of the Lord has rung out" (1 Thess. 1:7). Paul's awareness that God had in Jesus Christ "reconciled us to himself" was accompanied by a deep conviction that this same God had made him—and us—"agents of the reconciliation." (2 Cor. 5:18). Central to the meaning of the Christian's life is the experience of sharing Jesus Christ with others.

Young people in evangelical churches are aware that witnessing is expected not only of professional Christian workers and adults, but also of *them.* But our young people, for a variety of reasons, are not sharing Christ. The enthusiasm, the spontaneity, the naturalness of talking with others about a relationship with God that has deep personal meaning for us, isn't part of the normal experience of our Christian youth.

And this is of deep concern in youth ministry. Part of the meaning of being a Christian is found in identifying ourselves with Christ's great purpose, to bring persons into relationship with God, discovering in the Savior forgiveness of sins and freedom from bondage to sin's warping power. Because God reaches out to others to offer a great and free salvation, we, as God's children, are called to reach out to them also, sharing with them God's invitation to the present experience of eternal life.

The gospel is reality. Our call as agents of reconciliation is reality. So youth cannot know life in its full abundance until they find identity with the divine and compelling reality that is the good news of Jesus Christ—for all.

In a three-year study involving over three thousand teens and twenties in evangelical churches in this country and

Canada, a number of barriers to personal evangelism—this sharing of Christ's life with others—were discovered.[1] Over 95 percent of the teens indicated that *they* (not just adults) ought to witness. But most of them honestly admitted that they were not, in person-to-person confrontation, speaking with others about personal relationship to Jesus Christ. The young people had been *told* they *ought* to witness; but rather than responding to the church's exhortation, they found a number of reasons why they could not. The demand of "ought" was unable to motivate response, even when youth accepted the demand as reasonable and right.

What were some of the reasons youth advanced for failure to witness? The reason most often mentioned was fear. There was a deep concern for what other kids would think. Potential ridicule, fear of making a fool of oneself, uncertainty about acceptance if they should speak of Jesus Christ in personal relationship terms, all loomed large in their decisions to remain silent. Knowing the power of the peer group (see chapters 2 and 5), and youths' need to belong, we can be sympathetic with such doubts and fears.

A second reason youth advanced was lack of "know-how." "I wouldn't know how to begin," or "I wouldn't know what to do if someone asked questions," or "I don't know enough Bible verses," appeared on the majority of papers. While teens could point to training classes in the church, to role-play experiences in youth group, and even to Sunday school units on "how to witness," they felt totally inadequate for the task. The concept of witness as a simple sharing of what Christ means to them as persons, of an introduction of one friend to another, seemed foreign.

A third problem that loomed large was a lack of relationship with non-Christians. Few teens who responded spoke of non-Christian *friends*. Many explicitly said they "didn't know any unsaved kids well enough to speak to them" about Christ. Like their elders, the association of Christian young people were often circumscribed by the church crowd. Knowing others than these as friends—the kind of friends who come over to your home or whom you hang around with when you have free time—was unusual.

---

[1] The study was done under my supervision by a number of successive graduate and undergraduate classes in youth ministry.

A final problem was a sense of aloneness. Nearly all the teens expressed a belief that other Christian young people ought to witness, too, but nearly all said also, "If I were to witness I'd be the only one around doing it." The obligation of involvement in personal evangelism is something all give lip service to. And something most do *not* carry over in action.

Each of these barriers is a serious one. Together they cut our young people off from an experience that is part of the meaning of a Christian's life. God has called us to Christ, to know Him and love Him, and to invite others to know and love Him, too. We find part of our identity as Christians through participating in Christ's own love for others and expressing that love to them in witness to our Savior and Lord. Anyone concerned that youth become involved as Christians in life must, then, seek to involve them in personal evangelism.

But as we minister with youth we need to recognize the barriers that exist. Rather than urging and demanding, "Witness!" we need to find ways to guide teens into a healthy experience of the sharing life.

How can we overcome the barrier? What's involved in leading teens to witness?

Motivation I have suggested before in this book that the "ought" motivation is both ineffectual and unchristian. What is capable of motivating teens to share Christ with others—and what motivation is appropriate?

In the first place, motivation is to be Christ's motivation: *love*. Christ died for us, because He *cared*. A few of the kids who responded to the study on which this chapter is based mentioned a love motivation: "I want to witness, because I want my friends to have what I have." When witnessing is seen as meeting the deepest need of a person we have come to care about, it is removed from the realm of "duty" and becomes "desire." And to the extent that we care about the persons we share Christ with, we begin to operate with the motivation of God.

Sometimes we "care" for people in the abstract. "Everybody ought to know" is a chorus we have often sung. And who can deny it? But God hasn't placed us next to everybody. He has placed us next to certain people and wants us to care concretely for *them*. So we are to develop concern for those we know and come to love them more as we get to know them better. Love not only *calls for* involvement with others; it *is called out* by involvement with others. So one of the first effective steps toward helping teens witness is helping them come to know, as friends, unsaved persons. Rather than fighting against involvement with non-Christians—as many evangelical churches still do—we need to encourage involvement and train our teens to develop love for kids who are still outside of Christ.

The suggestion that the church encourage Christian kids to develop friendship with non-Christians reflects a basic concept of communicating Christ. For all the impact of mass media on communication in our modern world, few young people are reached for Christ by impersonal, one-way communication. The older "Youth For Christ" rallies of the fifties that emphasized mass evangelism have been replaced by an "each one teach one" strategy. Today the most effective communicator of Jesus Christ to a young person is another young person who will love him and in person-to-person relationship share the reality of Christ. Thus, all that I said earlier about the importance of a model, of someone to incarnate the reality of biblical truths so they can be tested and seen to be real, is totally relevant to evangelism. And the primary context for communicating Christ is one formed by friendship.

Motivation for sharing Christ, then, grows out of developing personal relationships with non-Christians and learning to love them for Christ's sake.

The love motivation in witness is, however, as much vertical as horizontal. Love for others takes on evangelistic meaning only when it is balanced by love for Christ as well. Thus, an effective witnessing emphasis in youth ministry presupposes that, through involvement in Scripture and body relationships, young people are growing in their own relationship with the Lord. As one of my friends emphasizes, "Witness must be the overflow of a life that Jesus has filled up." Jesus said, "The man who believes in me, as the scripture said, will have rivers of living waters flowing from his inmost heart" (John 7:38).

A third aspect of motivation for witness is found in the fact that motivation grows *through experience*. In most cases involvement in an experience is a precondition for motivation.

Part of the freeing power of experiencing God's truth is that, as we become involved in reality, the Holy Spirit's touch testifies that this is the life—that this is "where it's at" for us. To many young people and adults, motivation for witness has come through being in a situation where you somehow *had* to speak out—and discovered in the speaking the excitement and joy that sharing Christ brings.

A final aspect of motivation is found in group support. The knowledge that others are witnessing too, the opportunity to share experiences, and the chance to pray together and encourage each other in this expression of the Christian life—all of these are vital. And so once again we are driven back to the body relationship, *the* context for support and encouragement and stimulation to live Christ's life in the world.

We can begin to build motivation for witness as a natural expression of the Christian's life, then, by (1) developing a balanced ministry in which Christian young people are growing in their own relationship with God; (2) encouraging personal involvement and the development of friendships with non-Christian kids; (3) providing opportunities to share Christ by "going along with" others, gradually becoming involved; and (4) providing a supportive body relationship with other Christian kids who are committed to and personally active in sharing Christ themselves.

Know-how — The basic solution to lack of witnessing know-how is also found in experience. One philosophy of education has it that persons should be provided with information *before* they become involved in situations where they need to use it. Another philosophy suggests that information should be provided as necessary, *concurrently* with involvement. There's little doubt that the latter is usually best for developing skill in witness. Training classes that focus on providing "techniques" before involvement in witnessing experiences often prove *demotivating*. It is best to seek to let witness experiences provide a "need to know" motivation that blends the learning with the living.

Lack of friends — I have already spoken of this final category. One of our greatest needs in youth ministry is to encourage the development of friendships with non-Christians on the campus and in the neighborhood—friendships that, when the teen is a growing believer, become the context for sharing Christ.

The need to encourage development of such friendships raises many questions of programming in the local church. We will look at such questions in the next section of this book and in PROBE. But for the moment it is important to note that the church definitely needs to correlate its programming of youth activities with those of the school and community. And the church needs to plan ways to support individuals in their campus involvements—ways that will help them find opportunities to share Christ with their friends.

Helping young people tell others about Christ and so become involved in a vital dimension of living the Christian life is one of the basic goals of effective youth ministry. There are many barriers to evangelism that cut evangelical youth off from this rewarding experience and thus from balanced growth as Christian persons. But the barriers can be overcome. Supported by a balanced ministry that meaningfully involves teens in Scripture and in body relationships with one another, young people can be guided into the sharing life.

PROBE

case histories
discussion questions
thought-provokers
resources

1. One area touched on in this chapter is that of structuring activities to support the sharing life. The following letter, written by Dave Roper, youth minister at Peninsula Bible Church in Palo Alto, California, describes an approach he developed and used through the sixties. It gives a valuable picture of a broad approach to programming to encourage outreach and evangelism.

   Dear Marshall:

   Thanks for your note and your interest in our ministry here at Peninsula Bible Church. I hope that we can be some help in supplying information for the project that you mentioned.

   In order to save time and cover all the bases, it would probably be best to use the same outline and categories you suggested. So here goes . . .

   I. Description of special evangelistic projects

   A. *Best Deal* — We take over the Young Life clubs in the area during the summer and operate under the name of *Best Deal*. We change the format somewhat, have swim parties, barbecues, hootenannies, what have you. We call them "parties with a purpose." We try to flex with the crowd, and do whatever interests them currently. Right now surfing is the fad, so we are planning a "seminar in the sand" (the kids call it a "screech at the beach"). What we do is immaterial.

The purpose is to expose non-Christian kids in the area to Jesus Christ.

During the winter we try to have two or three reunions before our *Best Deal* retreat after Christmas. Actually, this year we have been pressed for time and could have only one reunion. We feel that we should have had more, to keep our contacts hot.

We have to depend on the kids to bring their friends. We discourage their coming alone, but it happens anyway. We encourage them to be frontal and tell their non-Christian guests what it is all about. We have found pagan kids don't mind coming to a "religious" meeting if they are forewarned and if they expect to have a good time anyway, but they resent being brought under false pretenses.

Teenagers will put up with a lot if things are done on their level and in a *qualitative way*. I can't stress the latter too much! Everything has to be up to snuff with the high school crowd around here. Perhaps Mr. Hendricks has told you of the unique community that we serve. We draw predominantly from the Stanford community, and kids here are used to the *best*. I feel that this is true of the high school community across the country these days. Kids are bone tired of the half-hearted attempts of the church to reach them. They simply are not impressed. So, at least here on the coast, they stay away from church. It's tragic, but it's a simple fact of life. In order to reach them we have to win their respect and the right to tell them of Christ. In short, the principle seems to be—keep it at their level and keep it sharp!

The program of *Best Deal* is flexible, but our messages *are consistently on the person of Christ and His ability to meet every need that these kids face in their world.* We don't try to be brief or breezy, but to lay the facts on the line. Again, I am convinced that teenagers do not want to be entertained and pampered. They want to know how to get the most out of life. We just tell them which way the Lord is going, and if they want to have complete realization in their lives, they need to go with Him.

B. *Young Life* — During the school year we encourage our church kids to get behind their *Young Life* clubs in their own schools. *Young Life* has done a tremendous job here, and we want to support them in any way possible. We are not interested in peddling P.B.C. [Peninsula Bible Church], and it is immaterial what church they land in, as long as they are getting fed. So we encourage our youngsters to bring their friends to *Young Life,* and support their campaigners, and we find that our kids have really rallied around the thing. It seems silly to me to try to crank up a competing evangelistic effort in a high school where *Young Life* is already working. If they are weak, we can give them help, and I have found that they really appreciate it.

C. *International Dinners* — We have had these on the college level and decided last year to try one for the high school students (exchange students) in the area. This is not strictly an evangelistic effort, as we did not present a gospel message at the dinner, but it is an opportunity for our kids to form friendships that lead to opportunities. International students cannot be pushed, and there has to be a prolonged friendship before they open up, so we want to provide some sort of time where these friendships can be started. We are planning another next month. This one is to be a dinner—prepared by the internationals for us. It is shaping up to be real exciting. We keep them small and hand-pick our sharpest, more mature high school kids to be there.

D. *Snow trips* — A fellow here in the area has given us the use of his cabin in the Sierras for short weekend snow trips. We take along fifteen or twenty kids and spend the time skiing and loafing around the cabin. We try to take up several non-Christians for exposure to the Christian kids and personal contact with them. We have two of these trips planned for this winter.

E. *Wilderness camps* — I wish that I could do this full time. It's really simple. We take a handful of fellows and spend a week with them in the Sierras. We try to pick young people who are in need of some personal follow-up; we move in with a special invitation to go fishing with us and then *make hay*. Ray Stedman and Bob Smith started this here at P.B.C. about four or five years ago, and we are becoming more sold on it every year.

F. *Retreats* — We have high school retreats every winter. This year we held an outreach conference: a *Best Deal* retreat. It is nothing new or novel. We asked every Christian kid coming to bring a non-Christian buddy and if possible to pay his way. We have a few scholarships available if they need help. However, we use them only as a last resort. We feel it is a part of the Christian kids' ministry to the others to fork over the cash. These retreats run over a long weekend and are pretty much like any high school conference. We keep them free and uncluttered, usually having only two meetings a day, allowing plenty of time for counselors to move in on a personal basis. They are fun and highly productive, as they often seal decisions that have been on the back burner for months. Again, we try to get top resource people. Most of the counselors are kids from our college class or the *Young Life* volunteer staff. We import speakers from outside. There are a number of excellent camp sites in the Santa Cruz Mountains.

G. *Backyard conferences* — We are doing some thinking now on a new approach for this spring, utilizing what we call "backyard conferences." We got the idea from International Christian Leadership and their work with Christian businessmen and leaders in government. We are putting together a team of sharp high school kids to bring to breakfasts and evening meetings where they can give their testimony in an informal way, and then have a free-for-all discussion afterwards.

II. Evaluation of evangelistic projects

A. *Purpose and Goal* — We call these approaches "evangelistic aids," because we realize the real work of evangelism is done on a one-to-one basis, not by blasting away in a crowd. This is true at all age levels, but particularly with the high school gang. We want our own church kids to *use these programs as springboards into personal discussions about the Christian faith.* As they drive home or see their friends during the week, they may have an opportunity to refer to something that was said in a discussion or in a personal testimony and then relate it to their own experience. In short, we want to make it easier for our own kids to witness to their friends. Some teenagers make a decision for Christ through a message delivered to the group, but the largest percentage of decisions come from personal follow-up either by one of our kids or an adult leader.

B. *Problems* — Man . . . where do I start?

1. Gaining support of teenagers in the church. Teenagers are terribly ambivalent. They are scared silly at first—afraid of all sorts of things, but primarily afraid of failure. They think the program will be a flop and that they will be embarrassed. They think that no one will come. Then again, they think that they can do everything, and therefore thousands of kids will come and have a great time. So they must be involved. Let them plan the programs, suggest speakers, etc., and give them lots of adult help and reassurance. I'm sure you know this as well as I do. Anyway, get them involved and teach them how to walk by faith.

   Our biggest problem is that we just don't *really* expect God to do anything. (Since they can see through adults like a pane of glass, it doesn't take them long to be unbelieving believers, as well.) So you have to walk by faith and teach them that God is expecting them to move out and be used.

2. Attitudes of parents. If you start evangelizing, you are going to have pagan kids all over the church, and most Christians don't really want that. The natives get contaminated. We can thank the Lord for a group of people dedicated to the idea that God put us in this community to build bridges to non-Christian folk and bring these people into a relationship to Jesus Christ. It is refreshing to have the freedom to move and experiment and know people are behind you and praying for your kids.

3. Leadership. We have a real need for dedicated training leadership. I'm not talking about bow-tie cuties. We have a bunch of those here on the West Coast. I mean men who are willing to sweat and pray over high school kids, who will take the time to get on their wave length. I don't really know what makes a good youth worker. I usually go to a prospective worker with two lists of qualifications: one a list of *absolute* prerequisites, such as faithfulness, teachableness, harmoniousness, and personal spiritual experience; the other a list of *desirable* qualifications, such as training and experience. I think we can teach a person anything, but only the Holy Spirit can motivate. We look for the person who wants to move and has the necessary spiritual qualifications first, and then we go on from there.

4. Quality. There's always the tendency to let down our guard and get sloppy. It's the beginning of the end when we do. Did you ever listen to kids comment on one of their peers? Almost everything they say has to do with appearances. "That looks good" is a favorite expression. Things have to *look* good to a teenager. He is not so concerned with reality as with appearance. So we show him how the two are related. Things look good because they *are* good. This is hard to sell when we just slam something together at the last minute.

5. Church relationship. This is not really a good definitive term for what I have on my mind. What I am talking about is the ability to maintain an aloofness from your own church groups when you go out to reach pagan kids. Because the church's public image may be offensive, we have to divorce ourselves from any local church and just go after kids as interested members of the community. We never mention our local church at these programs, unless someone asks us where we come from or who is sponsoring the event. We are not trying to be devious but just want to allay any suspicions. We have to instruct our kids on this, as well. We are not interested primarily in getting kids to come to our church. *We want to win them to Christ first.* Our allegiance is to Him, not to any local church body. *We sell this hard.*

   There are a couple of things that run parallel to this. We have found that kids do end up here at P.B.C. as a result of these evangelistic activities. In fact, right now the hard core of our high school group is made up of kids who met the Lord the last couple of years. However, in order to integrate these raw kids into a church environment, we have to make several adjustments. We don't soft-pedal the teaching ministry, but we do try to be as nonchurchy as possible. We call our group the Koinonia Kampus Klub (not the P.B.C. High School Group.) We have little calling cards printed up with the name of the group. We pass them out to kids, if they are interested. We call our evening group "The Huddle," not a training hour. We don't get together and entertain each other on Sunday evenings. We meet to plan for action (hence the name "huddle"). We prepare for assignments—planning *Best Deal,* working on creative projects, preparing a children's church program, visiting kids that are out on the fringe, doing work around the church, and preparing a program for a rest home. The whole idea is that we want to challenge kids—not entertain them. We have a big banner on the wall of the high school room. The thing reaches from one wall to the other, and in bright red letters three feet high it says, "THE EXTRA MILE." That's our theme this year. We want to stretch these kids all over the place. Give them realistic, honest-to-goodness opportunities to minister and not just play church.

I'm sure there are other things I might say along these lines. There are plenty of problems, not the least of which is the initial inertia that you have to overcome. I think it is essential in youth work that we be flexible and keep our programs terminal. By that I mean that we give everything to one program for a while and then shake everything up and start over to rethink the whole system. We want to be free to try new approaches and allow the Lord to lead us into new areas of experience. I think unless we do that, we tend to get swept into some little eddy and miss the main stream of God's purpose for us. Frankly, we want to know where He is going, and we want to be part of the program He has mapped out. In short, we want to follow Him. To do this, I feel we must stay alert and be willing to flex as He directs.

2. Dave Roper also shares these insights into how to motivate young people to witness:

HOW TO MOVE TEENS TO WITNESS
by Dave Roper

We have taught classes on evangelism, we have scolded, we have pushed; we have done everything that we could possibly do, and we've never had any kids doing personal nose-to-nose evangelism until about two years ago. What forced the issue was that we finally decided that we had to start taking kids out with us—literally hanging them up and sticking them out there and *making* them witness. So we started using Campus Crusade's Community Surveys. We'd go out to the park and down to the beach and over on to Stanford Campus and Foothill Junior

College Campus. We took different kids with us as we had opportunity and just witnessed to people "cold turkey." Kids began to trust the Lord, and it was just amazing. In a period of about three months, we had over fifty college and high school kids who accepted the Lord; it was really exciting to see what the Lord was doing. The same thing has happened again this year. We're finding that some of our own kids now are taking their friends out, and they're beginning to survey and witness on their own.

I am gaining a greater appreciation for Campus Crusade's approach. We just teach kids to memorize the Four Spiritual Laws and we use their procedure right down the line with very little modification. All I can say is that it's done the job; we have kids who are vital and they are effective in their personal evangelism. They're fruitful, and this is a real encouragement to all of us. We have had at Log Cabin in the past six months about seventeen or eighteen boys trust the Lord.

It has been due totally to the ministry of our own young people. I frankly know of no other way to motivate teens to witness than to go out with them. What we do the first couple of times is let them sit in and then about halfway through a presentation we'll turn to one of the kids and say, "Now Joe, what does Jesus Christ mean to you?" Kids turn pea green and try to fall through the floor, but they *have* to witness and they stammer out something and it is usually pretty bad and it comes out pretty heavy and not too effective, but at least they have said something! They come away from there all excited: "Man, that's great! Let's do it again!" About three or four times like that and they're ready to take someone else out. We tell them after about the second trip out that we want them to memorize the Four Laws, and we drill them to make sure they know what they are talking about before we turn them loose. We also want to build into these kids the whole concept of their spiritual life and the witness of the indwelling Christ through them. Otherwise, it just becomes another effort in the flesh.

So we find that there are two corollary points that are kept in balance all the way through: not only do we want them out witnessing to their friends, but we want their witness to be the overflow of a life that God has filled.

15

THE SERVING LIFE

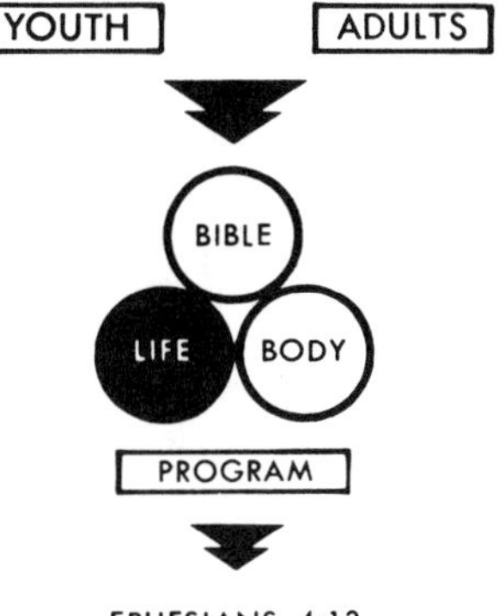

The evangelistic imperative is particularly clear in Scripture. But many people claim that God's call to service in the world, to "do good to all men," is not so clear. Denying that the church was called by God to be a social agency, they have little interest in ministries that are not directly evangelistic.

It's true that the church, as an organization, is not called to provide social services to the community. The church of the New Testament is an organism, Christ's body, and as such it exists for believers, a context in which they grow toward maturing in Christ. But the individual believer is called to involvement with others. Like the Father, who makes His rain fall on godly and ungodly alike, because He is love, the children are to care about people. We are to reach out to help them—because the God we represent is love.

In evangelism we need to take very seriously the concept that believers are to represent Christ in the world—that we are to be, as the very word "Christian" originally intimated, "little Christs." We are to live "so that the life of Jesus may be plainly seen in our mortal lives" (2 Cor. 4:11).

Being like Jesus necessarily involves us in the lives and concerns of others. The Bible says that we have "no high priest who cannot be touched with the feeling of our infirmities" (Heb. 4:15). Jesus is touched, and in His life on earth He was constantly touched, by human need. We may validly see His healings and miracles as divine acts that authenticated Him as God's messenger. But we dare not take them as cold, calculating acts in which the needy were used for His own purposes. The Bible constantly reminds us of this: "Jesus had compassion on them"; "Jesus reached out His hand and touched the leper"; "Jesus wept." God's loving heart was expressed in acts of mercy, in reaching out to others to become involved, to meet need.

Today, as representatives of His love, we too must be a people who can be touched—who have compassion, who reach out to others, who become involved, and who meet human need.

The impersonal "service project" is inadequate. I think most of us understand the kind of things I mean—things like collecting cans of food for a rescue mission we have never seen and never will see, except perhaps for a brief hour sitting on a platform in front of rows of tired and dirty men; making up a thanksgiving basket to be delivered by an embarrassed adult and a "teen representative" to a family who, while thankful, find the "charity" as painful to receive as it is awkward to give; and making the traditional visit to the local old folks home, where a small group of kids cluster together to sing for the assembled elders and give a testimony or two, and then, after short and smiling farewells, hurry back again to the world of youth.

These are terribly inadequate as expressions of God's love—not because the motive in planning them may not be right, nor because what is given may not meet a need. They are inadequate because such activities don't bring involvement with the others as persons.

Far better, as examples of ministries of God's love, are the following instances of involvement:

Steve Cory, son of Scripture Press editor Lloyd Cory, announces to his dad that he's decided to give up track so he can spend two more afternoons each week with the inner-city kids he's come to know while counseling at a summer camp.

As high schoolers, my wife and a friend gave up every Sunday afternoon to spend them with children in a children's ward in a Brooklyn, New York, county hospital. There they spent hours with the children, reading to them, talking, playing games, and telling flannelgraph stories.

Marlene LeFever, as a teen, joined several other girls from her church to spend Sunday afternoons in a home for delinquent girls, talking and listening, letting them know someone cared.

A MINISTRY OF CARING

The above examples of caring seem to me to include vital and necessary ingredients for Christian involvement in the serving life. What are these ingredients?

Personal involvement — In each of these cases, young Christians came face to face with persons whom they came to know and understand as they served them.

Involvement is important for both giver and receiver. So much of our "service" for others is impersonal and condescending. Giving "things" is often felt as a threat to the receiver's integrity, and the attitude of the giver is often questioned—whenever a closer relationship is possible. But when a person gives *himself,* when he builds a relationship in which he communicates his respect and concern for the other as a person, love is communicated. Persons who receive desperately need to feel love. For love is a great assertion of worth. A gift given in love does not subordinate the receiver to the giver. It exalts him. For it is evidence of his value as a person in the eyes of the giver.

Certainly this is what gospel love communicates to us. Whether we respond in faith or not, the gospel tells us that we are loved—that to God we are worth the price of Christ's own blood. If we are to represent this God adequately to others, we desperately need to affirm the value of the persons we contact and serve. We need to love them as we serve and so assure them that they are worth caring about—with no strings attached.

Personal involvement is important also for the giver. The Bible often speaks of Jesus as having been moved with compassion. Jesus *felt with* people in need. He understood their feelings and involved Himself with them.

One of the benefits to the Christian of his service to others (while surely not a primary motive for service) is that in coming to know and to feel with persons in need, his own heart is opened up to compassion. The Scripture says that "the love of God is shed abroad in our hearts" (Rom. 5:5 KJV). This is unquestionably important. As "God's obedient children," we are to be like our Father. We are to open ourselves up to experiences that are like the experiences of Jesus Christ, and we are to identify our own goals and purposes in life with His. "Interpersonal service," on the other hand, is tragically crippling to both the one who serves and the one who is served. Giving without love degrades the receiver. And serving without understanding and identifying with the one who is served is a hollow mockery of the love that Christ, our example, calls us to experience and to express.

Cost — In each of the examples of involved servant-ministry, expressing care for others was costly. It demanded a decision to give up personal comfort, time, or something else important to the giver.

Such cost is a necessary evidence of love. We know the love of God because He gave His Son. Real love demands demonstration, and the most meaningful demonstration involves a personal sacrifice on the part of the one who loves.

In the long run, of course, love means gain. We can never outgive God; the more we spend for others for His sake, the greater the blessing and joy we experience. But denial of self, accepting our share of the cross, is felt as sacrifice before we discover it is gain. It wasn't easy for Steve to give up his place on the high school team for the sake of the inner-city kids he'd come to care about. It wasn't easy for the teenage girls to give up Saturday or Sunday afternoon and give themselves at the children's ward and detention home. It is never easy to make the decision to surrender something that is ours for the sake of others. But it is just this kind of decision that meaningful service demands.

Understanding — I have already mentioned this above, but it is important enough to deserve separate emphasis. Serving others demands that we seek to understand them—that we learn to feel with them. Serving others is a two-way transaction. In it both we and the others give, and we both receive. Only service that involves us with others and leads to identification with them in their total situation approaches the servant ministry of Christ.

INVOLVING YOUTH IN SERVICE

As with many of the elements of youth ministry described in this book, it is difficult to *program* for involvement in service. Although the PROBE features following provide illustration of kinds of "service projects" teens may be involved in, and suggest resources, it is difficult to "plan" the kind of person-to-person ministry that our faith demands.

So what can we do? I believe that, as we minister with youth, we can be aware that the living of Christ's life calls us to care for other people and to express our concern in servant ministry. Each community, each situation, has its own unique opportunities and needs. And it is important that we make our young people aware of human need and involve them as persons in need, helping them interpret the experiences involvement brings and guiding them to discover in servant ministry who they are as Christians.

I am also convinced that the servant ministry that is participation in Jesus' kind of life with people is marked by person-to-person involvement, by a costly giving of ourselves and by a deepening understanding of and concern for persons.

Guiding youth into this involvement is part of our ministry with young people who are, after all, intended by God to grow toward the image and likeness of their Savior Jesus Christ.

PROBE

case histories
discussion questions
thought-provokers
resources

1. Books on youth ministry often provide suggested lists of service projects teens can undertake. Here is one such list from the book *Ways Youth Learn.*[1] Look through the listing and, as you do, ask yourself which of these have potential for involving young people in an experience of the servant-life as proposed in this chapter.

   a. *Helping in the church*

      1) Improving the church grounds and building.
      2) Participating in youth choir.
      3) Being an active member of the youth fellowship—helping in all activities; practicing friendliness; striving to reach unreached people.
      4) Equipping a game room in the church.
      5) Assisting the pastor by distributing materials, flowers, bulletins; telephone calls; running errands.
      6) Issuing invitations to strangers.
      7) Drawing and photocopying a map of the community giving directions to the church, and distributing to strangers.
      8) Visiting shut-ins; doing kind deeds for them such as reading to them or bringing music to them.
      9) Volunteering to drive cars to pick up shut-ins or others who could not otherwise attend. Baby-sitting for parents to go to activities in the church.
      10) Assisting with secretarial work of the church.

[1]Clarice M. Bowman, *Ways Youth Learn* (New York: Harper & Row, 1952), 125–26.

11) Holding services in institutions.

12) Writing up stories of church events for local newspapers or church papers.

13) Preparing some little-used room in the church as a chapel for individual prayer and small services.

14) Keeping the church building clean and attractive.

15) Caring for church hymnals and Bibles and books of worship.

16) Providing flowers.

17) Starting a costume wardrobe, collecting and classifying costumes for different types of dramatic productions.

18) Starting an art library—sorting, mounting, and filing pictures for ready use for teaching and worship purposes.

19) Making movable screens for church school rooms, particularly for children's rooms.

20) Assisting children's workers under their supervision) in storytelling, preparing equipment, gathering materials, and caring for children.

21) Maintaining fellowship with persons away from the home church through letters, bulletins, recordings, devotional aids, newssheets.

22) Faithfulness as a group in participating in the worship and general work of the church.

b. *Reaching unreached persons*

1) Finding who and where the unreached are. Making a house-to-house canvass or other type of community or school survey.

2) Publicizing church events (through personal word, telephone, posters, newspapers, bulletins, radio.)

3) Making provision for recreation regularly for youth and possibly also children's and/or adult groups; with a variety of activities, including the quiet and the active to appeal to different tastes and moods.

4) Making provision for the transportation of potential visitors.

5) Cooperating with youth fellowships of other churches and faiths.

6) Providing for services in closed churches.

7) Starting neighborhood prayer groups.

8) Starting outpost Sunday schools (under supervision of trained adult workers).

9) Developing an "enlistment" service to help newcomers find niches for participation.

10) Providing a lounge in the church building for reading, writing, or listening to music and for meeting friends under worthy auspices—for individuals who have no such place to go.

11) Visiting unreached persons in homes; assuring them of sincere, friendly interest, following up by bringing them to church activities.

12) Arranging an outdoor sing on Sunday afternoon in summer, especially for unchurched people, or in sections where such opportunities for friendly participation are rarely offered.

13) Arranging neighborhood gatherings for unchurched people to meet with friendly church people—for candymaking, packing boxes for relief, preparing for Christmas, etc.

14) Caroling—not necessarily only at Christmas but at other times as well.

c. *Activities for building brotherhood and world friendship*

1) Using special missions materials in denominational and interdenominational publications units, stories, activity ideas, party suggestions, music, drama).

2) Providing some bibliographies of missionaries and of peacemakers who have worked for brotherhood.

3) Encouraging hobbies that help to build awareness of the world (e.g., pen pals, stamp collecting, language study, making or collecting dolls of the nations, trips).

4) Setting up an "overseas workshop," a place where youth can meet to mend clothes, collect goods for relief, repair and make needed items.

5) Securing for showing among church people visuals or recordings to help deepen concern for others and build worldly-mindedness.

6) Inviting persons from other countries and missionaries within reach to counsel with the young people about world relations and possibly vocational missions work.

7) Setting up a world friendship library, corner, or shelf somewhere in the church (perhaps in the youth room) or in a basement.

8) Securing the interest of the librarian of the public library in arranging a special section or shelf of books dealing with international questions.

9) Getting in touch with commissions on world peace of the denomination for up-to-the-minute suggestions and materials, such as radio scripts that can be used to build confidence and inspire peace action among the masses.

10) Securing informational materials, including visual and auditory materials, from United Nations and possibly its branches such as UNESCO. Forming a United Nations club for securing needed information and discussing and disseminating it.

11) Starting a personal campaign to rid one's own speech of slurring words or phrases or jokes ridiculing other people.

12) Generally living as if all were one brotherhood, speaking that way, thinking that way, praying that way.

d. *Christian service action in lifting moral standards*

1) Seeing what recreational facilities and guidance are offered in the community to give youth from lower economic levels opportunities for fun and fellowship under worthy auspices and fostering higher ideals within them.

2) Getting the facts about attitudes and practices of youth in the community, schools, etc., as to cheating, stealing, boy-girl friendships, gambling, drinking, use of narcotics.

3) Calling together for consultation those likely to be most concerned and capable of offering help (church groups, civic agencies, character-building agencies, parents).

4) Making the total church program for youth so alive that it will help attract and hold the interest of unreached young persons; offering them jobs to do when they come so that they will feel needed and, thus, gain a foothold in becoming better selves; surrounding them with wholesome group relationships, strengthening their ideals; guiding them in understanding Jesus' teachings better and leading them to commitment.

e. *Christian service action in the local community*

1) Arousing interest in a community-wide recreation program for children, youth, and adults (including hobbies, crafts, outdoor activities, hikes, nature lore, folk games, other games, music, drama, intercultural festivals).

2) Working in institutions (typing, general work, leading games or crafts, playing piano, assisting with children, telling stories, coaching drama).

3) Conducting a Sunday-afternoon sing each week.

4) Growing flowers.

5) Supplying reading materials to jails and other institutions.

6) Helping harvest or gather perishable crops.

7) Having a "Lord's Acre" project.

8) Cooperating in a community survey.

9) Presenting plays or visual aids dealing with social problems.

10) Supporting a community project—such as a milk fund for babies (perhaps doing without refreshments at youth meetings, giving the money that would otherwise have been spent).

11) Investigating the treatment of criminals and delinquents—particularly of the younger ones—in the community.

12) Working to overcome juvenile delinquency.

13) Visiting the jails and detention homes and holding services.

14) Analyzing the liquor problem in the community and organizing strategically to work on it.

15) Encouraging citizens to vote.

16) Helping foreign-born people to secure naturalization papers.

17) Helping provide places for living and working for displaced persons.

18) Working for safety.

19) Helping prevent forest fires; replanting under direction.

20) Sending youth teams to needy small churches.

2. Many denominations offer opportunities for short-term missions service. In addition, other groups provide the back-up services and contacts that a local church youth missions team requires. Among such organizations are the following:

Bible Christian Union
Box 718
Lebanon, Pennsylvania 17042

Central American Mission
8625 La Prada Drive
Dallas, Texas 75228

The Evangelical Alliance Mission
P.O. Box 969
Wheaton, Illinois 60187

Gospel Missionary Union
10000 N. Oak
Kansas City, Missouri 64155

Grace Mission
2125 Martindale S.W.
Grand Rapids, Michigan 49509

Greater Europe Mission
P.O. Box 668
Wheaton, Illinois 60189

New Tribes Mission
Woodworth, Wisconsin 53194

Operation Mobilization
P.O. Box 148
Midland Park, New Jersey 07432

Regions Beyond Missionary Union
8102 Elberon Avenue
Philadelphia, Pennsylvania 19111

South America Mission, Inc.
5217 S. Military Trail
Lake Worth, Florida 33460

Teen Mission International
P.O. Box 1056
Merritt Island, Florida 32952

Unevangelized Fields Mission
P.O. Box 306
Bala-Cynwyd, Pennsylvania 19004

United Missionary Fellowship
P.O. Box 21-4095
Sacramento, California 95821

Word of Life International
Schroon Lake, New York 12870

Worldteam
P.O. Box 343038
Coral Gables, Florida 33134

The Worldwide Evangelization Crusade
P.O. Box A, 709 Pennsylvania
Fort Washington, Pennsylvania 19034

Youth for Christ (Project Serve)
P.O. Box 419
Wheaton, Illinois 60189

Part Four

PLANNING FOR MINISTRY

PROGRAMMING YOUTH MINISTRY

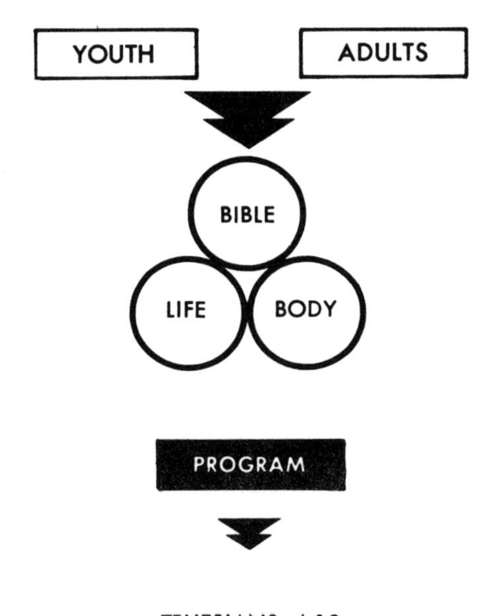

PROGRAMMING YOUTH MINISTRY

CHAPTERS

16

STRUCTURING FOR MINISTRY

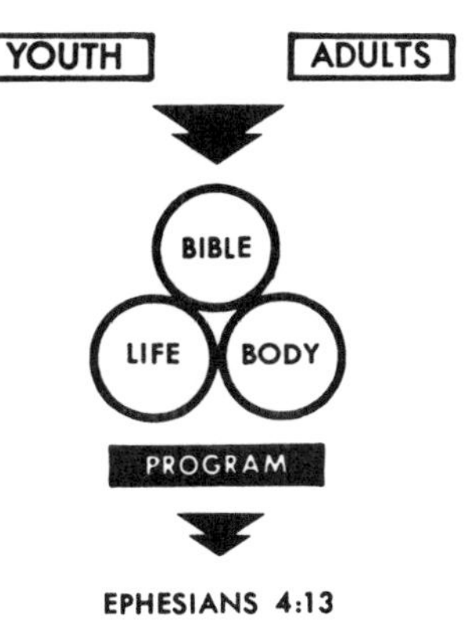

In a telephone interview[1] pastors told about their youth ministries and the dissatisfaction and failures that led to changes and experiments in nearly every church. New meeting times, new materials, new formats, and new group names were tried. The traditional time of the youth meeting was shifted from before to after the evening service, settings changed from churches to homes, etc. Some had dropped Sunday youth meetings altogether, while others held fast to the traditional approach. Speakers, films, packaged programs, discussions, and "tell it like it is" sessions were all being tried. In some churches socials had even replaced study and discussion.

The survey illuminates the common experience of many who minister with youth. Without clear concepts of goals, lacking a well-defined philosophy of ministry, experiment after experiment with programming is undertaken. And usually the result, after a brief surge of enthusiasm, is deeper discouragement and disinterest—followed by another desperate attempt to find something "new," "different," and, it is hoped, "successful."

But successful youth ministry isn't built on programs or gimmicks. Successful youth ministry requires involvement of youth people and adults in the three primary processes of ministry, and the development of programs that *facilitate involvement in these processes.*

The crucial issues in programming for ministry can be resolved into three: knowing the needs of the group and individuals, adopting a functional approach to youth programs and activities, and understanding the capabilities of available structural elements. The first of these is to be discussed in the following chapter on organization. The other two, functional programming and the capabilities of various structures, are the main concern of this chapter.

[1] Unpublished survey by Don and Martha MacCullough. Don is presently professor of Christian Education at Philadelphia College of the Bible.

I have just stated what seems to me the underlying, the basic, the utterly crucial central principle that is to guide us in programming for, or in structuring, youth ministry. This prime principle can be stated simply in the form of a question that we ought to ask about ourselves every activity or program we plan: *How does the proposed activity facilitate involvement of young people and adults in the three primary processes of ministry (i.e., Scripture, body, and life)?*

PROGRAM PLANNING CRITERIA

Too often youth activities in the local church simply happen, without clear purpose or function. Or the purpose may be a questionable one, having a negative impact. Socials and recreational activities are one part of the youth ministry in nearly all church programs, and are often carried on without thought of function. So the use of the proposed criterion, "Does the planned activity facilitate the three primary processes of ministry?" can be illustrated by an examination of different approaches to socials and recreation.

To illustrate this to my college classes I have obtained tape recordings from youth ministers in various parts of the country who have distinctively different approaches to social activities. Let me sketch three of them, each of which is represented in the practice of a particular church.

1. *The 100 percent philosophy* — This viewpoint expressed in the practice of a church in Maryland, regards meeting the social needs of Christian youth as one of the church's responsibilities. Christian teens, like all youth, are developing socially. They need to learn to relate effectively to the opposite sex; they need fun times together. They need to see that being a Christian doesn't cut them off from the fun things of life.

Thus, this church plans regular weekly social activities for its own teens, with the specific purpose that Christian kids have fun together, thus meeting their social needs and—by encouraging boy-girl contacts in the context of the church—promoting dating within the Christian community. In this church no "devotionals" or other spiritual emphases are "tacked on to the end" of socials. Socials are viewed as valid in themselves and as an integral part of the church's total ministry to the young people.

2. *The 70-30 percent philosophy* — This approach was adopted by a pastor who ministered in a large church in

Phoenix, Arizona. He determined to use socials creatively to involve more of his own teens in spiritual-growth activities and to build the group's status in the youth culture. He planned sharp and exciting weekly recreational and social evenings. These activities lasted about three hours and featured sports, games, swimming, etc. The last hour of the evening was given to poolside Bible studies or films or special speakers.

Over a three-year period the program drew more and more kids from the church and outside it. And the reputation of that church for having class activities actually gave teens who attended it higher status in the campus world! And, of course, the more kids that were attracted by the social activities, the more were present for the spiritual.

In this church, then, socials were not viewed as ends in themselves, but as means to several definite ends: to attract greater numbers for Bible study and other spiritual activities, to build the status of the group in the community, and, as a result, to help members of the group feel a sense of pride in belonging.

(3) *The 0 percent philosophy* — This philosophy, represented by a church in California, states flatly that the meeting of social needs is not a primary responsibility of the spiritual leadership of the church. Rather than planning socials, the youth leadership encourages parents to accept this responsibility and open their homes to groups of their children's friends. Although this stand has brought pressure from parents who want social activities provided by the church, it has been firmly maintained.

For one reason, in this church there is a consistent emphasis on involvement with non-Christian youth. The leadership *doesn't want* Christian kids to develop friendship *only* with other Christians. So it refuses to compete with public school social and recreational programs, feeling that these are part of the "world" that Christians are to be "in" while not "of." Rejection of responsibility for the social life of youth, then, is balanced by acceptance of responsibility to help them live Christ "in the world" in which they are challenged to become involved.

There are, however, infrequent socials—of two types, and for distinct purposes. One type of social is evangelistic, and for this all stops are pulled out, as the church plans exciting and unusual activities to attract non-Christians. Christian kids are encouraged to invite their friends; there is gospel presentation;

and the main burden of follow-up evangelism rests on the kids themselves.

A second type of social is simple, inexpensive, and also functional. It is designed to bring youth and their adult leaders together in a relaxed and informal atmosphere where they can get to know each other as persons as they play and talk together. The focus of this social is "getting acquainted."

In each of these approaches, the leader is *aware of his purpose in providing the activity*. There's no "Let's do it because we've done it before," or ". . . because the other churches do it." The function of the activity is determined in providing and planning it.

Each of these approaches might be valid in a given local situation. That is, to some extent the approach one takes is conditioned by the needs and present state of growth of the kids in the group.

Then too, each approach has broad implications for the overall direction of the ministry. For instance, what are the long-range implications of the 100 percent philosophy?—the one that sees the church as "responsible to meet the social needs of Christian teens." What happens if the contacts of Christians are increasingly focused on and limited to other Christians?

In many churches such ingrownness develops with adults as well as with youth. All of life revolves around the church and church activities, and all friendships are with other Christians. But when the church becomes our world, contact with the world for which Christ died is too often broken! Our "separation" easily becomes a semimonastic *isolation*.

The church as God's transforming community must function to equip the believer to live in the world and communicate Christ to the world. I have seen too many people from evangelical churches whose social lives have been so focused on Christian friends and church activities that they have not come to know non-Christians as persons and are, in fact, uncertain and frightened about relating to them. In the long run, I am deeply concerned about the impact of this first philosophy on the direction of our ministry.

However, we can perhaps agree on these three thoughts. Each approach may have a valid role in a given ministry at a particular stage in its development. The role given to a particular activity (whatever it may be) should be understood and purposefully planned by the leadership. Each activity must be evaluated in the light of its long-range implications and its relationship to other elements in the youth ministry. (Thus, for example, the 0 percent philosophy, which encourages involvement in school activities, may not be appropriate if steps to help the kids become involved in Scripture and body relationship have not been taken, and if they are, therefore, unready to share Christ.)

With this said, let's return to the main issue in programming (which was stated earlier). In everything we must ask ourselves: "How does the proposed activity facilitate involvement of youth and adults in the three processes of ministry?"

We can apply this approach to social/recreational activities as to any others. Looking at the three primary processes broken down into the elements I have indicated in earlier chapters, we see:

Process Area	*Process Elements*
Scripture	being open and self-revealing being honest grasping the meaning of Scripture for our lives making response to God in worship in faith/obedience etc.
Body	intimate knowing of others being self-revealing bearing one another's burdens praying for, showing love to one another accepting and encouraging one another motivating etc.
Life	evaluating experiences expressing shared concerns seeking to grasp reality (Scripture) responding in obedient trust sharing Christ (witness) serving others etc.

Our questions, then, are twofold. First, what process elements can be facilitated by socials and recreation? Second, what kinds of social activities are facilitating?

I think it is clear that the social philosophy presented as the last of the three, the 0 percent philosophy, is directly related to sharing Christ, and that socials can, as used in the California church, also give support to kids in witnessing efforts. It is also possible to see an indirect relationship to processes of body relationships. While the deep sharing and coming to know one another as persons that is at the heart of body ministry doesn't normally happen in the social and recreational context, it is still true that Christians need to see and know each other in many different situations. Sharing good times with others is one way of getting to know them as persons, and of sharing life.

So again, as in the California church, socials may have a function in providing informal settings where youths and adult leaders can get acquainted with each other. But while socials, which tend to maintain relationships on a rather superficial level, may have an indirect "body-building" function, they are not central or crucial to that process.

Centrality — I have suggested so far that we begin to think about elements in youth ministry by first attempting to relate each proposed activity to our model of ministry. That is, by asking whether or not a particular activity or structure or program actually involves young people and adults together in one of the three basic processes of ministry.

I have also suggested that we break down each process area into process elements: specific activities that characterize or constitute involvement in the processes.

Finally I suggested that some things we do in youth ministry have a direct impact on primary processes, while other things have an indirect impact, and still others have no impact at all. In making this last distinction, we move to the question of the *relative importance* of the things we plan and do in youth ministry. My suggestion here is a simple one: our primary concern is to provide for and involve our youth in those activities that have the most direct relationship to elements of the three processes.

On this basis, it is easy to say that socials are *relatively less important* than, for instance, retreats at which teens are involved with each other in mutual self-revelation and welcoming (Rom. 14:1). This is not, of course, to suggest that in planning a retreat we leave no time for games or fun. It is simply to point out that in planning *any* youth activity, we need to have its purpose clearly in mind and relate that purpose to the controlling concept of the nature of our ministry. Socials for socials' sake hardly fits this conception of youth ministry.

Specific activities — It is important here to note that the full range of things done in any youth ministry is available to the leader who seeks to minister in the pattern developed in this book. Youth leaders may still use films, or drama, or service projects, etc. Youth meetings may at times feature speakers. *But the function of these activities may very well differ from their function in the "normal" youth program.*

For example, films are often used by church youth groups. Too often a film is merely show, and after it is over comments are made about it or applications drawn from it. But films, like drama, have the unique capability of capturing and crystallizing a life issue so that youth can sense it and, seeing it portrayed in the film, begin to deal with it. Too often a film attempts to deal with the issue in a cloture pattern. That is, the film seeks to present a problem and then to present in its conclusion the Christian "answer." Rather than creating an open-ended situation that can stimulate the kind of probing and sharing that characterizes both body and life ministry processes, the film maker feels compelled to make a presentation and then give his answer.

But in youth ministry we are much more concerned about encouraging teens to explore their own lives and experiences, to discuss and define issues, and to find their own answers in Christ than we are about having them hear what a film maker has to say. When these purposes are kept in mind, when we have as a goal the use of a film to launch teens in one of these processes, then we *use the film differently from the way it is used in most churches*. When the film approaches a climax, and the life issue has been stated but not resolved, we stop the film. And we challenge our teens to explore the issue, its relationship to their own lives, to suggest a possible range of solutions, to relate them to the Christian revelation, and to make personal decisions and commitments.

Having specific goals in mind helps us evaluate the function of each youth ministry activity and to plan how to use resources creatively and purposively.

In summary, then, I have suggested that in structuring youth ministries we have several clear guidelines to follow and that all of them are derived directly from our philosophy of youth ministry itself. These guidelines are the following:

1. Plan activities and programs with a definite purpose in view.

2. Measure the purpose by this test: How does this planned activity facilitate involvement of youth and adults in the three primary processes of youth ministry?

3. Determine carefully the elements that are integral to involvement in each of the three processes (see p. 271).

4. Give priority to activities that directly facilitate involvement of youth and adults in these process elements.

5. Use resources (such as films) creatively, to involve youth and adults actively in the process elements.

PROGRAM STRUCTURES

By program structures I am thinking of those situations in which youth and adults get together—in the most simple term: "meetings." In most churches the program is developed around several continuing, or permanent, meeting structures. Thus, a church will have a regular Sunday-school program, a regular Sunday-evening youth meeting, a regular youth choir, a regular Wednesday-night youth prayer meeting, regular monthly or weekly socials, etc. The tendency even in churches with limited youth programs is to center the ministry around the regular continuing programs (usually Sunday school and Youth Group) and to supplement these with infrequent or irregular retreats, camp programs, and/or service and evangelistic projects.

I am convinced that in general this approach to ministry is unhealthy. We ought to be constantly evaluating and constantly flexible in our programming. To a great extent this means that the major weight of our ministry may better be carried by *short-term program structures*.

Let's say, for instance, that we determine that *the* primary need of kids in Community Church is to come to know and trust one another, building toward a true body relationship. So, for the first quarter of the church year, September-November, we are going to focus on involving kids in process elements that contribute to body development. How might we do this?

Let's start off with a three-day "before school" retreat. Sort of as a last fling and launching combined. We go off to a camp with our adult and college-age leaders and plan rather intensive "getting-to-know-you" activities (perhaps along the lines suggested in the retreat on pp. 233–39). For this we break the kids down into groups that correspond to the Sunday-school classes they will be meeting in during the new school year.

When we get back home, we want to continue to build relationships in these groups, so we replace our regular Sunday school curriculum (for this quarter) with Lyman Coleman's *Serendipity,* a renewal-oriented program that helps kids get involved with each other by building on familiar Bible stories and concepts (see pp. 132–33). Also for this quarter we plan *body* meetings for the whole group (all who will attend), meeting together Sunday evenings. In these we focus on discovering from Scripture how Christians are to love and support each other, and then we invite the kids to share needs and perceptions right there and to receive from others in the group those ministries they have been reading about.

These two programs are open to all the youth in the church, though not all kids will take part.

At the same time, youth leaders want to begin building leadership in the youth group, and so there is an open invitation to kids who want to meet with them at 6:30 one morning a week before school. They meet at a secluded spot, perhaps a coffee shop or restaurant, and on different mornings the leaders get together with groups from the different high schools that group members attend. In the meetings, leaders seek to get to know the kids, encourage them to pray for each other and share needs, and lead a short Bible study—for which each is asked to prepare and to which each contributes.

Adult leaders also spend time with those who will lead the Sunday morning group discussions, talking about and praying about individual teens in each group. planning how to help each individual in the coming week's study and sharing. Much time is spent during these months with the youth leadership staff, to build with them the same kind of body relationship that is being worked toward in the youth group itself.

If the leaders see special needs, they can develop short-term programs to meet them. Normally these will grow out of the expressed and thus-discovered needs of the teens. Are a number of kids concerned about dating relationships, or parent/teen conflicts? Perhaps a Friday evening, Saturday "overnight" at the church, using films and role plays to help focus issues and stimulate sharing and discussion will be appropriate. It is not necessary in a program like this that *all* the youth show up; it is enough that we are providing for those who sense a need and have a desire to respond.

The next quarter we may shift our emphasis. Say that during the Sunday school hour we return to our regular curriculum for the quarter. Sunday nights we continue the body meeting approach, which the kids who come are appreciating, and this develops into a team meeting. Because the kids have become enthusiastic about sharing Christ in the high school, we switch the early-morning prayer breakfast to afternoon sessions, when we have more time with the kids, and work with individuals and groups from each high school to plan outreach strategy. Part of our strategy may involve a New Year's retreat that focuses on how relationship with Christ can "overflow" to touch others' lives. And among the things we plan on the retreat is a four-day Easter evangelistic camp, the "ticket" to which is at least one non-Christian friend to accompany each attending teen from our group.

And the next quarter? Perhaps something else: elective doctrinal and "how-to-study-your-Bible" classes during Sunday school hour, Sunday evening outreach team meetings to continue evangelism, special small-group "counseling" sessions with all the teens of the church, in which leaders meet with three or four at a time, perhaps a preparatory program for a summer missions program, etc.

The particular program, activities, and approaches any youth leader develops will be dependent on the growth and the needs of the youth—as a group and as individuals—at a particular time. In fact, all I have tried to illustrate with the foregoing is simply this: youth programming must be *flexible* and it must be *responsive* to the needs of youth. For flexible, responsive programming, it is important to think in terms of short-term—not long-term—structures.

It is important to be ready and willing to change—as long as all changes are related (1) to the needs of the youth with whom you are ministering and (2) to the basic philosophy of youth ministry, which provides a theologically derived direction for ministry.

PROBE

case histories
discussion questions
thought-provokers
resources

1. Several terms are used in specific and special ways in this chapter. If they are to prove serviceable tools for programming, they should be understood clearly.

To check your grasp of the concepts expressed in each of the following, jot down a brief definition of it now, expressing your present understanding. Then check back over the chapter and develop revised definitions.

a. the "prime principle" in program planning

b. the three primary processes

c. process elements

d. central activities

e. program structures

f. flexible and responsive programming

2. I provided on page 277 a rather sketchy chart, showing some of the process elements in each of the three primary process areas. You will note in looking at the chart that the process elements listed are actually activities youth are engaged in—activities that lead to growth in the process areas.

   This chart is not an exhaustive one by any means. There are additional activities that may be said to be characteristic of involvement in each process area. In planning youth ministries, we need a clear idea of variety and range, as well as type, of process elements in which we should seek to involve our teens. So it should be particularly helpful for you to develop your own chart of process elements. For help in developing a more comprehensive list, you may want to reread the sections of this book that deal with each of the three primary processes (Scripture, body, and life).

3. One final practical task may help you evaluate the present state and direction of your current ministry with youth. Why not complete the following chart (p. 284) and include on it additional process elements developed in the PROBE 2 study?

   This chart lets you see visually the process elements for which your present structures seem to provide.

   In the next chapter I will have more to say about evaluating the effectiveness of involvement in the processes. But at this point, I will only ask, Are youth given opportunity for involvement in key elements of the three primary processes through your present program?

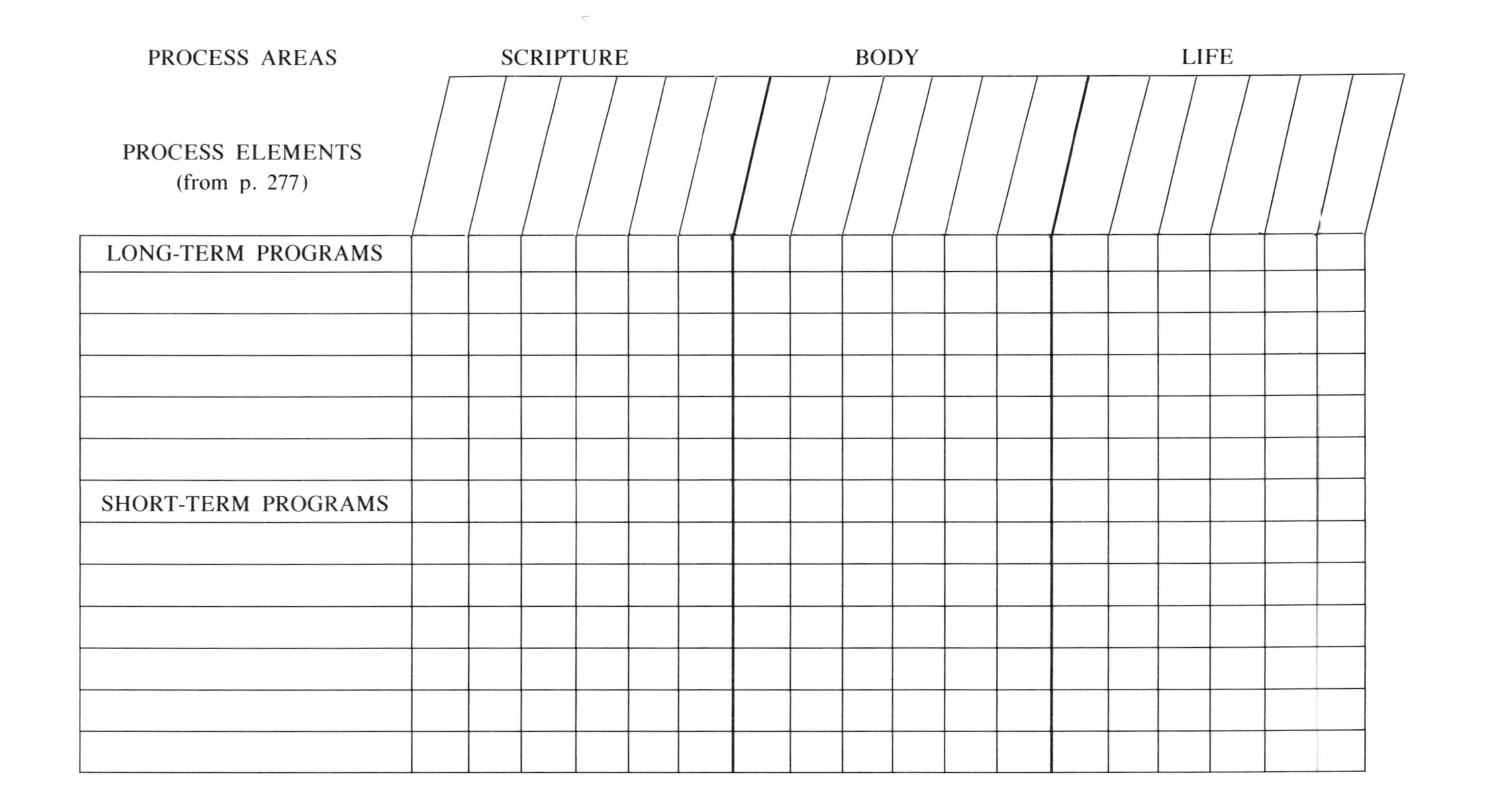
PROCESS AREAS
SCRIPTURE
BODY
LIFE
PROCESS ELEMENTS
(from p. 277)
LONG-TERM PROGRAMS
SHORT-TERM PROGRAMS

17

ORGANIZING FOR GROWTH

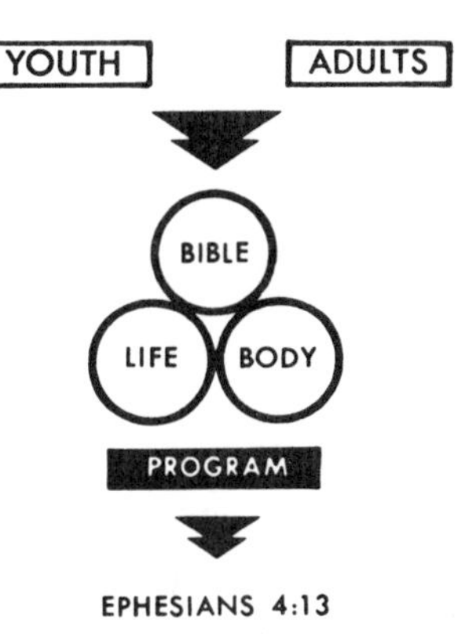

In the previous chapter we looked at some of the program structures that can support youths' involvement in the three primary processes of ministry. It was suggested that we need to view programs and structures in a distinctly functional way, always testing what we are doing by our purpose in youth ministry and always ready to respond flexibly to meet developing needs in the group and in individuals.

This last thought is a particularly important one. It implies a feedback system that keeps us informed of where teens are in their growth as Christians and as persons. It implies an organization that uniquely facilitates communications within the group and has persons, not the planning of programs, as its main concern.

How do we organize our ministry for this kind of growth—the growth of youth as Christian persons? What concepts and principles can guide us here?

There are several kinds of organizational structures for church youth groups that are currently popular. One approach has the youth elect officers who represent them and who, with the youth sponsor(s), plan activities and programs. In this *representative form* of organization, as in our representative form of government, the assumption is that interests and needs will be communicated to the leaders by group members, who then act in their behalf. This assumption is all too often unwarranted—in youth groups as well as in government. Too often teen officers are not in close touch with other kids in the group. Many leaders will even develop negative feelings about them when they fail to respond to the plans made for them and when their "spirituality" may seem to flag. Even in the best of circumstances, the officers' concerns are focused on planning and motivating others for involvement in program activities. And as the officers represent the group, involvement with the officers in fact seems to blind adult leaders to the need for contact and communication with all group members.

A second approach to organization features a *planning group* system. In this popular form of organization, the group is divided into teams, each of which is responsible to plan and put on programs for the others in the youth group and perhaps to plan other activities. The idea here is to involve the whole group by spreading responsibility for group meetings and giving everyone a chance to develop various "leadership" skills by taking different roles in the teen meetings.

This approach, pioneered by a Christian-education publisher and currently the organizational base on which a number of published youth materials are planned, also has a number of weaknesses. For one thing, once again the focus of the organization is on programs and meetings. And group leaders are cast as motivators in planning, being expected to urge others to take part in the meetings. But—and this is an important point—as publishers of such materials are presently becoming aware, high schoolers are not any longer responsive to this approach. Although there may be value in taking this approach with young teens (junior highs), most older teens (particularly those who have been organized on this plan as young teens) are openly disinterested.

Because in practice this form of organization channels the attention of the gathered planning groups toward programs (rather than into the three primary processes of ministry), little meaningful communication takes place in the planning group settings. If you doubt this assertion, check the suggested time allotted and the tasks to be accomplished in such meetings, as outlined in published materials.

Often the sample program materials themselves that publishers provide give excellent seed thoughts and helps for involving youth in exploration of various significant issues. Such materials ought to be purchased and made a part of the youth leader's resource library. However, attempting to build a youth ministry on a steady diet of such programs week after week is tragically self-defeating. And organizing youth to facilitate the production of such programs (the planning-group approach) is also, in the long run, self-defeating.

A third approach to organization brings adults and youth together in a "youth council." Although still part of a representative system, youth councils often function on policy level, seeking to consider the broader needs and directions of the ministry. Still, communication channels are seldom clear. Although youth members may be elected from various organizations (e.g., one from each Sunday school class, two from the youth group, one from the youth choir, etc.), they are too often viewed as representing these organizations rather than as being channels between persons. And little opportunity is given in classes or groups to hear reports of council members or to request information on the feelings and needs of the kids. Even when such opportunity is given, the questions of concern are normally: "How do you feel about this program?" or ". . . that plan?" or ". . . our Sunday school classes?" etc.

Somehow each form of organization that I have mentioned seems (1) to view as adequate the communication from youth through *representatives;* (2) to put elected leaders in roles where they make decisions about, and seek to gain general support for, programs and meetings; and (3) to focus attention on the program plans rather than on persons.

Strikingly, none of these characteristics seems related to the nature of spiritual leadership as discussed in chapters 7–9! Even when these approaches to organizations "work," they tend to train the most concerned of our Christian youth for organizational roles rather than for spiritual leadership.

I am aware that many will disagree with what I have been saying in this chapter. They will object, "But it isn't *necessarily* so! Elected officers, or planning group leaders, can be trained to function in the spiritual leadership way. This criticism of the ways we have organized youth groups isn't really valid."

To this objection I must express both agreement and disagreement. Theoretically, elected officers or group leaders *can* be trained to function in different ways—just the ways I am going to suggest in this chapter. But practically, they are not. The fact remains that these organizational forms are *primarily oriented to programming, not to personal ministry*. No one who has sat in on meetings of youth group officers can help but be aware that the focus of conversation and concern is group meetings, what to do in them, how to gain the cooperation of the group to attend them, which teen will call so and so or take this or that responsibility, and so on. But youth should not be taught to focus their concern on the planning and maintenance of youth programs. They should be taught to love and minister to persons. They should not be trained to see the church as an organization but to experience the church as an organism.

What I suggest, in fact, is that we do away with officers and elected (or appointed) teen leaders and organize the youth group on entirely different principles than those of the representative, program-oriented, organizational role patterns the discussed forms imply.

AN ORGANIC APPROACH TO ORGANIZATION

I have just suggested that we reject contemporary organizational patterns for the youth group and reorganize on entirely different principles. It is helpful to spell out some of the principles on which this reorganization is to be based, particularly to make more clear the contrasts between organic and contemporary forms of organization and, thus, the compelling reasons for reorganization.

Contrast one: responsive versus representative leadership. It is true that one of our tasks in ministry with youth is to develop Christian leaders. We must provide a context for maximum growth, so that the spiritual gifts God has given each believing teen may surface, be recognized, and develop. We should also realize that not every one of the youth in a church will respond to the opportunities to grow that a youth ministry provides. A number will remain untouched.

There are a variety of reasons for this. Some teens may be "verbal Christians." They have heard the gospel from childhood, they know all the right words, but they have never responded personally to Jesus Christ. With others, a lack of response may simply be unreadiness. Some Christian teens who avoid opportunities for full dedication to Christ in high school respond enthusiastically as collegians or in young adulthood. God has His own time for each of us. And there are other reasons, but whatever they are, the fact remains that in any youth ministry there will be some youth ready to respond and others who remain on the fringe, involved minimally, but seemingly untouched and unready for discipleship.

In most churches *the primary strategic error in youth ministry is to organize to minister primarily to the contact group and to largely ignore the core group.*

These two groups are represented in the diagram at the right. As indicated, in most churches the *core group* will, particularly in the beginning of a ministry, be considerably smaller than that of the fringe group. This latter group, labeled the *contact group,* is made up of teens with whom the church has regular contact through one or more programs and for whom church activities must be provided, but who have not yet responded to the invitation to full discipleship.

One of the reasons for this is that in most churches leaders still naïvely expect to have a spiritual impact on kids in and through *meetings*—not in and through persons. Thus, programs and the organization of the group itself focus on gaining hearings with the contact group, and much of what the officers and adult leaders discuss decides what kinds of programs will motivate and interest the fringe kids.

The fact is, however, that the most significant group is the core group—the teens who are already responsive to the Lord and who can be led into disciplined lives. *And the most effective way to reach fringe kids in the contact group and lead them into the core is by the impact of loving contacts with the core teens.* Contact group teens are to be *drawn* into the core, not *dragged* in by more and better programs.

An organic organizational structure, then, is based on the fact that life is most effectively communicated through life. Such a structure focuses on building up kids in the core group in order that they may spread dedication through the group by the kindling power of their own love for Jesus and one another. In a very real sense, *the core kids are the teen leaders.* But their leadership is not going to be of an "elected representative" type. It is going to be the servant-leader, example type, discussed in chapters 7–9.

Thus, we now can see something of what is meant by a *responsive* leadership rather than a *representative* leadership We need to view as our leaders those kids who respond to Christ in true discipleship, not those who are elected by members of the group.

This responsive leadership is not exclusive. It is open to everyone in the group. That is, anyone in the contact group should be able to move into the core group *at his own choice*. We make provision for this by inviting all to core meetings but, at the same time, insist on a level of dedication and discipleship that makes membership both costly and meaningful. (By this I mean spelling out clearly our expectations for those who choose to take part in our core sessions. In some cases we may consider an early prayer/Bible study breakfast a core meeting, or perhaps an evening session where kids share what they have discovered in personal Bible study that each member of the group is expected to complete before attending.) As I mentioned, much of the time and the majority of the personal contacts of the adult leadership should be invested in core-group activities and development of relationships with those who respond by choosing to accept the disciplines of core-group membership.

This, then, is one of the principles on which our organization of the youth in youth ministry is to be based. We seek to develop a responsive, not a representative, leadership.

Contrast two: person versus program orientation. In the new organizational structure, we seek to orient those who respond to the invitation to leadership to persons, not to programs. By this I mean that we do not try to make the kids responsible for the programs we plan (though individuals may be invited to take various planning responsibilities). The development of programs, the planning of retreats, etc., are the responsibility of the adult leadership, in response to needs that youth reveal. What we seek in our core gatherings is to develop in teens a sense of responsibility and a love for other teens. This love is not exclusively exercised in the core group, but the teens are encouraged to love and get to know, to share with and pray for, kids in the contact group and non-Christians on the campus.

In keeping our focus on encouragement of core teens to love others, we are helping them see that the Christian is only indirectly concerned with church activities—but deeply concerned with the persons who make up Christ's body. And, thus, the major topic of conversation, and the major burden of prayer, as far as the group as a whole is concerned, is the persons that make up the group. By taking responsibility for programming and motivating attendance at meetings of youth, we are free to help them develop a concern and sense of responsibility for persons. And never think that there is no difference between *indirect* concern for persons ("We want to get everyone out to this retreat so they will grow closer to Christ") and *direct* concern for persons ("Ken's really shook about school just now. He wants to come, but he's afraid he'll flunk out if . . ."). There *is* a difference. A tremendous one.

Contrast three: communication versus control patterns. Each of the organizational patterns I criticized earlier was essentially a control pattern. Youth were involved as leaders and given control functions, if not to make final decisions about programs and plans, at least to influence other teens and gain their cooperation or attendance.

The organizational form I am suggesting is concerned that the youth be given a communication function—not a control function. That is, that the primary function of kids in the core group is not to make decisions about "what next" (although they will have the *greatest* impact on decisions, in providing needed feedback), but to share with each other and the adult leadership all they know of the needs and concerns of one another, and to contact group kids.

I just noted that the organizational pattern I am suggesting is oriented to persons, not programs, and that the kids in the core group (the true leaders) become involved in knowing and loving contact group kids. What is learned of their needs and interests, their ideas and attitudes, their suggestions and criticisms, is shared in core meetings with a view to loving and praying for them and finding ways to draw them closer to the Lord. As needs are shared, the adult leaders (who are also involved with individuals in the contact as well as the core group) develop quite an accurate impression of the needs of the larger group and seek to meet these needs in a variety of ways and through a variety of program structures. *It was only because I envisioned this kind of feedback through the youth organization that I could suggest in the last chapter that we think in terms of ministry structures that are responsive and flexible—and, thus, short-term.* Only when there is a communication system that lets us know where the group as a whole and individuals are as persons can we hope to minister to needs, guided all the while by our overall concept of the nature of youth ministry.

The organization we need for youth ministry, then, is one that provides for open communication lines, not for youth's involvement in programming control.

ORGANIC ORGANIZATION OUTLINED

With some of the assumptions about the nature of our organization explained, we can turn to an overview of organic organization itself and the function of the various elements. The organizational pattern is diagramed in Figure 9 and shows the position of the youth leader, the adult leadership core, the teen core, the contact group, and the world-setting in which the group is placed.

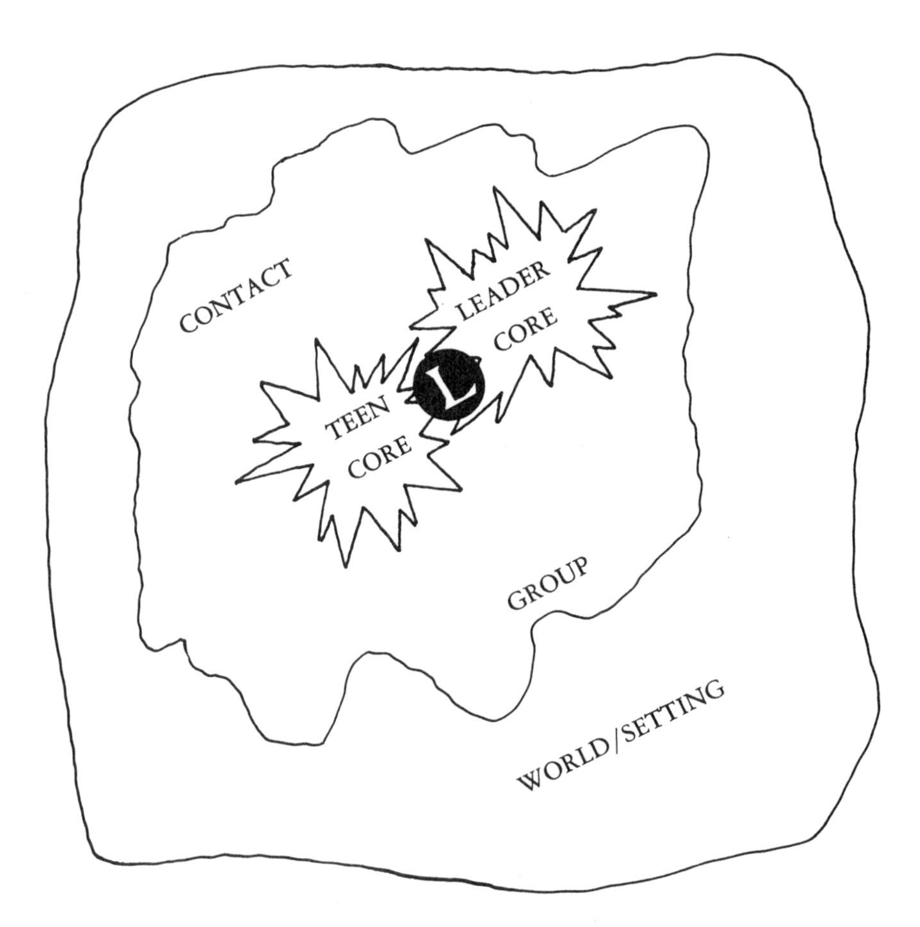

Figure 9
Elements in an "Organic Organization" Pattern

The leader — As I suggested earlier in this book, the leader in any Christian ministry is central to its development.

This is true whether the leader is a pastor, one of several elders in the New Testament pattern of multiple lay leadership, a youth minister, or a "head sponsor." The leader is central, because in the biblical pattern he sets the tone for the group, providing the example and demonstrating in "going before" the others in love and self-revelation the realities of the Christian life.

As leader he needs to set the example both for the adult leader core and for the teen core, as well as maintain relationships with kids in the contact group and non-Christians in the youth world-setting.

The leader's time is spent investing his life in others, in motivating and encouraging discipleship primarily in his leader core and teen core. Strategically, he seeks to reach the whole group and the world around by igniting response to Christ in these two key groups.

Although it helps if the person who is the leader has an awareness of the many resources and options open to him in terms of materials and activities and structures for youth ministry, it is essential that he have a clear grasp of the principles and processes of youth ministry. For ultimately the guidance of the program and the development of its structures in response to discovered needs is his responsibility.

Teen core — The teen core, as noted above, is formed of youth who respond to the open invitation to go on in discipleship with Christ. Through the example of the adult leadership, core teens are guided to focus their love for one another, for others in the contact group, and for kids in the world. Through sharing in the core meetings, they come to sense their responsibility for all the others in the body and provide the kind of information about the group and individuals in it that is necessary to guide the adult leadership in planning the overall program.

The leader core — The leader core is made up of all adults (and in many cases college students) who minister with youth. Ideally, this includes all associated with youth ministry in any agency, for youth ministry should be considered as a whole in the local church, not divided into "Sunday school" and "youth group" organizations with separate staffs and usually, separate philosophies.

While members of the leader core may have different roles in the ministry, such as "teacher" or as "leader" of kids going to a particular high school, they are still to function primarily in the biblical servant-leader role. That is, they are to be examples, sharing themselves with the teens and being involved with them in the three primary processes of ministry—in Scripture, in body, and in life.

Here, I may stress again, the role of the overall leader is crucial. For much of his time will have to be spent with the adult leader core, helping them to think in terms of persons, not programs, and leading them to the kind of body relationship with one another that they seek to foster among the youth.

Finally, let me add that the leader core shares with the youth director or head sponsor responsibility for developing the program structures through which the needs of the group and individuals are to be met.

Contact group — As noted, this group is the "fringe group"—teens who are associated with the church and attend some of the youth activities, but who have not responded to the challenge to discipleship as have the core kids. Their failure to respond in no way indicates that they should be disregarded in planning the youth ministry or that the activities they do attend should be discontinued. In fact, as the core group is developed, the contact group becomes the primary recruiting ground for disciples. So at all times a concern for the contact group kids as individuals, a love for them, and an attitude of honest welcoming and acceptance of them needs to be maintained. Also, the adult leadership will show concern by seeking to develop personal relationships with contact group kids as well as encouraging core kids to build such relationships.

World-setting — The world-setting of the youth group is the campus and neighborhood world in which the young people live daily, and in which they meet non-Christian teens. Thus, the world/setting, although shaped by the general attitudes and values of youth culture, is viewed primarily as the *persons* who move in it. And so the goal of the church youth ministry is clear: to reach out into the world-setting to share Jesus Christ with teens, and to draw them into His body as they respond in saving faith to Him. Therefore, the primary approach to teens in the world is the same as the approach to kids in the contact group at church. Young people who are growing in the Lord reach out with His love to them—to share themselves, and to care.

At times, as discussed in chapter 15, individuals or the group may minister love in service. But always, in individual contact, each will seek to love others and so share Jesus Christ with them.

This very loose organization, then, *is designed for communication of life by reaching out to persons with love.* Reserving program-planning for the adult leadership, organic organization of youth ministry frees youth to focus the concern of a responsive teen leadership on persons, communicating the needs of individuals to one another and to the adult leaders while, at the same time, communicating to individuals in the contact group and world-setting the love of God.

EVALUATION

One final advantage of the organic organization as developed in this chapter resides in its provision for constant evaluation of the ministry.

Evaluation in Christian education has historically been conducted on two levels, whereas in fact the truly meaningful level of evaluation is a third. This means that we have had no truly meaningful way to evaluate what we have been doing in our church for many, many years.

Level one evaluation is in terms of "programs provided." You may have seen such guides, which are often used in denominational evaluation booklets (and even, with some slight modification, in this book!). This guide simply asks, "Do you have a departmental Sunday school?" "Do you have one teacher for every six children in the primary through junior high departments?" "Do you have a children's-church program?"

It is obvious that questions of this kind simply do not speak to the *effectiveness* of programs but rather assume that if a church provides certain activities and conditions, effective ministry will take place.

I mentioned that there is a chart of this type in this book. Look back on page 284, and you will note that you were asked to analyze (another word for evaluate) the programs you provide in your present youth ministry by checking process elements that presumably take place in your various long-term and short-term programs. It should be clear that, while such a chart can help you see what you may *not* be doing, it can tell you very little about what you *are* doing. Simply because an opportunity to interact with Scripture in a particular way, for example, is provided, does not mean that anyone in that situation is so interacting, or that any are responding.

Evaluation on this level tells one nothing either of the present state of the practice in an organization or of the results in persons' lives.

Level two evaluation is in terms of "good practice." You can also find examples of this kind of evaluation guide in Christian education materials and publications. "Does the teacher provide opportunity for the student to talk?" "What percentage of the time is teacher talk and what percentage student talk?" "Are questions open-ended to stimulate discussion, or do they simply require a yes or no answer?"

This kind of evaluation is also carried out by observation, as when a supervisor in the public school system watches a "practice teacher," or a consultant visits a Sunday school to observe.

At best this kind of evaluation can point up weaknesses in practice and suggest methods and techniques for improving the quality of the teaching or leading. But again this kind of evaluation says nothing about results. One can't tell what is happening in the life of an individual by observing class or group practices. And because this kind of evaluation cannot give us answers about effectiveness or about needed changes in our ministry, it is not what we need.

Level three evaluation is concerned with what is going on in persons. It involves a revelation of needs and a revelation of growth.

There have been some attempts to assess needs and changes in persons, normally through self-report questionnaires. Although these may be helpful at times, they encourage response only to the questions that are asked. And too often these may be the wrong questions! Also such forms do not provide for continuous appraisal.

Both a broader self-revelation and continuous appraisal are very important for youth ministry. Too often the only way we learn the questions we should ask of youth is *after* they have told us their experiences and concerns. If we are to attempt flexible and responsive structuring in youth programs and activities, we need continuous feedback. We need to know when something we have done has helped, and how much it has helped, and we need to know when we have failed. We need to know what needs are surfacing *now,* how deeply these are felt, and by how many. We need, in short, a continuous flow of deeply personal information that can be gained only by a sharing of lives in response to love.

The organization I have suggested, then, has the advantage in maintaining the kind of *personal* communication lines discussed, of providing youth leadership with a unique flow of the kind of data that permits constant evaluation of the state of the ministry.

Other contemporary forms of organization simply do not provide for effective level-three evaluation.

DOES ORGANIC ORGANIZATION WORK?

Many raise very practical and, on the surface, valid objections to ministry concepts that I have presented in other books. I am sure these same objections will be raised to this book, and to this chapter in particular. "But," they say, "does it work? Isn't this all 'ivory tower' stuff?" And others comment, "If only he'd work with youth in a church instead of in a college, he'd find out why it's impossible to do what he's talking about."

I appreciate these objections and the element of validity they contain. I am not now serving a church as pastor or youth minister, and so I can't point with pride to a particular success of "my method." I do, however, have several reasons for believing that these particular objections are not actually valid, and in fact make nothing that I have said in this book or others of less value than if I were presently ministering in a church. But because, as I said, the objections are raised and do seem to have some validity, it seems to me worthwhile to take a moment to answer them.

First, the pragmatic test is hardly a final one. Because something "worked" for me doesn't mean it would "work" for you. Each of us has different gifts, each ministers in different situations. Therefore I could hardly promote a particular system just because it worked for me. That would be totally insufficient reason to argue that you ought to adopt my approach.

Second, what I have tried to present in this book is *principles*. This is, in the technical sense of the term, a "theoretical" book. It develops a philosophy of youth ministry; it does not give you five easy steps to success with youth!

As a theoretical book, a book on philosophy of youth ministry, it pays more attention to *why* we develop our ministry in certain ways than to *how* we do specific things. I have tried to provide practical ideas and resources in the PROBE sections, but this is definitely not a book with forty gimmicks that will increase your attendance at the youth group.

As a theoretical work, then, it has to be judged on theoretical grounds. Simply saying, "I don't think it will work," or "I think you'd have a hard time doing it yourself," is hardly a basis for rejecting or accepting a philosophy of ministry. No one, in fact, suggests that *any* approach to youth ministry is easy. Or that any guarantees success. God is the great Actor in our ministries, and His Spirit is the One who touches lives and hearts. The basic question we need to ask of a philosophy of ministry is not, "Does it look easy?" but "*Is it in harmony with the way God works?*"

Third, then, is this: Is it theologically and biblically sound? To me, this is the most significant consideration of all. For in all I have written I have tried to understand and explore God's written revelation and to express what He has shown us of His body and the nature of the ministry to which we are called.

I am, I confess, very much disturbed by people who ask only, "Are you doing it?" and overlook the central and crucial issue: Is this the pattern of ministry God has revealed?

How long must we Evangelicals, who pride ourselves in our high view of Scripture, resist seeking in God's Word direction for our ministries while querulously complaining that anything that does seek to explore Scripture for guidelines "looks hard"?

I must confess that as a fallible and limited human being, I cannot guarantee that in this book I have at all times caught and expressed the thoughts of God. That is far beyond me. So I am and must remain open to correction on the basis of possibly having misunderstood or misapplied what Scripture is saying. But at the same time I must decisively reject objections that excuse failure to examine one's own ministry under the authority of Scripture by suggesting that, since another is not currently involved in a particular ministry, his view may automatically be rejected.

Finally, I must also say that the basic approach to youth ministry developed in this book *does* work. I personally know men in youth ministry whose works are built on the biblical principles developed here and whose impact on young people, some of whom I also know, has brought about some of the most exciting and vital renewals in our country. A few of these men are quoted in this book or are used as examples in PROBE features. Each of them is building his ministry on what he has seen in the Word of God as guiding principles and each has discovered both that a biblically based youth ministry *is* hard and that God is a faithful and a trustworthy leader.

May we all be willing to trust Him.

SUMMARY

In summary, then, I have developed in this chapter an organizational pattern that is closely linked with what has been said in the rest of the book about the nature of leadership and the nature of the three primary processes of ministry. In a very real sense, this chapter and the rest of the book depend on each other. Only when a ministry is designed to involve youth in Scripture, in body relationship, and in life, will the organization I have suggested prove effective. And, conversely, only an organic type of organization will support and encourage the three processes of ministry.

PROBE

case histories
discussion questions
thought-provokers
resources

1. As in the preceding chapter, certain terms and concepts are crucial for understanding the approach I suggest. So take a moment to jot down your own definition of the following, and then work back through the chapter to develop sharper, final definitions.

    a. representative leadership

    b. responsive versus representative leadership

    c. person versus program orientation

    d. communication versus control pattern

    e. core group

    f. contact group

    g. level-three evaluation

2. I suggested in this chapter that teen "leaders" in most organizational settings do in fact focus on program concerns, not people concerns.

    If you are presently ministering with youth, check me out by listing, right now, the topics of conversation in your last three meetings with teen officers. Also jot down an estimate of the time given to the discussion of each.

How much of the interaction was oriented to program-planning or ways to get kids to cooperate with programs, and how much to considering group members as individuals and showing concern for them.

3. In this chapter I suggested that there are two core groups with which the youth leader needs to invest himself. The first is the adult leader core, and the second the youth core, made up of kids who respond to the challenge to discipleship.

   In most churches, this latter core group will be small. In your church, who do you think would be ready to respond now? List names, if possible.

   How can you go about developing them into biblical servant-leaders? Have any ideas?

4. It is probably difficult to grasp just what I am suggesting when I recommend that we take various responsibilities of youth and accept them ourselves. This is particularly difficult when so much of youth ministry literature seems to suggest the opposite—giving youth responsibility—and when good business management practices insist on delegation.

   But I believe that what I have suggested is important and that we should at least understand who is involved. Perhaps it is easiest to make the distinctions needed in terms of kind of responsibility we give youth. In youth ministry literature, the usual responsibility that is given to youth is *program* responsibility. In this setting the leader acts as a coach and helps the youth do their jobs. But the kind of responsibility we need to be concerned with is *people* responsibility, and this is not directly related to "jobs."

   It is probably easiest to see what I am suggesting by looking at the two approaches in operation, in the planning of a retreat in the normal "delegate responsibility" pattern, and then in the suggested "adult accept responsibility" pattern.

Retreat planning: approach one

In the fall the group's officers had laid out an annual calendar, and a retreat was scheduled for Easter vacation. In November at a biweekly officers' meeting, several committees were appointed to prepare for the retreat. There was a transportation committee, a program committee, a site committee, an entertainment committee, and a publicity committee. Committee chairmen were invited to meet with Mr. Swanson, the youth minister, before December to get help for starting on their jobs.

Ted, chairman of the transportation committee, was given places to check for bus rental, and he and Mr. Swanson discussed the advantages and disadvantages of using cars. Ted was then expected to determine costs, to poll the kids and their parents to see how everyone felt about using cars, and to see if adult drivers might be available. He could then make recommendations to the full committee.

The program committee gathered at Mr. Swanson's home and went through his resource files. They checked materials from several publishers and looked over books that others had used as bases for retreats. Finally they decided on a topic presented in various parts that teens would have, signing up the selected kids for their parts and seeing to it that they were prepared.

Entertainment and publicity committee chairpersons also had their turn. In the chat with Mr. Swanson what they were to do was laid out and a calendar of due dates was set up. The site committee chairman was given a list of eight camps and retreat centers within a few hundred miles of the church and told to write or phone each for brochures and to check availability. He was to be ready with his recommendations by the next scheduled meeting, because time was slipping away fast.

As a good delegator, Mr. Swanson regularly checked on the progress of his committees and repeatedly told his kids that if they had any problems, they should be sure to see him. He also praised them liberally when they were working well. But, as usually is the case, there were some who just didn't get the job done. Disappointed but not dismayed, Mr. Swanson worked especially hard the last week and a half before the retreat to catch upon the loose ends, and everything seemed to go off pretty well.

Retreat planning: approach two

Spring was the traditional time for a retreat at Staub Memorial Church; so in early September, Carl, the youth minister, had reserved a camp in lower Wisconsin for the Easter break. Now in January he was sitting around his living room with the fifteen kids who made up the committed core he'd been building toward since he came to Staub a year and a half before.

He brought up the subject of the retreat casually and asked the kids what they felt the retreat ought to accomplish. They had some of the usual ideas at first: a "deeper walk," maybe a focus on personal evangelism, maybe something on getting involved in better Bible study. But Carl led them to probe for needs. What did they feel their own greatest needs were just then? How about the other kids in the group? As they talked, he encouraged them to think of individuals they knew. What were their needs? Where were they spiritually? And how about the group as a whole? What did the whole group—not just the gang gathered there that night—really need?

About an hour and forty minutes later some things were beginning to come clear. The whole gang was agreed that what everyone needed—they themselves as well as the others who were not so involved—was to experience more of the unity the Bible says we have in Christ. The fringe kids needed to be drawn in and to know the love and acceptance that was beginning to mean so much to those who had responded to Carl's ministry. And the core kids needed to be reminded that they were all one in Christ and that they needed help to resist the temptation to look at kids on the fringe as "outsiders."

With the need defined, they spent nearly half an hour praying about what had been discussed, looking to God to meet the needs they felt.

Carl resisted the temptation to set up "committees." Instead, he began in the following weeks to encourage all the kids to get closer to the others in preparation for the retreat and to pray for individuals, both that they'd come and that God would meet each one there. Carl took on the responsibility to plan the program himself. This wasn't to be a packaged program. He dug into his resource files and tried to tailor the program to fit the specific needs of his group and to fit the activities to the kinds of things they liked and responded to. This kind of expertise was something none of the kids he worked with had as yet developed, and he didn't expect them to take on responsibilities for which they were not prepared. (After the retreat Carl planned to sit down with three or four of the key kids and evaluate the retreat. In the evaluation, he would take them through his planning process and consider with them why some things had been effective and why some had not.)

Although he had made arrangements in September for the retreat center, Carl drove up on Saturday with Roger to look it over. On the way they stopped off at two other camps and talked about the advantages and disadvantages of the different settings. Carl didn't make Roger responsible for selecting a site, but he wanted him, as a member of the group, to know how to select a retreat center and to understand the criteria that were important to use. What is more, on the trip he and Roger had hours for getting to know each other on a deeper level.

While publicity was primarily handled through person-to-person contact, Carl knew the importance of creating excitement and group expectancy. About a month before the retreat he invited several of the most creative kids (fringe as well as core) to his home for a poster party. Carl discussed with the guys and gals what they wanted the retreat to accomplish. They talked over how to appeal to most of the gang and then they set to work creating ways to communicate and "sell." As the posters took shape, three of the girls spontaneously developed a hilarious skit and were asked to put it on in Sunday school. Pizza and prayer climaxed the evening, and the dozen who left Carl's house that night were now enthusiastic retreat boosters.

Carl did more work than Mr. Swanson had done. And it took him more time. But the retreat had greater impact, not only on the weekend itself, but in all the times of preparation and the ministries with individuals they had occasioned.

Evaluation

These two sketches illustrate the differences that I feel are important in the two approaches to leadership. And they illustrate what I mean when I say adult leaders should *take on* rather than *delegate* responsibilities in planning and programming.

Note that in the first setting, teens were given jobs to do that had only indirect relationship to people. These were jobs "for the Lord," perhaps, but with dubious connections to *ministry. Teens were asked to do jobs for which they were inadequately prepared. The best of explanation and direction falls far short of the kind of training that the "do-it-with-them" approach of apprenticeship provides.*

In delegating Mr. Swanson forced his relationship with the kids into a performance-based pattern. He was not and could not be viewed as "friend and example" in this leadership role, where he was setting himself up as "boss" and demonstrating the boss role in checking upon their performance. (While checking up on others *is* necessary and valuable in ministry, it is important initially to make the checking up in terms of spiritual growth and responsibility. The performance ["job"] relationship is best held off until a deep personal relationship is firmly established.)

In the second setting Carl involved his kids in the deepest concerns in planning: discovery and statement of need, prayer that God might work in meeting needs, and sharing the responsibility to draw others toward the Lord. Carl's focus was on involving teens, not in the "job" responsibilities, but in the "people" responsibilities.

Carl took responsibility for planning and programming elements that only he was equipped to do well. But he worked to equip others—not by having them do, but by involving them with him in evaluation and in conversations on trips like the one he took with Roger.

Carl did not try to "do it all himself," but instead he attempted to plan with the kids. He did not just delegate and check up, forcing preparation into the "job" category. He involved himself and, by being there, set a tone and directions, demonstrating his desire to associate with the group.

Carl had extra time with various individuals and groups and by keeping his focus on persons, he further developed his ministering relationship with them.

Part Five

THE PRODUCT OF MINISTRY

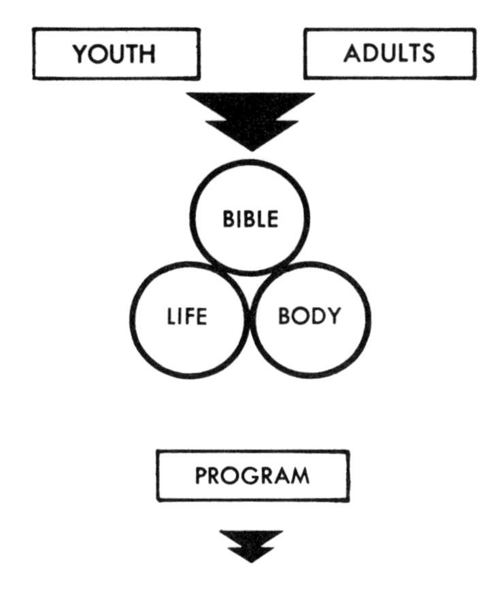

THE PRODUCT OF MINISTRY

CHAPTER

18. GROWTH, TOGETHER

18

GROWTH, TOGETHER

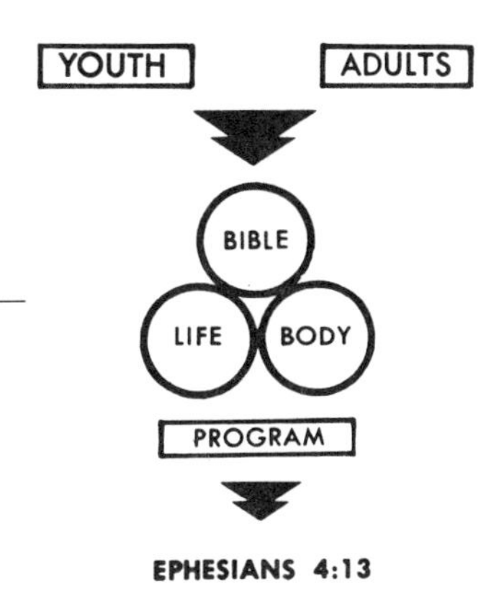

The apostle Paul stated that Christ gave a variety of gifts to be used in the ministry of the church. "Some he made his messengers, some prophets, some he gave the power to guide and teach his people. His gifts were made that Christians might be properly equipped for their service [ministering work], that the whole body might be built up until the time comes when, in the unity of common faith and common knowledge of the Son of God, we arrive at real maturity—that measure of development which is meant by 'the fullness of Christ.'

"We are not meant to remain as children at the mercy of every chance wind of teaching and the jockeying of men who are expert in the crafty presentation of lies. But we are meant to hold firmly to the truth in love, and to grow up in every way into Christ, the head. For it is from the head that the whole body, as a harmonious structure knit together by the joints with which it is provided, grows by the proper functioning of individual parts to its full maturity in love" (Eph. 4:11–16).

Yes, Ephesians says it. Growth, together, to maturity is both the product and the goal of the body of Christ; thus, it should be for youth ministry as well.

In a real sense, this short passage brings together nearly all that I have been saying in this book. It focuses God's philosophy of ministry on its goal—growth toward maturity in Christ.

Note the various thrusts of the passage. God gives leaders to His church, leaders who are to guide and teach His people. But these leaders are not bosses or dictators. They are servants who exist to equip and activate believers for *their* ministering works. It is through the functioning of all believers—of each as an individual part of the body—that the body of Christ grows to its full maturity in love.

God has grouped Christians together, called us to union with each other as a body. It is "in body" that we grow. It is in the unity of a common faith and common knowledge of Christ that we are built up toward real maturity.

Thus, the Christian leader seeks to develop love among believers—love, the gift that frees us to experience our unity. Not all respond immediately. So the leader works most closely with those who do respond, that they may grow and by their love draw others more toward Christ and into a greater—a more evident and active—unity.

The body is a harmonious structure, growing as each individual makes a personal contribution. So the Christian leader seeks to develop openness and honesty—the context in which love can be given and received, the context for gift ministry. Because believers are to hold to the truth in love, the leader seeks to involve the youth in Scripture. Because we are to express "the fullness of Christ," the leader guides them to share and explore their daily lives, that they may grow up into Him "in every way." And because a "full maturity in love" means expressing the fullness of Christ to others, the leader helps them share the gospel with others and to live as Christ lived in the world—as a loving servant.

Youth ministry is concerned with persons and seeks to help individuals grow in Christ in company with other growing believers, for so God has ordained. And our approach to ministry must reflect both the divine purpose and the divine pattern.

Only when we understand the goal to which Christ calls us and grasp the tremendous resources He has provided in His Word, His body, and His Spirit—only then can we conform our efforts to Him and know the joy of those who live and minister in full accord with His will.

PROBE

case histories
discussion questions
thought–provokers
resources

One final suggestion. Now, at the end of this book, try "putting it all together" by developing a ministry strategy of your own. Here's how.

Suppose that you have been invited to a typical local church as minister to youth. Briefly describe (drawing on your own experience) the situation you find: size of the group, present structures, attitudes of kids and adults, etc. Then write out a tentative three-year plan, stating goals for every six-month period and giving details on how you expect to move to reach them. Feel free to go back over any section of this book, but develop *your own* plan as thoroughly, thoughtfully, and carefully as you can.

INDEXES

Subject Index

Scripture Index